ANTIQUES
ROADSHOW
Experts on Objects

Edited by
Christopher Lewis

BBC BOOKS

The contributors would like to thank the following for
their help and advice: Alan Brett, Martin Golland,
Esther Jagger, Douglas Nie, Mike Scott, and
Lindsey and Robert Tilney.

The information given in this book on the care of
antiques is offered in good faith, but BBC Books and the
contributors cannot take responsibility for any accident,
damage or loss caused as a result of following
their advice.

Published by BBC Books
A division of BBC Enterprises Limited
Woodlands, 80 Wood Lane, London W12 0TT

First published 1987
© The contributors 1987
ISBN 0 563 20628 4 (hardback)
ISBN 0 563 20602 0 (paperback)

Designed by Bob Gordon
Typeset in Sabon by Ace Filmsetting Ltd, Frome,
Somerset
Colour separations by Technik Litho Plates Ltd,
Berkhamsted
Printed and bound in England by W. S. Cowell Ltd,
Ipswich, Suffolk

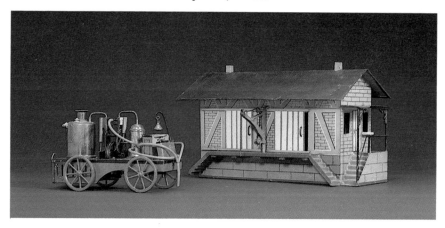

*Above German tinplate toys. A fire
engine driven by spirit-fired steam
piston, made by Gebrüder Bing about
1900, and a railway warehouse of about
1902 by Märklin.*

*Previous page Guernsey silver
punchbowl, about 1700.*

CONTENTS

FOREWORD

Hugh Scully with a Roadshow *customer and her fairground horse.*

In the late spring of 1977 a group of people, most of whom had never met, let alone worked together, travelled from all over Britain to the town hall in Hereford to make a television programme under the working title *Antiques Roadshow*. Few of them had been in front of a camera before. They were experts on antiques but had no knowledge of broadcasting, and to make their task even more daunting there was to be no script or opportunity for rehearsal.

The odds against success were certainly high, especially since the programme was dependent on that most unpredictable group 'the general public'. Would they turn up in sufficient numbers to make the exercise worthwhile, and if they did, would they bring with them antiques of interest and value? In the event, several hundred people came to the town hall that day and the small production team from the BBC in Bristol, led by producer Robin Drake, returned home reasonably satisfied with what had been achieved.

The Hereford show was what is known in broadcasting as a 'pilot', the all-important halfway stage between an idea and a firm commission from a channel controller. Few programmes about art and antiques enjoy mass popular appeal, and there was a certain scepticism about the prospects for the new show. Not even its most enthusiastic advocates would have dared to predict that the programme might eventually attract an audience of over fourteen million people, but at least the Hereford show was good enough to win a series of eight programmes on BBC1. That series, with Arthur Negus as the resident expert, was transmitted in the spring of 1979.

Since then, of course, the *Roadshow* has become a familiar and immensely popular feature of the television schedules, with an audience that increases each year. It is particularly appropriate that this book should be published to coincide with the programme's tenth anniversary.

I am often asked to account for the immense popularity of the *Roadshow*, and always reply with one word: 'People.' It is unquestionably our customers, with their brown paper parcels and bulging shopping bags and great expectations, who make the programme such riveting viewing. I remember so many individuals who have contributed to the great success and sheer fun of the *Roadshow*. There was the lady who came to see us utterly convinced that she had a painting by Constable. Our expert told her that it was, alas, a copy. She argued her case with some vigour, and millions of people subsequently enjoyed the colourful bout between the two evenly matched opponents — matched, that is, in verbal if not art historical expertise. Remembered, too, is the gentleman in Scotland who had much to tell us about his collection, but allowed his fondness for Scotland's national drink to inhibit his ability to explain. There was the army padre, a former prisoner of war, who brought along two old tin cans welded together to form a crude chalice for the celebration of communion for his fellow prisoners. I remember the young boy who so delighted Arthur Negus with his collection of carpenter's working tools; and the hapless couple in Bath whose dog had put its paw through the oil painting they were about to bring to the *Roadshow*. Yes, they are the stars of the show, and the programme relies much on their charm, good humour and occasional eccentricity.

Then, of course, there are the antiques. Is there a never-ending supply? Will we not soon run out of places to visit and things to discover? I think not. Britain is uniquely fortunate in that it has not suffered invasion in nearly a thousand years, and even the Civil War did not result in the plundering that happened as a consequence of war and revolution in other parts of Europe. We have a rich and still largely unspoiled heritage. Much of it is in private homes all over Britain, in a sense waiting to be discovered.

The third essential element in the success of the show is the great knowledge of the experts, as you will discover when you read and enjoy their contributions to this book. Many television professionals envy their easy conversational style and ability to convey information in a relaxed, informal and totally unpompous way. Now, for the first time, they bring that style to a book, much of it based on the things they have seen during their travels with the *Roadshow*.

To them all, our thanks. To you, our hope that this *Antiques Roadshow* book will provide as much pleasure as the television series that has provided its inspiration.

Hugh Scully
London, 1987

Introduction

When I first approached the authors of this book for an idea of their contributions, it rapidly became clear that any kind of comprehensive coverage of the subject matter of the *Antiques Road-show* would be impossible. There is just so much. We see everything from beads to brass beds, from eighteenth-century dinner services to modern china with 'dishwasher-proof' on the back, and from tinplate toys to the plastics of the fifties. So we ended up choosing subjects which are representative of many different fields, but which particularly appeal to the expert concerned. Thus in the field of furniture John Bly writes about chairs because of his personal delight at the social manners they portray. Michael Clayton confines his vast knowledge of silver and metalwork to a chapter on the many varieties of provincial silver. And Hilary Kay chooses three disparate topics from the wide and amorphous field of 'collectables'.

We have tried to be more comprehensive about porcelain and pottery. Far and away, this is the largest category of item brought to the *Roadshow*. Everyone, it seems, has an old plate or dish of some sort. On many occasions we have been brought the entire contents of the parlour display cabinet, each piece separately wrapped and packed in grocery boxes. Several of our experts have combined to span five hundred years of manufacture from Britain, Ireland, the Continent, China and Japan, giving a useful introduction to this fascinating area of collecting.

Richard Dadd, Artist's Halt in the Desert. *This was the watercolour that re-emerged at the Barnstaple* Roadshow *after being missing for more than a hundred years.*

A George III bombé marquetry commode, the finest piece of furniture seen in the first ten years of the Roadshow.

In the four years that I have been producing the programme, I have never ceased to marvel at the enthusiasm and good humour of the people who attend. Six weeks before the event, we advertise in the local newspapers and by poster. People with small items are just asked to bring them along on the day. Those with larger pieces like furniture, outsized pots or even suits of armour are asked to send a photograph. If it looks interesting, one of our team will visit the owner by appointment and then, if examination confirms that we might use it in the programme, arrange transport to the hall. Occasionally we see something else in the owner's home which interests us, and we suggest that that comes in too. Other than these few items, there is no 'planting' of juicy objects at the *Roadshow* to be casually discovered later on. Our experts genuinely don't know what treasures await them when the doors are opened and the people file in.

Everyone is funnelled through our reception desk where knowledgeable eyes quickly scan their offerings. We have two purposes in mind: first to channel them to the right expert, and second to give early warning of particular items of local interest which we might wish to use to reflect our travels round the country. The team of experts waiting to examine their treasures is composed of members of auction houses, consultants, dealers and museum curators. From a pool of about sixty, up to twenty or so join us each week, ensuring a range of expertise to deal with the thousands of objects we see.

At the porcelain table there may be three or four experts swopping opinions and advice, surrounded by piles of old newspapers and a crowd of interested onlookers. I always think the atmosphere is like an Oriental bazaar, though of course no one is buying or selling. This non-commercial aspect is one of the reasons why people bring us their possessions. They know we will give them an honest opinion, uncoloured by any interest in offering to buy, sell or deal. Most *Roadshow* customers see the occasion simply as an opportunity to learn about their treasures in order to enjoy them the more.

On most occasions it is the experts who suggest the pieces they would like to record for the actual programme. Sometimes a glimpse will be enough for them to know they have found something interesting. In other cases a thorough examination will be necessary, discussion with colleagues, even a telephone call or two to confirm the identification. Nothing is ever said to the customer until the recording itself; we pride ourselves on retaining the essential spontaneity of the interview.

Over the years we have certainly had some memorable finds. A lost Victorian watercolour by Richard Dadd turned up at Barnstaple. It had been missing since an exhibition in Manchester in 1857 and its existence was known only from a description given in the exhibition catalogue. I remember the expert who recognised it approaching me across the crowded floor, clutching a ragged-

John Bly examines the valuable Irish peat buckets that had been converted into part of a hi-fi system.

looking piece of paper – the painting. 'I think,' he said, the perspiration standing out in beads on his forehead, 'that this is it – the jackpot!' It was later sold to the British Museum for over £100,000.

Another lucky customer had bought for £400 a secondhand hi-fi set which included a pair of loudspeakers unusually mounted in attractive wooden buckets. When he saw a similar bucket in a glossy magazine, he came hotfoot to the *Roadshow*, where John Bly told him he had a pair of Irish peat buckets worth £2500 – considerably more than the entire hi-fi. Another customer was not so lucky. Her pair of Worcester spill vases were of high quality, but one had been extensively restored after the cleaning lady had knocked it off the mantelpiece. That accident had reduced their value by £1000.

My fondest memory is of a man from Sunderland who noticed a damp patch in his ceiling. He clambered up into the loft and found himself standing on a piece of sodden board – a painting, as he discovered when he dried it off. It was an English pastoral scene of a stream running through woods, and was not particularly to his taste. So he put it in the back of his wardrobe, where it stayed for several years. His wife, keen to regain the space, suggested that if she painted a few daffodils in the foreground it might look a lot better. They might even consider hanging it on the wall. Instead, her husband deflected her enthusiasm to the frame, to which she applied a thick coat of cream paint. Then they heard that the *Roadshow* was coming to town. This news coincided with a call from a knocker – a door-to-door dealer – who offered them £50 for the painting *and* a teaset they owned. Fortunately they decided to go first to the *Roadshow*, where the teaset was valued at £50 and the painting at £4000! It was by Alfred de Bréanski, an artist of some quality whose work has become much sought after.

Valuation is, of course, an imprecise art. 'Is that all?' said an irate firearms collector when told that his pistol was worth only £200. Well, yes, but if he had had the pair they would have been worth £600, and if in their original box with all the accessories, even more. There are all sorts of qualifications and variables which can affect a valuation. For a start, what sort of valuation is it? For insurance, probate, selling or buying? In what condition is the item? In some categories condition can mean the difference between a few pounds and thousands. And is the item in fashion at the moment? Valuation is at best an educated guess by an expert well qualified to make it. Experts have access to the latest auction prices for similar items. They have a 'feel' for the rightness or wrongness of an item, gained through long experience of handling and comparing objects.

Auction prices are perhaps the fairest way of quantifying value because they are a sort of public valuation, though always subject to unpredictability. Were there enough people at the auction? Were they the right people? Were two of them particularly keen to get the item? All these factors can unsettle the results. It should be remembered that the majority of buyers at auction are dealers, and buying in antique shops may be more expensive to allow for their mark-up; not always, though, and buying from a reputable dealer gives a guarantee which may well be worth the difference.

So valuation must be qualified. It is impossible to be precise in many cases, and you will often hear an expert leave a wide margin for error. £4000–6000, for example, is more a guide to the range you might expect than something you could take to your bank manager.

Do we spoil the enjoyment of hitherto unrecognised treasures by valuing them? I know of no instance when we have, though a high figure may raise questions of security and insurance. Few people coming to a *Roadshow* would thank us for not telling them what they came to find out. In the Isle of Man a farmer's wife came to the show with a particularly fine English commode, looking like a small chest of drawers with a curved front and ormolu mounts. Our furniture expert knew at once that he was looking at the best piece of furniture we had ever seen at the show, and he booked the item for recording. In the meantime the lady had confided that things were pretty difficult at home just now. There was the farm to run, and her husband was in hospital with a heart attack; she too was due in any day for an eye operation. How, we wondered, would she take the news that her commode was worth £35,000-plus? Would it be the last straw? Wasn't ignorance bliss? Fortunately common sense prevailed. She had come for a valuation, and we ought to give it to her. For all we knew, the good news might be just the piece of luck she needed at the time. The expert did take the precaution of asking her to sit down before telling her the price. 'No wonder!' she said, duly flabbergasted. 'I'll never sell it, though, for sentimental reasons.' A few months later she changed her mind; the commode went to London and made a hammer price of £50,000. Did we spoil it for her? I don't think she would say so, and the commode, of course, will now be recognised and preserved as the valuable and beautiful work of art that it is.

Travelling with the *Roadshow* is always fun. As one expert put it, 'It's like belonging to a club of old friends.' It's hard work too, with many an expert losing his voice at the end of the day from a surfeit of Victorian fairings or photographic reproductions believed to be lost masterpieces. But we never turn people away. Everyone and everything is seen. Everyone gets the service. That's the deal we make with the public when they come – and that's how those missing masterpieces are found.

Christopher Lewis
Executive Producer
ANTIQUES ROADSHOW

ENGLISH CHAIRS

JOHN BLY

Most chairs are easily portable, so as well as dining chairs we see on the *Roadshow* hall chairs and spinning chairs, garden chairs and children's chairs, rockers and miniatures and every variety of stool – once we were even shown a one-legged milking stool! But unless any of these is extremely unusual or part of a set, it is unlikely to be of great value. Nevertheless it is always worth finding out. One pair of small chairs (p. 52), which looked more suitable for an Arabian tent than a home in England, were a mystery to their owner. They turned out to have been made to an Art Nouveau design by Carlo Bugatti and were worth nearly £1000.

So how do we tell? What are we looking for? I try to remember that antique chairs so often look like the people who first used them. Cromwellian chairs are austere, but those made during Charles II's reign are fussy, with lots of frills and fringes. A good mid-eighteenth-century chair looks every inch the English squire, while a delicate shield-back of the 1790s reminds one of an elegant dandy. Of course, this rule does not always apply – but as a quick guide to dating it has served me well over the years.

My first lesson in looking at chairs this way came when I joined our family business and my father sent me out on the road to buy as best I could. After four years working in London I thought, like most young people, that I knew it all, but I soon got into trouble. One day I bought a chair and tied it on to the top of my car, to arrive home looking like Steptoe with his cart. As I pulled into the yard, my father came out of his office and with great compassion said, 'I want you to give me four reasons why you shouldn't have bought that chair', and when I couldn't provide even one he started to explain. It was basically a Hepplewhite period chair which had been altered several times. The upholstery was out of period, the back was too tall, the seat was too narrow and the arms

Top of page *Hepplewhite period mahogany chair of about 1786. The straight legs taper to a spade toe, and the back is starting to show the influence of Classical design.*

were the wrong height. 'It's a Georgian gentleman turned into a Victorian spinster,' he said. This was such a logical approach and such an interesting way to learn that I was hooked.

We don't get many seventeenth-century chairs brought into the *Roadshow*, and when one does appear it is usually a disappointment for the owner – age is no criterion of value, and the fact that a chair is three hundred years old does not necessarily mean that it is worth a great deal of money. But try explaining that to someone who has waited patiently in a *Roadshow* queue. To the specialist, however, these early chairs are always interesting, irrespective of their value. Peculiarities in their carving and decoration can give a precise provenance such as a county, village or even a maker, and their construction forms the basis for all future development.

There are many stories regarding the history of the chair, and how it developed from a stool with the addition of a back. This isn't strictly true, because we have had chairs and thrones for as long as we've had stools. Nevertheless, the simplest seventeenth-century chairs are known as back stools, and are made in the same way as the stool – that is, with a mortise and tenon joint, hence joined or 'joint' stools. This type of construction has no glue, each joint being secured with willow pegs, driven through. These pegs are rarely cut off on the inside, and visible of course only when you turn the chair upside down. Now this may look a little untidy, but you should never trim them back or cut off the ends – you could be destroying an important clue to age and authenticity.

Below right *The country squire type of good mid-eighteenth-century mahogany chair. The back is pierced and swept up at the corners, and the seat has straight rails.*

Below *George I walnut chair of about 1720. The strong curvilinear lines of the back are repeated in the seat rail.*

Early George III chair of about 1765. The legs are still square in section and still have stretchers.

Another guide is the timber. Until the late seventeenth century, oak was the primary wood. By the 1690s this had been superseded by walnut, and by the 1750s this in turn had been replaced by mahogany. The age of classicism at the end of the eighteenth century saw the use of more exotic timbers, such as rosewood and satinwood, and by the 1820s oak and walnut were returning to favour. The best Victorian chairs were made of rosewood, mahogany or walnut.

Seventeenth-century chairs had a very sensible arrangement of supporting stretchers, which joined the legs together in an H shape some two-thirds of the way down. On better chairs a front rail was added, usually shaped and curved. A carved X was an alternative form of stretcher during the William and Mary period. However, by the 1730s most good fashionable chairs had no side or centre stretchers at all; they returned again with the straight-leg chairs of the 1750s, and remained popular thereafter in certain areas of manufacture.

Stretchers were an integral part of the Windsor chair, particularly during the nineteenth century, and variations in their structure can affect the value. A Windsor chair with a bowed or crinoline stretcher is more desirable than one with a plain H pattern. And if all the stretchers and legs are in yew wood to match the back, the chair can be worth several hundred pounds more.

The original Windsor-type chair was used in the garden and the earliest examples were painted, usually dark green. They were generally of plain turned stick construction and can easily be mistaken or overlooked as being of no merit. There is a very specialised market in such chairs, but it is important that they retain as much of the original paint as possible. I had such a chair once which I loved dearly; it was covered with several layers of paint which had worn away on the seat and on the edges of the arms, and to me it looked wonderful. A friend staying with us for a weekend thought he would give me a surprise by cleaning some furniture, so he stripped and waxed my chair – and spoilt it forever. He also reduced its value by at least three-quarters! So never attempt to strip or clean anything until you have made sure you will do no harm.

In terms of design, the Queen Anne period was like the calm before the storm. For a short while, good middle-class furniture had a graceful, dependable quality. The backs and arm supports to chairs were curvilinear and the legs had prominent knees which graduated down to an inswept ankle to terminate in a ball and claw foot or a pad foot. The leg we call cabriole, but it is something of a misnomer. Cabriole was actually a French dancing term, meaning a bound or leap, and it was used to describe the legs on French furniture which ended in a cloven hoof foot. British furniture-makers did not adopt the foot as a decorative feature, but kept the shape of the leg, and so we have a happy compromise of designs and a rather attractive word to describe the style.

There are wonderful wing chairs from the early eighteenth century – the wings or ears were introduced to shield the sitter from the draughts which were so common in English houses. When viewing sales or looking in shops, you may find that the under canvas of these chairs is ripped out. Don't be put off: it has been done in order to establish, beneath its upholstery, what the chair is made of and how old it is. Makers in the eighteenth century soon found that if they were going to upholster chairs fully, so that only the legs and stretchers would show, there was little point in using expensive timber to construct the entire frame. The show wood, as it was called, might be of walnut, mahogany or even oak, whereas the rails and the rest of the frame would be of beech. I remember one customer on a *Roadshow* being terribly disappointed to find that the fine walnut back legs of his chair were abruptly spliced on to a cheap beech frame 3–4 inches up inside the cover, and it was some time before I could persuade him that this was in fact a very good sign and did not in any way indicate shoddy manufacture. However, if you own such a chair it is important that before you start stripping anything away you have it looked at by an expert. Certainly no recovering or repairing should be undertaken on such furniture until you have had this advice, because a good Queen Anne period wing chair will be worth many thousands of pounds.

The curving lines of the 1720s gradually became overdecorated and carved with simulated rockwork, waterfalls, shells and all manner of fanciful scrolls. These were applied in greater or lesser degree according to the importance of the piece, and it is such decorative features that we use to assess the quality and date of chairs from the mid-eighteenth century. Another guide came with the Chinese revival – called the 'Second Chinoiserie' – which saw the application of Chinese fences, bridges, mythological birds and figures, creating an alternative to the Baroque and Rococo extravagances. Even a small Chinese motif such as a pierced corner bracket or rail can add considerable interest and value to a chair today. The same can be said of the Gothick taste of the 1760s, with its cluster column legs, pointed arches and crocketed spires – copying the main styles of our ecclesiastical architecture.

Fine examples of this period, be they Rococo, Chinese or Gothick, are extremely rare and valuable. But do beware – they were all much copied and mass-produced in the late nineteenth century.

My personal favourites from the eighteenth century are those pieces which are not overdecorated but have just sufficient elaboration to give the impression that the maker enjoyed his work. The chair on p. 11 (right) is to me a perfect example of the country squire type of chair I mentioned earlier; I have a particular fondness for it as it was purchased by my father in the 1920s. It is hard to believe that he actually got a reprimand from his father for buying such an unsaleable item. However, that is what it proved to

Late eighteenth-century satinwood chair of about 1795. The back has a Classical vase shape, and the decoration is now painted rather than carved.

be, and so it went into my grandfather's office – and it's been there ever since! Like a great many things brought along to the *Roadshow*, it doesn't have an enormous commercial value now, but as a piece of our family history to me it is priceless.

The 1750s saw the start of the period of English furniture which has for years been recognised as 'Chippendale'. A remarkable craftsman in his own right, Thomas Chippendale produced the first book of designs devoted entirely to furniture. *The Gentleman and Cabinet-Maker's Director*, published in 1754, contained 160 fine line drawings which cabinet-makers around the country could copy according to their skills and the wealth of their patrons. The brilliant part was that he provided drawings of chairs, cabinets and so on, giving the option of an expensive or a cheaper version. A chair was shown with a carved cabriole leg on one side and a plain, straight leg on the other. His interpretations of current designs became so popular that his contribution to the history of English furniture outshines that of his contemporaries. Dining chairs of this period, particularly the straight leg type, were made in enormous numbers. These were constructed with three basic types of seat – a solid wood seat with a cushion, a drop-in upholstered seat, or an overstuffed seat, where the material covers the seat rails all the way round. Of the three types, the solid seat is by far the most unusual but not the most fashionable, and so it may represent a real bargain for the chair buyer today.

A word of warning about the drop-in seat: beware of recovering the seat yourself without first taking off the last cover. It might look an easy do-it-yourself job, but you may make the seat too bulky to drop into the seat frame. This will force the seat rails apart, and once this has happened you will need an expert to repair the frame.

By the 1770s the Classical designs of Robert Adam were being adopted by the leading furniture makers and designers. We tend to label the last twenty-five years of the eighteenth century as being 'Hepplewhite' and 'Sheraton' in that order. Both men published pattern books which, like Chippendale's *Director*, received wide coverage. Their eminence in the history of English furniture may be explained by the fact that they present us with possibly the best references to the changing styles, for neither was prolific in actual output of furniture. In fact, while we know that George Hepplewhite was a respected cabinet-maker and that Thomas Sheraton trained to be one, so far no known piece of furniture has been found that is attributable to Sheraton's hand; I'm afraid those pieces claiming to be 'signed by Mr Sheraton' will continue to be viewed with some suspicion.

Some of the most charming examples of chairs can be found during the transition from Chippendale to Hepplewhite and Sheraton designs. In deference to the new Classicism, the legs of such chairs were given a slight taper, sometimes ending in a spade foot, and the top of the back was deeply curved in serpentine form

Regency mahogany dining chair of about 1810, showing Grecian influence.

14

Victorian high-back upholstered chair with a good walnut frame. A delightful but prim maiden aunt?

CARE AND REPAIR
—— 1 ——
- Keep all good furniture away from direct sunlight and radiators to prevent bleaching, drying and warping. Avoid too dry an atmosphere.
- Use good wax polish and avoid sprays.
- Don't apply too much wax, and use a small brush to clean corners.

to make what we call a camel back. On finer examples, the backs were often curved to simulate Prince of Wales feathers or a bunch of wheatsheaves. Both of these are of great interest to a collector, for it is said that a chair with Prince of Wales feathers indicated support for the Prince, and a bunch of wheatsheaves support for the King – George III, known as 'Farmer George'. The next stage was to sweep the back uprights inwards to form a waist, above which the heart- or shield-shaped back can also be seen as the silhouette of a perfect Classical vase.

By the end of the eighteenth century, turned legs and sabre legs were popular for dining chairs, and by 1810 they had virtually taken over from the square, tapered variety. The mark of a good sabre leg is that the toe will protrude in front of the seat rail, indicating quality of design and manufacture. A poor sabre leg has a less generous curve which, although following the fashion in principle, shows greater concern for economy in that it required less timber. Basically the sabre leg changed little during the next thirty years, but the turned legs got heavier as the period progressed, and we draw on this fact for accurate dating.

The early 1800s saw furniture design once again influenced by outside events as Britain went through a period of patriotic fervour during the Napoleonic Wars. Many chairs were decorated with simulated rope or cable backs, anchors and other marine subjects – a reference to the importance of the Navy (this was the time of Nelson's victory at Trafalgar). These decorations were often joyfully mixed with Neo-Classical and Egyptian motifs, in a style we now recognise as Regency.

Now I am sure that the historically minded will immediately say that the Regency lasted only from 1811 until 1820. True, but this was the 'political' Regency. 'Antique' Regency describes the period when the Prince of Wales and his circle of friends determined a style of furniture and interior decoration which was totally distinct from that prescribed by Robert Adam and his contemporaries. In short, the younger generation of wealthy aristocrats rebelled against the refined, accepted designs and patronised bolder and much more aggressive styles. The most elaborate and outrageous examples we call High-Style Regency. I have been lucky enough to have had two or three pieces of this type brought along to the *Roadshow*, and I have for a long time believed that this period has yet to yield some very exciting finds.

Designs for chairs after 1820 show bulkier outlines and a swing away from Classicism to a revival of the eighteenth-century scroll and foliate decoration. This, combined with a Gothic revival, continued well into the Victorian era. By the 1850s there were over fifty thousand people employed in the furniture industry, many of whom were in the upholstery side of chair making. Upholstery can be an important guide to when a chair was made. As early as the 1830s coiled springs were being produced in quantity in Birmingham for chairs, settees and bedding. And it was from this period

Satinwood Classical revival chair of about 1890. The carving is enriched with various inlays including mother of pearl.

CARE AND REPAIR
— 2 —

- Don't sit on a chair which has a loose frame. Reglue loose joints as soon as possible, using water-soluble glue.
- When recovering a drop-in seat always remove old coverings. A build-up of material may force the joints apart, and repair is expensive!

that the fully sprung seat became popular. To accommodate the springs, the upholstery webbing was stretched across the bottom edge of the seat rail. Prior to this the webbing went across the top of the seat rail, which is what my father meant about the upholstery on my chair being out of period. Another change at this time was the use of braid or gimp to finish the edges of upholstery, rather than close nailing – that is, using large, dome-headed pins to give the appearance of a beaded edge.

As the Victorian period progressed, the chair took on the appearance of an elderly great-aunt; delightful, interesting, reliable, but rarely elegant in the late eighteenth-century manner. Meanwhile the manufacturers experimented with materials as well as style, and chairs were made of cast iron, papier mâché and even coal. But novelty gave way to practicability and wood remained the most popular material for furniture construction. Oak, walnut, mahogany, rosewood, all the fruitwoods, beech, birch and many others were utilised. In the latter part of the nineteenth century the timber indicates the quality of the chair rather than its date.

The curvilinear salon or parlour chair which developed during the 1860s into the 'balloon back' was the last great innovation of the period. This usually has shaped legs similar to the earlier cabriole style, and a lot of people confuse them with 'Queen Anne'. This is an area in which some of the greatest disappointments occur. Owners discover that the set of 'Queen Anne' chairs they have prized so highly is only Victorian and not, after all, worth a fortune. Today, however, any set of chairs is expensive, and if you are starting from scratch why not try collecting odd ones or pairs to build up a harlequin set? It is great fun, and can be an interesting and affordable way of learning about antiques.

If you really have set your heart on buying a pure set, make sure that they all match precisely and that there are not too many replacement pieces in each chair. This could indicate that the set has been dismantled and enlarged. If, for example, four chairs have been taken to pieces and a right front leg taken from one, a left front leg from another and so on, each old piece being replaced by a new one, there will be enough spare old legs and backs left over to make another chair, thus turning a set of four into a set of five. Genuine repairs and replacements may be necessary and are quite acceptable, but consistency of replacements is something to look out for.

By the end of the century, design had got further complicated by the popularity of revivals of earlier periods. The designs of Chippendale, true Queen Anne, Hepplewhite, Sheraton, Robert Adam and even Regency all came back, sometimes separately, sometimes mixed together, but all slightly modified, and it is these modifications which the trained eye can spot and quickly identify . . . which is where I began. If only I had known all this twenty-five years ago, I might never have bought that chair!

DOLLS AND TEDDY BEARS

HILARY KAY

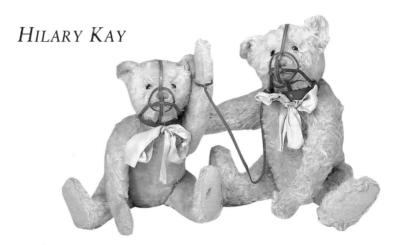

In the early *Roadshow* recordings seven and eight years ago very few dolls were brought in; now the scene is quite different. It is no doubt a reflection of the growing number of collectors, newspaper and magazine articles, and well-publicised saleroom results. More recent *Roadshows* have drawn dolls by the pramful, from vinyl 'Cup Final' dolls dressed from head to foot in the colours of last year's winning team to the highly desirable and valuable wooden dolls from the reign of William and Mary.

The earliest dolls were ancient Egyptian; wooden models of female figures, they may not have been made strictly as playthings. It is the figures with articulated legs and/or arms which are now generally regarded as being made for a child's use. Clay or terracotta dolls with moving limbs have survived from ancient Greece and Rome, and the numbers discovered indicate that the habit of giving children dolls as toys was widespread. Clearly boys as well as girls played with them, since some represented soldiers rather than female figures.

In fifteenth- and sixteenth-century Europe evidence of dollmaking and ownership is seen only in portraits, which occasionally show a child holding a carved wooden doll; both dolls and owners wear scaled-down adult dress of the period. These elaborate dolls were for the children of the nobility, and were probably imported from Germany to England. Fine wooden dolls were, however, made in this country in the seventeenth century. Perhaps the best-known early English wooden dolls are the pair christened Lord and Lady Clapham, now at the Victoria and Albert Museum in London.

Wooden dolls made before 1800 are very scarce indeed, but on one *Roadshow* I had the good fortune to be brought a fine example from the 1730s. She had survived the centuries in extraordinarily

Top of page *Two early teddy bears with humped backs made by Steiff in Germany about 1913.*

18

good condition, still dressed in her crisp original costume. The head and body were of wood turned in one piece, to which legs were joined by a slot-and-groove system at the base of the torso; her arms, whch ended in fairly crudely modelled hands, were joined to the top of the torso by thin strips of leather. The delicately carved wooden head had been covered with a layer of gesso (a paste of whiting and parchment, then largely used as a smooth base for painting or gilding furniture), which had been painted to imitate a lifelike pallor. Her present owners had acquired the doll by descent through the family.

Very few wooden dolls of this date and style are still in private hands; those most likely to be seen, owned or remembered today are the 'Dutch' dolls from the later nineteenth century (since many of these dolls were made in Germany the word 'Dutch' could have originally been 'Deutsch' – in a similar way to the term used to describe a primitive American style of art and furniture called 'Pennsylvania Dutch', also meaning 'Deutsch'). These wooden dolls were very different from their eighteenth-century ancestors, however. They were rather crudely turned, and the elongated heads had a triangular sliver of wood inserted into the face to represent a nose. Only the head and lower arms and legs were painted – straight on to the wood, without a layer of gesso between. These German dolls were made in huge numbers and in a wide variety of sizes – some small enough to sleep comfortably in a matchbox, whilst others stood a majestic 20 inches high.

Also from Germany, and dating from the end of the seventeenth century to the mid-nineteenth century, were dolls made from papier mâché (see p. 113). Few seventeenth- and eighteenth-century papier mâché dolls exist today, but greater numbers were produced in the nineteenth century and so more have survived the test of time. Sometimes described as Biedermeier (the Austrian and German decorative style of the 1820s and 1830s, inspired by the French Empire style), these particular dolls can be recognised by the detailed moulding of the complicated coiffures of the time. The heads, moulded in one piece with the neck and shoulders, were then mounted on to bodies of stitched white leather or kid with lower legs and lower arms of carved and painted wood.

Another medium widely used since early times was wax. It had advantages over wood in that its pourability allowed the doll to be easily moulded with good detail and to be tinted in flesh tones. Real hair inserted into the head enhanced the effect. In the production of dolls' heads wax was used in a variety of ways. Sometimes a block of solid wax would be carved and moulded to shape. 'Poured wax' shoulder heads were made by pouring melted wax into a mould and allowing it to set for a few moments before the surplus was emptied out; the cast head was removed from the mould so that detailed features such as eyes could be hand finished, and finally the 'shoulder head' would be mounted on a stitched cloth or kid body. England became particularly well

Rare George II wooden doll of about 1750. Her wig is made of real blonde hair.

German doll of about 1850, with head and shoulders made of china and the rest of kid.

known for producing fine poured wax dolls in the mid-nineteenth century; some of the best were made by Madame Montanari, who had some of her wares on display at the Great Exhibition in 1851, and Henry Peirotti, also London-based. Both manufacturers specialised in beautifully modelled heads and limbs, some requiring two or three pourings to produce the final lifelike flesh tint. Indeed, it was not until the introduction of heads in unglazed porcelain (called parian or bisque) later in the century that greater realism could be produced than was possible with wax.

Although one London factory was producing about twenty thousand cheap wax dolls a week in 1871, some examples were exquisite and sold for sums in the region of £50. Bearing in mind that at this period a doctor or similar professional man was earning about £5 a week, a doll of this quality represented a huge investment and children were seldom allowed to hold and play with one unless supervised.

Dolls with glazed ceramic heads had been made in the eighteenth century, but they only became widely popular in the second quarter of the nineteenth century. Manufactured largely in Germany by a moulded process, they could be mass-produced with ease. The earliest, made before 1800, still looked like models of adults, but as the nineteenth century progressed the faces became more podgy and childlike. Eventually these dolls became very stereotyped and were produced cheaply in such large numbers that a great many survive intact today. But their shiny faces were not really lifelike, and in the mid-nineteenth century dolls with heads of unglazed porcelain superseded them.

This highly adaptable medium had almost infinite modelling possibilities, and manufacturers produced ladies with extravagant moulded hairstyles or delicate hats and bonnets, sometimes including details of jewellery and costume moulded on the throat and chest; baby and child dolls were also produced. Originating mostly from Germany, but widely exported, particularly to England, these dolls cornered the market until the French began to make bisque dolls of outstanding quality in the 1860s and 1870s.

The early French dolls of this period, usually sold with a complete outfit or even a wardrobe of clothes, displayed every fashion device and accessory which would have been worn by well-to-do ladies of the day. Their makers include Mademoiselle Huret, Simonne, Gaultier, Bru and Jumeau. Heads and shoulder plates of fine bisque were mounted on to stitched white kid bodies; the lower legs and arms were originally made of bisque, but later papier mâché limbs were used with ball joints at the shoulders, elbows, hips and knees. The most notable features of French-made dolls are the fine-quality bisque used in their manufacture and their hypnotic and lifelike eyes; the Jumeau dolls also had heavy, lustrous eyebrows.

The producer of the *Roadshow* received a letter from a young viewer before one recording, telling him of her collection of dolls.

Bisque-headed doll with a jointed composition body, made in Germany about 1890.

Jumeau bisque-headed doll, with typical large eyes and heavy eyebrows, made in France about 1880.

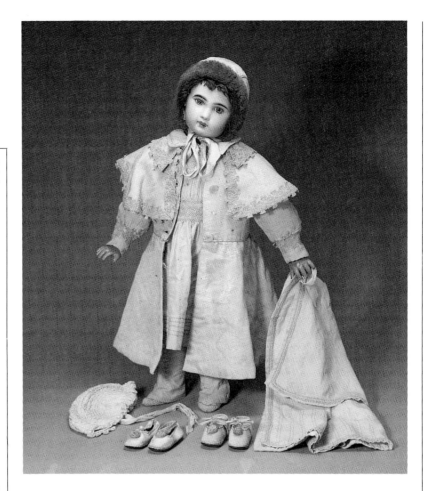

CARE AND REPAIR

∾

- Don't wet hair or eyelashes.
- Don't wet composition hands and feet.
- Wipe ceramic or biscuit dolls' heads with cotton wool wrung out in soapy water.
- Dust kid and fabric dolls' bodies, and teddies, with a soft brush or use the upholstery nozzle of a vacuum cleaner.
- Don't attempt to clean dolls' clothes without seeking expert advice.
- Don't use modern chemicals of any description on old teddies.
- Store in acid-free tissue in a box containing an insecticide block. Don't use polythene, which attracts mould.
- For storage, pad dolls' clothes with acid-free tissue to prevent creasing.
- Store wax dolls away from heat and out of direct sunlight because they can melt or crack.
- For restoration, and if in any doubt, consult a specialist.

For expert advice contact the Bethnal Green Museum of Childhood, Cambridge Heath Road, London E2 9PH.

Amongst several others, she brought in a scarce French fashion doll, beautifully dressed, with a fine bisque head. It had been handed down to her from a great-aunt. Although surprised at the likely saleroom value of the doll, Anastasia was already very interested in collecting dolls and was delighted that she already owned the type of doll which many collectors would regard as their best piece.

In 1899 most of the French dollmakers joined forces to form the Société de la Fabrication des Bébés et Jouets (SFBJ) when it was realised through bitter experience that the high quality of French dolls could not compete successfully with German quantity. Perhaps the most extravagant of the French dolls were those which were mechanised to provide unaided movement. These included simple clockwork mechanisms mounted so that a doll's legs operate in a walking motion, whilst others had small phonograph talking machines mounted within their chest cavities and were accompanied by interchangeable cylinders playing different nursery rhymes. Others moved their arms to 'blow kisses' whilst murmuring 'Mama' or 'Papa'.

The German factories concentrated on producing faces which became increasingly naturalistic; heads with Oriental, mulatto and negro features were made, as well as novelties such as dolls with two or more faces which rotated to change expression. The heads were mounted in bodies of papier mâché, with wooden limbs jointed at the shoulders, elbows, hips and knees.

The search for realism led to the production of so-called 'character' faces which depicted an expression, rather than the bland and soulless faces of some of the earlier dolls. Portrait dolls followed, with facial features sometimes modelled on young relatives of the dollmakers; these faces were popular, but far fewer portrait or character dolls were produced than the more predictably 'pretty' dolls. The scarcity of the character dolls means that they can be worth significantly more. I once found a doll with a distinctly petulant expression in the storeroom of a toy shop; she was very scarce indeed, and realised £25,000 not long ago. Clients are frequently surprised when I ask them to tell me whether their dolls are pretty or ugly, but the difference in rarity and value can be extraordinary.

The makers of bisque-headed dolls are relatively easy to identify since most manufacturers impressed their details on to the back of the head; Jumeau, however, tended to use a rubber stamp instead,

Above German bisque-headed character doll, made about 1909 by Kammer and Reinhardt.

usually in blue or red ink. Usually the indented marks were in the form of a series of numbers and letters, which can be deciphered from collector's guides. Sometimes the doll's wig may partially cover some of the relevant details; if so, take great care when gently lifting the wig to reveal the missing parts. On dolls whose head and neck are made together, the manufacture details will often be impressed on the outer side of the shoulder plate, or (more irritatingly) on the inside of the shoulder plate, hidden by the stitched kid body. Wax dolls are seldom identified by the maker, but if identifiable at all the mark would be stamped or signed somewhere on the body rather than on the head.

As the twentieth century progressed, other materials began to be used. Celluloid, invented in 1869, was used in dollmaking from about 1875 and continued well into the twentieth century. After the Second World War vinyl became the commonest medium. Felt was used widely earlier this century once it had been discovered that after treatment it could be easily and permanently moulded. The exponents of this particular process included Lenci, Chad Valley and Norah Wellings, whilst the German company of Steiff produced dolls of stuffed and stitched felt. But Steiff is today much better known as the company which produced the first and most collectable teddy bears.

Group of German dolls made for a doll's house about 1890. They are dressed to look like a family and their servants.

Steiff teddy bear of about 1907, covered in blond plush.

On a hunting trip in Mississippi in 1902 the US President, Theodore (Teddy) Roosevelt, refused to shoot a bear cub – the only game seen. The newspapers cashed in on this story, particularly the *Washington Post* which printed a cartoon which was syndicated across the country. Bears of every type and style became widely popular and toy bears poured into the shops. At the wedding of Roosevelt's daughter in 1906 the tables were decorated with small bears made by Steiff, described by a wedding guest as a new breed of bear called 'teddy bears'.

The bears made up to about the First World War were realistically modelled, with long bodies and comparatively short legs, long arms and feet, a humped back and a long muzzle (p. 18). The fabric was often long-fibred plush in delicately shaded colours, and the bears were produced in a wide variety of sizes from small 6–10 inch ones to giants of 24 inches and over. Stuffed with slim wood shavings and often with a 'voice' or growl mounted inside the chest, these bears made quite fierce additions to the nursery.

As the years passed, the shape of teddies changed quite drastically as they became softer and more cuddly. After about 1910 the limbs began to look much more human, with longer legs and smaller feet. The hump on the bear's back started to shrink, and by about 1920 it had gone entirely. The muzzle became less pronounced and more rounded, and plush in vivid yellows, orange and rusts began to be used increasingly. The plush itself became less lustrous and thick; sparser and sometimes even curly-fibred pelts were used. The wood shaving stuffing was still used extensively up to the 1920s, after which kapok, with its softer, more comforting feel, became more popular.

After Steiff's success other factories in Germany, such as Bing and Schuco, produced bears and soft toys. These companies often made bears with internal clockwork motors which enabled them to somersault or walk. Schuco went on to produce tiny teddy novelties in bright crimson and violet plush; their hinged stomach would open to reveal diminutive powder compacts, or a removable head would conceal a small scent bottle.

Teddies have recently become extremely popular with collectors, particularly if they are very early and have survived in good condition. Usually bears come to me with rather sad faces, their plush worn and their noses pushed to one side where they have been regularly and fiercely hugged; some even carry operation scars, undertaken in sympathy with a young owner who may have once had his or her appendix out! One particular teddy bear was different, though, and fulfilled every criterion of top collectors. Originally bought in 1904 for the grand sum of 19s 6d, he was considered far too expensive for a child to play with and stood in a glass case. Eventually, many years later, he was brought in for auction wearing his original price tag. As a result of his absolutely mint condition and early date of manufacture he realised over £5000 for his lucky owner!

PROVINCIAL SILVER

MICHAEL CLAYTON

Michael Clayton with a Roadshow *customer.*

Top of page *Tazza, made in Ipswich in 1560 probably to hold communion bread.*

When you are a specialist in any subject – I dislike the word 'expert' – you are assumed to know a good deal about it. But you never know it all, and the fascination never palls because somewhere, some day, someone will present you with an oddity – and maybe also a rarity – that breaks all the rules in the world of 'English' silver. This often means something made in the provinces, Ireland, Scotland, or the one-time colonies such as North America, Jamaica, India, Hong Kong or South Africa. All these places had two things in common at some stage in their development: they were a long way from any large urban centre, and the people living there wanted to own up-to-date silver, similar to what they had seen in the houses of others. There is nothing new in wanting to keep up with the Joneses! Consequently there is an amazing variety of provincial silver, good, bad and indifferent objects, some of it even rather old-fashioned either because the silversmith was elderly, or because his client simply wanted a copy of something which was itself old-fashioned.

I have always hoped that one day a really spectacular piece from the provinces or the colonies would appear on the *Roadshow*, but as yet the best – so far as I am concerned – was a Norwich communion cup of about 1570. Like so many ecclesiastical pieces this had been divorced from its church by long years of being 'looked after' in the safe at the 'big house', and eventually forgotten or even given away unknowingly by the squire several generations later, when fashion had changed and perhaps a new cup had been given in place of the one assumed to be lost. This habit of refashioning or replacing both church and secular silver must be remembered when reading inscriptions, because the old inscription was sometimes re-engraved on the new-fashioned piece. Until the nineteenth century it was quite usual to refashion silver and,

A set of three casters for sugar, dry mustard and ginger or pepper, made by Gabriel Felling of Bruton, Somerset, in the sixteenth century.

Chocolate pot by R. Williamson of Leeds, about 1700.

indeed, regard it as an extension of one's bank account. To a certain extent this attitude lingers today, but now it is called buying for investment.

By comparison with the huge quantity of surviving London-made silver, very little provincial silver is still in existence. In terms of quality some items compare very favourably with their London equivalents, and the few sixteenth-century larger pieces even surpass them. Amongst the products of various country silversmiths some particularly fine examples are the magnificent set of three casters by Gabriel Felling of Bruton in Somerset (above). A number of pieces came from Leeds, including a remarkable, though not unique, chocolate pot by one of the Williamsons. Almost certainly made in Chester is the badge of the Company of Smiths given by Prince Arthur, eldest son of Henry VII, in 1499, ostensibly to mark their attention to him when his horse needed a new shoe at short notice. The largest piece of silver made in Chester is a punchbowl of 1686.

Although spoon making, so widespread in the sixteenth and seventeenth centuries, seems to have become the specialist area of production for only a few centres by the eighteenth century, very large basting spoons are to be found from almost all the provincial centres. This is perhaps because in cooking the wear and tear on a tinned or silvered spoon soon revealed the copper interior which,

Coffee pot of about 1720 by Richard Hutchinson of Colchester.

even if it did not poison the food, certainly did not help the flavour. These spoons, 15–18 inches long, are as a result often well worn. They used to form a subject for collecting on their own. Now, sadly, as with so much else their value has rocketed, but they can still be considered both decorative and useful. The production of forks was always very specialised, and although a few rare examples survive from provincial towns during the 1740s, notably Aberdeen, the majority are London-made, with some competition from Exeter and Glasgow during the early 1800s.

Bristol was the second city of the kingdom until the mid-seventeenth century, yet only a handful of spoons survive from earlier than the eighteenth century. Norwich, Chester and York, almost equally important centres, supported thriving guilds of goldsmiths – the name by which silversmiths always liked to be known – and a number of large and important pieces still remain. In contrast Coventry, almost as important, can claim not a single piece. At least one standing bowl of 1570 exists, made in Exeter by Richard Hilliard. Along with Barnstaple, Exeter had the advantage of nearby silver and lead mines; but, truth to tell, enormous quantities of lead and some silver were also found in the Mendip Hills between Bath and Bristol. The proximity to a supply of raw materials also applied to Chester, Edinburgh and Glasgow, where the mines in the Leadhills produced not only silver but gold as well. Thus the Earl of Morton presented the King of France with 'a very fair deepe bason of naturall gold gotten within this Kingdom of Scotland' (undoubtedly made more attractive by being filled with gold pieces). The crown of Scotland, remodelled by James Mossman in Edinburgh in 1540, has always been said to be of gold from the same source. There were also lesser mines available to York, but certainly not to Norwich – yet it is from this city that the largest and finest pieces survive, dating from the sixteenth century.

Like London, Norwich was a great commercial centre, relatively close to the Continent and receptive to many of the latest fashions. Ipswich, Hull and Newcastle all traded with the Continent, though the silversmiths of Ipswich had succumbed by the late seventeenth century to competition from Norwich and London, leaving a few local men such as Richard Hutchinson in Colchester making a precarious living in the 1730s. During the Middle Ages Bury St Edmunds must have been a thriving centre: like other monastic towns it would have encouraged the production of devotional objects and, almost certainly, secular ones also for sale to pilgrims.

Strangely, whilst the Reformation and Henry VIII's need for ready cash worked to the detriment of the vast treasures of the monasteries (already considerably depleted by politically adroit sacristans during the previous twenty years), it also contributed to the wellbeing of those opportunist goldsmiths prepared to undertake the conversion from chalice and paten to communion cup and cover, following various royal decrees during the reigns of

This communion cup made by Lawrence Stratford of Dorchester in about 1575 has typical Elizabethan decoration.

Elizabeth I and James I. A number of goldsmiths, such as the Gilbert family in Ipswich, Lawrence Stratford in Dorchester and William Mutton in Chester, seem to have made a corner for themselves in this 'replacement' church plate. Mutton was fiercely Protestant – perhaps he really enjoyed breaking and melting the 'Papist' cups of his predecessors – but he certainly got bored with producing identical cups for every parochial client, and the variety of decoration and detail on his products is remarkable. Exeter and York made the most of these same opportunities, and large numbers of these communion pieces remain.

The majority of pieces surviving from the sixteenth and early seventeenth centuries, either from London or the provinces, are spoons. Barnstaple, in particular, specialised in a peculiar form known as a 'Buddha' knop. This strange, half-female finial may owe its origin to a misinterpretation of a Continental original, or be a debased form of the 'maidenhead' or virgin spoon. York also produced spoons, some of which survive; likewise Edinburgh, though with regional variations. None the less, it is not until after the Civil War of 1642–6 that surviving pieces of wrought provincial plate are found of the sort which we might see on the *Antiques Roadshow*. These can take many forms, but the majority have some sort of connection with eating and drinking, more often the latter, and include jugs, mugs, tankards, beakers and tumbler cups – at the Peterborough *Roadshow* in 1986 we saw one of these tumbler cups.

So far I have only talked about those pieces which can be ascribed to particular centres, but there are many other towns and cities which undoubtedly supported silversmiths of whom we know no more than their names. Yet there are pieces still extant, with as yet unidentified marks, which it may one day be possible to ascribe to a particular silversmith, maybe from some previously unconsidered centre. For example, there are still in existence a pair of silver-mounted drinking horns made in Chesterfield in 1574. Sadly these have no marks at all, but they remain with the family for whom they were made. Perhaps the family papers may one day reveal the name of that sixteenth-century goldsmith.

Another major city was Lincoln, and during the Middle Ages so was Durham. Yet nothing from these centres survives, although Lincoln was at one stage credited with the mark of a fleur-de-lys. Durham, the centre of a semi-autonomous prince-bishopric and thus a County Palatine (like Chester) with mighty lords nearby at Lumley, Raby and Middleham, had every reason to support at least one full-time silversmith. However it is from Newcastle-upon-Tyne and Gateshead, not Durham, that a steady stream of silver proceeds during the late seventeenth and early eighteenth centuries, and quite possibly may also have done so from earlier times.

The great noblemen close to the court, the source of fashion, would not have cared for 'provincial' workmanship, though their

CARE AND REPAIR

~

For silver and silver plate

- Don't use abrasive silver polishes.
- Don't over-polish or polish too often, or you will wear the silver away. Take special care with hallmarks.
- Use a soft toothbrush to polish corners, decorative details and awkward bits.
- When polishing silver mounts, e.g. on tea caddies, don't get polish on the wood or other surfaces.
- After cleaning, wash silver thoroughly, ensuring that no chemicals remain inside hollow handles etc.
- Don't put silver in a dishwasher. Wash in hot soapy water and dry with a soft cloth. Never immerse knife handles.
- Contact with salt, rubber bands or plastic damages silver.
- Store in acid-free tissue paper.
- Leave a sugar cube in silver tea or coffee pots to absorb metallic odours.
- Dents can easily be repaired by a specialist.

household stewards may have found it necessary to order copies of pieces needed in a hurry without recourse to the Laird. This is especially so as one travels north to the Border and Scotland, where in most areas communications were still difficult even in the early nineteenth century.

So far as Ireland was concerned, Dublin produced magnificent silver, fully up to the standards of London, until the mid-eighteenth century. After that time the quality declines somewhat, though the richness of decoration and almost ridiculous weight of metal employed, particularly during the economic crises of the early nineteenth century, defy rational explanation – a very Irish situation. During the eighteenth century Cork (the last port of call *en route* to America) supported a number of silversmiths, and silver was also manufactured in Kinsale, Limerick, Galway and Belfast. The sad economic and political history of Ireland explains the lack of more eighteenth-century provincial survivals. English settlers and absentee landlords did not usually order their plate in Ireland, and if they did it was in Dublin, where they clustered about the court of the Viceroy. Yet it is from Ireland that one finds more gold snuff boxes marking the gift of the freedom of a city than from anywhere else in the British Isles. Indeed, if one includes these boxes there are probably more wrought gold pieces from Ireland than from England and Scotland.

Solid gold is very rare (silver gilt is not), and fewer than one hundred pieces survive from earlier than 1800. A number of these were race prizes, usually simple so that the recipient obtained the maximum 'weight of bullion' with as little as possible lost upon cost of fashion (workmanship). Because the local silversmith tended to be given old-fashioned pieces to melt and rework (which were seldom gold), most of the larger surviving gold objects are of London origin. Quite often the earlier ones bear only a maker's mark, on the doubtful ground that being special commissions (and this was also argued for silver) they did not need to be submitted for assay at the nearest 'hall'. This logic also avoided any duty due to the Crown!

Proximity to an approved Goldsmiths' Hall was a very real problem for many a provincial maker until the mid-eighteenth century. The ancient centres, fully aware of their declining influence as the new manufacturing towns of Sheffield and Birmingham grew up, were very jealous indeed of the old-established rights of assay (from French *essayer*, to try). They fought hard to have Parliament reject the petition of these two emerging centres, who wanted assay offices of their own because of the inconvenience of sending pieces to London, Newcastle or Chester, not to mention the problem of security in the days when hijacking by highwaymen was a very real possibility. In the end offices were set up in both towns in 1773. The committee concerned met at the Crown and Anchor tavern in London. Was it chance that Sheffield chose a crown as its mark, leaving Birmingham – in the very centre

William III tankard hallmarked at Norwich, 1701.

of England – with a most unsuitable anchor? York, having revived its assay office in the 1770s, soon faded away. Chester hung on until 1962, but from 1870 relied almost entirely upon Birmingham manufacturers, who found that the public would pay a little more for Chester-marked silver than for that from 'Brum'.

In Scotland the heyday of provincial silver seems to have been during the first decades of the nineteenth century, most often for fiddle pattern table silver. The silversmiths – once thought to be itinerant tinkers – of Dumfries, Greenock, Paisley, Dundee, Montrose, Perth, Arbroath, Banff, Inverness, Tain, Thurso and even further north all supplied a steady demand for these pieces. Very occasionally they made something larger, such as a quaich (a Scottish drinking bowl), a wine funnel, a cake basket or, very rarely, a gold presentation box, for which they probably demanded the equivalent weight in gold guineas before they would even begin the work. Glasgow, Edinburgh and Aberdeen were, of course, considerable centres and, until the Act of Union of England with Scotland in 1707, Edinburgh silver was fully equal to that of London and Dublin.

The manufacture of porcelain on the Continent during the 1740s had a serious effect upon silver products. Changing habits such as the drinking of tea, coffee and chocolate rather than beer or ale amongst the 'silvered' classes caused a further decline in demand for such things as large jugs and tankards. Tea and coffee pots, which had been produced in huge numbers during the first half of the eighteenth century – even from towns as far apart as Banff and Liverpool – suffered from the porcelain competition, so much so that by the middle of the century silver teapots were quite uncommon.

However, porcelain was equally expensive, and it was breakable. In time the pendulum seems to have swung back again, so that by 1775 the silver teapot was once again all the rage. At least one pair (for black and green tea) were made in York in the 1780s, and a number of tea caddies are also known from Glasgow, Aberdeen and Chester. Glass had the same effect on the production of spirit or dram cups; silver beakers were ousted by glass tumblers. Salt cellars, like table silver, were very largely made by a few London specialists, and provincial examples are comparatively rare. Most provincial makers were called upon to make baluster-shaped casters (for sugar, pepper and dry mustard) from time to time, and occasionally whole sets with cruet frames; examples are known from both Aberdeen and Chester. Dishes and plates, together with covered vegetable dishes and soup tureens, were only rarely produced outside London, although sauce boats are known from Newcastle and a very specialised circular form, with its handle at right angles to the lip spout, was made in Exeter. This centre also produced some particularly fine teapots and coffee pots, often the work of Pentecost Symonds during the reigns of George I and II. Brandy saucepans were popular everywhere!

Beaker by Thomas Dare II of Taunton. Despite showing the date 1646 it was made in about 1665.

Tortoiseshell chest containing three George III silver tea caddies, made by David Smith and Robert Sharp, London, 1763.

Eighteenth-century mounts for swords and occasionally pistols are found from a number of Scottish burghs; they were usually direct copies of the normal weapon of the day. Scots regalia, plaid brooches, even sporrans and dirks were widely made, especially after the visit of George IV to Scotland in 1822.

Improved communications worked against the local man, as did the competition from the relative mass production of Birmingham and Sheffield during the late eighteenth century. This was especially true once Sheffield plating – carried on in Birmingham by Matthew Boulton on an even greater scale – came into common use from 1760; it meant that more and more the local man was obliged to order up pieces from such centres rather than make them. Edinburgh makers, and even some Londoners, were not above overstriking the Birmingham or Sheffield hallmarks. Indeed Mr Lothian of Edinburgh wrote to Mr Boulton in Birmingham in such wise that he received the following reply: 'You ask us to supply unmarked plate [the eighteenth century referred to silver like this]. This is, of course, against the law, but we will always try to oblige a client!' Most so-called Edinburgh-marked candlesticks, and those from Glasgow, of the late eighteenth and early nineteenth centuries bear marks which are double struck and rather blurred! In short, provincial makers could only survive where communications were poor and while mass production remained a thing of the future. By 1840 this was no longer so. The railways were about to cause an upheaval greater even than the canals had done previously. Provincial silver making had died.

TEA CADDIES

JOHN
BLY

From a collection of tea caddies you can see all the changes in design which occurred during the eighteenth and nineteenth centuries. You can plot our social history over three hundred years and trace the development and decline of materials like china or papier mâché – or you can simply keep tea in them.

I am glad to say that at least one tea caddy is brought in to every *Roadshow*, and among the best I have ever seen was one decorated with filigree and contained within its original case; it was a box inside a box. The result was a state of nearly perfect preservation, and the colours and gold edges to the decoration were quite dazzling. Unfortunately, I got so wound up with excitement that my long and thorough history of the tea caddy ended up on the cutting room floor. So, to make amends, here it is.

One of the first records of tea is in a letter dated 1613, sent from one agent of the East India Company to another in China requesting 'a pot of the best sort of chaw'. Known to us firstly as 'chaw', in China as 'teka' and in other Eastern countries as 'tee' or 'tay', it was first drunk in England for its medicinal qualities – it was said to be good for 'clearing the sight and expelling infection'. Also recommended for a hangover, it was mentioned by Samuel Pepys, who records that his wife made tea on the advice of the potticary (chemist), who claimed it was 'good for her cold and defluxions'.

Because of heavy duties and shipping costs, tea was extremely expensive. In 1665, a Mr Thomas Garway advertised that he had tea for sale from 16s to 50s a pound. Lord Bristol's 'Expence Book' for 1690 contains an entry that reads: 'Paid to Medina ye Jew for a tea-table and two pairs of china cupps, £10.00' and later '£2.00 for half pond [pound] of Kieser tea'. By 1719 the cost of East India Company tea had gone down to about 85p a pound, but this was still very expensive. However, despite these fantastic prices – or

Top of page Nineteenth-century buhl caddy with brass and tortoiseshell marquetry.

Opposite Collectable tea caddies representative of the late eighteenth and early nineteenth centuries. The most desirable is the pear-shaped caddy.

CARE AND REPAIR

— ∿ —

- For polishing wooden caddies, see pp. 16–17.
- Keep tortoiseshell away from sunlight, which destroys its colour and surface, and wipe very occasionally with almond oil to enhance appearance. Repairs are for experts only.
- Don't wet mother of pearl inlay.
- Use nothing but a soft dusting brush on buhl. For any other work seek expert advice.
- Polish Tunbridge ware with good wax polish. Repairs are best left to specialists.
- Don't wet enamel. Dust with a soft brush, and leave all repairs to specialists.
- Damaged or missing wooden veneer is usually best repaired by specialists.
- For ivory see p. 137.
- For papier mâché see p. 116.
- For silver see p. 29.

perhaps because of them – tea drinking became part of the every-day round in high social circles. The Duchess of Lauderdale was one of the first ladies to give tea parties for her friends, and records show that in 1679 her private closet at Ham House in Surrey contained a carved and gilt tea table and a Japan box holding tea and sweetmeats.

The word 'caddy' is actually a corruption of 'catty' (the Malayan *kati*), which is a measured amount of tea weighing about about $1\frac{1}{3}$ lb. The tea was packed into containers which, when full, weighed one *kati*, and a number of these were then packed into a chest. This chest is one of three main types of tea container which we now collectively call caddies.

In chronological order, the first is the tea canister, a bottle-type holder in tin, pewter, silver or china; generally speaking, it was rectangular in shape with a turret top. Sometimes the whole top panel, turret and all, was made to slide off. Alternatively, the bottom panel could be removed. This was for easy filling; for emptying you merely took the top off the turret.

The second type is the tea chest, some of which were made to contain two or three canisters, together with sugar nips, mote spoon and teaspoons. The mote spoon, another collectable object, has a pierced bowl about the same size as a teaspoon at one end and a spiked barb at the other. The pierced bowl acts as a strainer when removing motes of tea from the surface of the cup, and the spike is used to clean the leaves from inside the teapot spout.

The third type is the caddy itself, which is basically any tea box. By the time the word was adopted late in the eighteenth century it could be of any shape, material or size. It is to this vast selection that most of the existing examples belong today. Because tea was still an expensive luxury these caddies were always kept locked.

In the 1750s, Chippendale's *Gentleman and Cabinet-Maker's Director* showed designs for tea chests and caddies which were made in huge numbers. For this reason, it is still possible to buy a totally genuine, if small, piece of eighteenth-century furniture in the Chippendale style for a surprisingly low price. The most popular is rectangular, often in mahogany, the edges carved with a quarter section moulding known as a 'caddy moulding', and with a hinged lid which had a cast and gilt metal handle. The whole thing stands on four small bracket feet, either straight-cornered or curved in ogee form – the latter would be a slightly up-market version. The next stage in luxury is one of these caddies with a secret drawer which slides out from the side at the base. Best of all is one with bombé sides – looking rather like a rectangular or square baluster. At this period the chests containing canisters are often of shagreen, a type of leather or fine morocco; the best have silver mounts at each corner, silver feet and handle, and a silver escutcheon round the lock. More rarely the chest may be deco-rated with either tortoiseshell or ivory, and rarer still is enamel (opposite).

Enamel casket containing three matching caddies, made in south Staffordshire about 1770.

Enamelling is similar in appearance to porcelain, with the benefit of a metal foundation. This is either an alloy or a metal such as copper, bronze, silver or gold, which is dipped and fired repeatedly until the required thickness of enamel is reached. In England painted enamel objects were produced in great numbers in the Midlands, particularly in Bilston, Wednesbury and Birmingham. Some were made at Liverpool, and for a short while, from 1753 to 1756, at a factory in York House, Battersea, London. Like porcelain, enamel is fragile and is prone to damage over the years. Condition is important, and values are high, so always get specialist advice when buying or selling, particularly before having enamel restored; an ancient break is much better than a bad repair.

Two important guides to the age and provenance of a caddy are the feet and the metal mounts. Most tea chests had little feet — either wooden bracket feet or metal ones of ball and claw, or animal foot, pattern. If no feet were intended, the underneath had a baize covering. On the better examples, this was always inset slightly from the outer edge, with a narrow strip of wood creating a border, so the edges of the material didn't show when the caddy stood on the table. Always check for signs of original feet having been removed. There may be discoloration where the wood and glue of a bracket foot would have kept the surface fresher and paler than the rest, or small screw holes which would have oxidised and gone black where metal feet were screwed on. Also check that the feet are original. A border for a felt base or signs of a material covering would indicate that they are not.

During the last quarter of the eighteenth century feet were used less and less as the shape of caddies became more varied. They were round, elliptical, octagonal and hexagonal as well as rectangular and square, and as the shapes became more influenced by Classical designs the surfaces were inlaid or painted rather than carved. Inlay of the Adam period marked a revival of the seventeenth-century practice of marquetry, with formal swags, festoons and oval panels created out of the exotic timbers now being imported. Satinwood, rosewood, kingwood, zebra, coromandel, thuya and amboyna were all employed, sometimes in their natural state, sometimes dyed to a range of colours. It is hard to believe how bright the marquetry was until you find a panel inside a lid or compartment where no light has eroded the startling yellows, greens, reds and blues.

The use of exotic veneers was extended to all types of furniture, and I remember many years ago a well-known dealer and close friend buying a wonderful table, the top of which was decorated in this way. It was such a fine example that he placed an advertisement with a photograph of the table in one of the trade magazines, stating that he wished to purchase similar period furniture 'decorated with erotic veneers'. This naturally prompted much hilarity, but only two replies. One was from someone wishing to sell such a table, and another from a colleague who said he had no such erotic furniture, but could offer a cup of tea and a suggestive biscuit any time he cared to call!

One type of caddy that turns up surprisingly regularly is the sort finely decorated with curled paper or filigree. The finest examples of these date from between 1780 and 1800, but some poorer-quality ones were made up to the late Regency period. The effect was achieved with strips of paper, some coloured, all with a gilt edge and about ¼ inch wide. These strips were curled as if between finger and thumb into spring-like coils to create ovals, rounds, formal borders and frames, as well as foliate stems and flowers. They were stuck edgeways on to the surface of the caddy and the corners and edges were built up to the level of the paper with wood or ivory mouldings. Oval panels of porcelain, ivory and enamel were sometimes incorporated into the design, and I have seen several on which the filigree has been protected with thin glass, retained by the corner moulding.

Tea caddy decorated with curled paper filigree in the style popular between about 1790 and 1810.

Interior of a rosewood tea caddy of about 1830, showing compartments for different kinds of tea and a glass bowl.

Tortoiseshell and mother of pearl were two other materials used as veneers to great effect. When backed with different colours, tortoiseshell can be made to look green, yellow, red and brown, of which green is the most sought after at the moment.

Ivory was applied in smallish pieces, usually strips, and interspersed with black beading. Eighteenth-century ivory caddies are rather small and charming and, like green tortoiseshell, very much in demand.

A gift of a box of tea was always welcome, particularly if it came in a pretty caddy, and without doubt the most novel caddies of the period are in the form of fruit, turned and carved out of appropriate timber. These apples and pears can command a very high price today, but beware – they were desirable objects before other caddies became collectable, and were therefore copied long enough ago for the fakes to have acquired a convincing patina. As well as applewood for an apple and pearwood for a pear, sycamore and burr beech were often used to make plum and melon shapes. During the nineteenth century they remained popular and were made with the advantage of steam power, which allowed harder woods such as lignum vitae and boxwood to be used. The best ones will have some of the original colour, like a rouged apple or yellow-green on a melon. Any damage such as a broken stalk can detract quite considerably from the value, and this is one kind of caddy you should not try to repair yourself.

A development of tortoiseshell came after 1815, when a French marquetry cutter, Louis Gaigneur, came to London and revived the French art of buhl (p. 32), so named after the eighteenth-century master of the craft, André Charles Boulle. It comprised the use of brass and tortoiseshell, and later rosewood, cut like marquetry; a sheet of each material was prepared and glued one to the other; a design was then cut through it with a jig saw and the two

Bow-fronted tortoiseshell caddy of about 1820.

separated, creating two panels of design, one with brass background and tortoiseshell pattern, and the other vice versa. This bright and attractive effect immediately became popular for small objects for the dining, writing and dressing table, as well as for larger items of furniture. It retained its popularity until the 1860s.

The 1820s saw a great change in the shape of tea caddies. The sides tapered in and down from the waist and feet returned to the corners of the rectangular body. These feet were usually of stamped and gilded brass in the form of lions' paws, or of turned and ebonised wood. Ring handles were added to the sides rather than the top and were made either of stamped brass in the form of a basket of fruit, or of turned wood.

Mahogany with ebonised stringing, or slightly later walnut, were the most popular woods for tea caddies before 1835. These caddies usually hold two or sometimes four well-fitting boxes, which are sometimes marked G and B for Green and Bohea tea. In the centre is a space for one or two glass bowls, which are usually considered to be provided for blending the tea (p. 37). I say that with some reservation, because on one occasion I had just finished explaining the use of the blending bowl to a *Roadshow* customer when a colleague came up and showed me a cabinet-maker's price list of 1910, in which a list of optional extras for a tea caddy included a glass bowl 'for sugar'!

The teapoy (opposite) is the next stage of caddy, although strictly speaking this has come about only through association. We think of a teapoy as a tea chest on legs, containing up to four boxes and two bowls, whereas the earliest references to teapoys describe a 'small three legged table or stand or any tripod'. George Smith's book *Household Furniture*, published in 1808, contains a design for a teapoy which is a small occasional table on centre column support and platform base, 'used in drawing rooms to prevent the company rising from their seats when taking refreshments'. Being used for refreshments and having a name like 'teapoy', the association is not hard to understand. The item we think of as a teapoy is similar to worktables of the period, and both these and tea caddies were ideal subjects for the papier mâché maker and japanner.

As early as 1778 Horace Walpole purchased a papier mâché tea chest for just over £3, which was really quite a lot of money. Papier mâché caddies conformed in shape and decoration with the rest and remained popular until the decline of the papier mâché industry at the end of the nineteenth century.

There is a tremendous gap in value between the unusual, desirable caddy and the plain, rectangular boxes made in their thousands between the 1790s and the 1870s. But there is one type which is both plentiful in supply and for the most part fairly solid in price – the Tunbridge ware caddy. Tunbridge ware is characterised by a decorative surface treatment in wood which originated in Tunbridge Wells. It looks like mosaic, with pictures and borders created out of thin fragments no bigger in section than a matchstick. The effect was achieved by gluing together an arrangement of thin sticks so that the ends showed the desired pattern, rather like letters through a stick of rock. The whole block was then cut by a machine similar in principle to a bacon slicer, and the resulting flakes were glued to the object to be decorated. The unique aspect of Tunbridge ware is that only naturally coloured woods were used; they were not dyed. Such woods as barberry and nutmeg as well as native oak and imported purplewood, brazil orange, zebra and ebony were the most popular.

Any caddy with a Tunbridge ware picture of an ancient building is very desirable. Some flower panels also are good news, but beware of paying or expecting too much money for the type that has two bands like ribbon running across the top down the front and back. These are attractive pieces with which to start a collection, however, because there are too many of them about to be very valuable and expensive yet.

Of all the charming stories I have heard, one of the best concerned a tea caddy made in about 1835 in the form of a miniature pedestal sideboard. The top of each end 'cupboard' opened to disclose F and G (Fine and Green) tea canisters, and the centre space contained a bowl. There is always conjecture over these small pieces of furniture – were they travellers' samples or apprentice pieces? The answer is long enough for a chapter on its own, but this particular caddy was made in the north of England, where, the owner claimed, when furniture was commissioned for a newly married couple a miniature of one of the pieces was made as a gift from the manufacturers to be presented to the bride at the wedding. The one I was looking at was a family treasure, traceable back to that happy wedding day over 150 years ago, and utterly impossible to value.

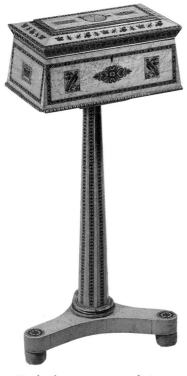

Tunbridge ware teapoy dating from about 1830.

JEWELLERY

JAMES COLLINGRIDGE

James Collingridge examines a piece of jewellery brought in to the Roadshow.

On the *Roadshow* I never cease to be amazed at the conglomeration of items that have accrued over the years in people's jewel boxes, in particular those that have been bequeathed by older members of the family. Those little boxes can contain everything from old buttons to diamonds. On one occasion I found a carved green bead which to the owner's astonishment was an emerald, and later sold at auction for £2700.

Buttons have small value except in sets (usually of six). However, it is worth bearing in mind that if they are made of precious metal and of good design, a pair can always be turned into earrings or cufflinks, and a single one possibly adapted to a ring top, tie pin or pendant.

Inevitably, at the bottom of the jewel box I will find one or more of the small silver brooches that were mass-produced at the end of the last century. Machine stamped and normally hand-decorated, they bear the fashionable names of the era or 'Mother', 'Baby', 'Forget Me Not' and other endearments, including the ever-popular 'Mizpah', a Hebrew word translated as 'God watch between me and thee when we are absent from each other.' These were originally designed for sale as cheap jewellery to factory girls, and cost only a few pence when new. They still do not have any great commercial value since there are thousands of survivors. However, for those who are interested they can form the basis of a reasonably priced collection.

No jewel box would be complete without the usual tangle of chains and pendants, the majority of which date from the Edwardian era. As a rule they are stamped in light and airy scroll designs in 9 carat gold and set with semi-precious stones or sometimes coloured glass. Whilst mass-produced, they have of late become quite popular and frequently sell in the region of £100 at auction.

Top of page A mid-nineteenth-century cameo.

That so much mourning jewellery should continue to turn up is hardly surprising. One only has to read the inscriptions on the various pieces, and indeed on eighteenth- and nineteenth-century gravestones, to realise that in those days of limited hygiene and unsophisticated medicine death was ever present, even for the very young. Although most memorial jewellery which appears on the *Roadshow* is from the nineteenth and late eighteenth centuries, the practice seems to have started in the seventeenth century and occasionally an early item is brought in, usually decorated with a skull and crossbones or of coffin shape (known as a memento mori). These are hardly in today's taste – and I would say, with some hesitation, strictly for the collector. The reason for my hesitation is that once on a phone-in programme I made a sweeping statement that mourning jewellery was out of fashion and no longer worn, only to be told that the enquirer wore her brooch every day! Much wiser now, I realise that, provided one can overlook their associations, even the pieces constructed entirely of plaited human hair are extremely well made and a great deal has gone into their design – in particular items such as long drop earrings. Not for my taste are bracelets and necklaces, although these often have exceptionally good gold clasps and terminals.

Look at any Victorian portraits or early photographs, and at the throats of the high-necked dresses of the period, and you will notice large mourning brooches. Sought after today, they were usually made in gold or, for the less well-off, in rolled gold. For the most part they were decorated in black enamel with a locket inset into the back – intended not for a photograph or portrait but rather for a lock of the loved one's hair. Often, where a hair locket was originally set in front, it has been removed by a twentieth-century owner and replaced with a gemstone. In the late eighteenth and early nineteenth centuries lockets and pendants were inset with miniatures on one side and a plaited lock of hair on the other. Sometimes the hair was arranged in a spray interspersed with seed pearls against a background of opal glass. The second half of the century saw the introduction of photography, and miniatures were replaced with hand-coloured photographs.

It was the practice of the rich to make a bequest leaving a memento of a ring to the bereaved. This would be in the form of a gold band enamelled in black with the deceased's name, age and date of death. Sometimes this appears in the form of engraving on the inside of the ring, presumably to cut the cost of enamelling. I have always been fascinated by such details, and though on the whole they do not have any bearing on value, they do make an interesting study. Of course any association with a historical event or famous person would have an important bearing on the value.

Whilst mainly black enamel was used, and obviously pandered to the morbid taste of our forebears, one occasionally comes across white enamel mourning jewellery. This was intended to signify the virginal state of the unmarried, and from the point of

Victorian black mourning brooch set in gold with pearls.

Nineteenth-century gold and enamel pendant, set with chrysolite and a central garnet.

CARE AND REPAIR
—— 1 ——

○ Keep all jewellery in a compartmentalised, padded box or roll, and never let one piece rub against another.
○ Wind chains and pendants around a piece of paper to keep them unkinked and untangled.

See also p. 44.

view of wearing these pieces are perhaps more in keeping with today's styles.

Mourning rings are commonly hallmarked, bearing the same date letter as the silver of any given year, and so can be precisely dated. However, many of the other items do not have distinguishing marks and can be made of either gold or rolled gold. It does take quite a lot of experience to spot the difference between gold and rolled gold, and it is always wise to take advice. It is tragic to come across a brooch that has been taken to a back-street jeweller for testing, and a large piece scraped off for nitric acid to be applied, when, to the experienced eye, the item is so obviously rolled gold. The way the test works is that the acid will not attack the gold. As rolled gold is a form of gold plating on base metal, it is necessary to remove part of the surface by scraping before applying the acid. Once applied, the acid will attack the base metal and does leave some damage, however carefully done. Since most of the gold used in the last century was surface treated, either way such a test can ruin a whole piece. The surface treatment consisted of dipping the item in an acid bath containing saltpetre and water to burn off the other constituents in the gold alloy. This resulted in a texture of fine gold on the surface, which gives the item a lovely bloom and its character, but is often mistaken by the uninitiated as brass. Mercury gilding was also used in the last century, producing a similar effect. As the fumes given off by this treatment caused the early demise of most of the workmen, however, this method of gilding was outlawed. Most of the brooches produced in the middle of the last century were treated in this way and are chunky in appearance, although light in weight. The fashion of the time dictated that they were decorated with wirework and granulations and invariably had a locket for hair or a portrait in the back. They are quite commonly found in a fitted case with matching earrings, termed a demi-parure, and are highly sought after today.

Earrings are always very much in demand. Those dating from the last century would have been for pierced ears, and any Victorian earrings with screw tops have invariably been adapted. This does of course detract from their value. Most ear clips date from the 1920s and at present are not quite as popular at auction as the long drops of the Victorian era.

Most costume jewellery, as the name implies, was never intended to be worn as anything other than fashion jewellery. That made in the late nineteenth or early twentieth centuries has little or no resale value, unless it is by a known maker. Usually constructed of stamped and gilded metal and set with glass, it is very subject to chafing in a jewel box. Some of the earlier paste-set items, however, can bring as much at auction as the pieces they are intended to simulate.

A valuation day always brings with it a crop of pearls which fall into three categories – imitation, cultured and natural. The first, as with costume jewellery, have little or no resale value. High prices

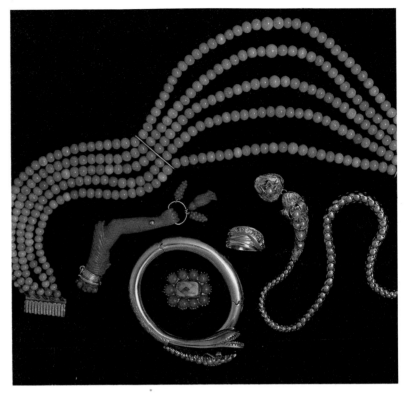

Right *A selection of gold and coral Victorian jewellery.*

Below *Early twentieth-century fob watch in a gold and enamel case set with pearls, valued more highly as jewellery than as a watch.*

can be paid for natural pearls. However, the mediocre will realise very little more than their cultured pearl counterparts. Arguments often arise regarding natural and cultured pearls. The experienced eye can frequently detect the difference, but on occasion it is necessary to refer pearls to a laboratory for X-ray testing.

The reason for this is that the outer skin or nacre of both the natural and cultured pearl is identical. A pearl is formed by an irritant within the oyster, which will then cover the irritant with a thin coating of nacre and continue to do so throughout its life. Obviously the longer the irritant is within the oyster, the bigger the pearl will become; and the more the coating, the better the quality of the pearl, provided that it is even and not misshapen (known as baroque). Having discovered this, the Japanese – it is in Japan that most of the cultured pearls originate – decided to cut short the length of time it takes to form a pearl by inserting into the oyster a mother-of-pearl bead of a similar material to the pearl. It only differs by the grain, which is straight, whereas that of the pearl is concentric. This shows up quite clearly under X-ray. In a lesser-quality cultured pearl – one that has not been left in the oyster for a long time – the outer layer of skin is relatively thin and can wear off, revealing the mother-of-pearl core. However, in a natural pearl the layers are the same throughout. Most imitation pearls are hollow glass beads coated on the interior with a substance made from fish scales.

CARE AND REPAIR
2

○ Cameos are easily cracked, so keep them away from other jewellery and avoid extremes of temperature.
○ Diamonds can chip and crack, so don't bang your rings down hard, and avoid extremes of temperature.
○ Keep amethysts, zircons and opals away from heat, which can crack or fade them.
○ Pearls are improved by contact with the skin.
○ Clean pieces set with diamonds (which attract grease), rubies and sapphires with proprietary jewellery cleaner (or gin if you can bear to!)
○ Don't put pearls, turquoises, opals or any pieces with stones in a closed setting (one with a back) into liquid.
○ All repairs should be professionally done.

See also p. 42.

Art Nouveau belt buckle designed by Archibald Knox for Liberty's, 1904.

Although not particularly hygienic, a very old method employed by traders to test for authenticity is to rub a pearl very gently against one's teeth. Natural and cultured pearls will have a gritty feel, whereas glass beads will be entirely smooth. Sadly, whilst cultured pearls brought the wearing of pearls to the masses, they also had a detrimental effect on the sale of natural pearls, bringing the price down considerably; only the very best now command high prices in the salerooms.

What of the value of jewellery? To the large-bosomed lady who throws out her chest for me to admire a pendant, asking at the same time 'What do you think of this?', it may seem a relatively easy task to arrive at a value. Unfortunately, it is not as simple as all that. Is it old or new? Is it machine- or hand-made? Is it a precious metal, precious stones or imitation? These are some of the things which the jeweller must examine carefully through a magnifying glass.

Having made an assessment, a retail jeweller will take into account what his regular supplier will charge for a similar item, plus his profit margin and value-added tax. An auctioneer will give an opinion on what he feels the item will raise on a given day. All too frequently, having given an opinion, I am informed that I am quite wrong and that the local jeweller has said that the item is worth three or four times as much. The answer is invariably that he has quoted a price at which the piece would sell in the shop window. This can be broken down into manufacturing costs, manufacturer's profit, retailer's profit – which in most cases are more than 100 per cent – and of course value-added tax. Whilst the mark-up price on a piece of jewellery may at first seem excessive, when one takes into account the overheads involved in running a high-risk business it is not really surprising.

Jewellery can be an investment, albeit a long-term one, much as some stocks and shares. In my view it should be bought for the purpose for which it is made: adornment and enjoyment. If you are tempted to buy for investment, as with all other commodities go for the best you can afford and seek the advice of a reputable retailer or auction house.

When the crowds have thinned at an *Antiques Roadshow*, we specialists get a chance to have a word with each other before the long journey home. The standard question crops up, 'Did you see anything good today?' For me it may well not have been a good day in respect of the items that I saw, but as always the characters who came along more than made up for that. The real gem I saw one day was the little old lady who came along with her granny's brooch. Although she was able to tell me more of its history than I could possibly know, she was not the slightest bit concerned about its low value, exclaiming: 'Goodness me, as much as that!', when told it was worth about £50. When your paymaster is the DHSS, a £50 brooch can be worth a lot more to you than a £1 million painting to the owner of a stately home.

ART NOUVEAU

ERIC KNOWLES

Eric Knowles hoping for some good Art Nouveau at the Roadshow's Miscellaneous *table.*

Top of page Modern copies of this WMF *pewter table mirror turn up everywhere, so beware!*

Why is it that whenever the town of Accrington turns up in conversation, back comes the standard retort 'Accrington Stanley'? The next time you hear the name mentioned, forget the football club and say 'Accrington Tiffany.' The reason is that that town in industrial Lancashire houses one of the best-kept secrets of the art world – the finest public collection outside the United States of glass by the American Art Nouveau designer Louis Comfort Tiffany.

The collection was left to the town by Joseph Briggs, a local lad who made good. Briggs left these shores early this century for the United States, where he found employment with the firm of Tiffany – not with the silver and jewellery side of the business, but with the glassmaking and architectural interior design concern. Louis Comfort Tiffany, the head of the company, was then regarded on both sides of the Atlantic as the high priest of taste in the world of decorative and applied arts.

It seems that the two men got on well, and eventually Briggs rose to become an important cog in the Tiffany machine. The march of time, however, waits for no man. Tiffany's company seemed to be entrenched in the spirit of 1900 and, by the arrival of the 1920s and Art Deco, had little in the way of novelty to offer its clients. When the business closed, those items remaining on the shelves which previously had been priced in dollars were sold for the same amounts in cents. Briggs returned to England with an extensive collection, half of which he donated to his native town while giving the other half away to his various relations.

Several years ago I came across one of the family pieces at a valuation day in Nottinghamshire. It was a wall clock composed of a mosaic which included various iridescent and coloured glass segments. The object was possibly the work of Briggs himself, who

Above *Silver and enamel tankard by Archibald Knox, made for Liberty's.*

Above *Gallé cameo glass vase decorated with an iris.*

Opposite *Of all the wonderful objects created by Tiffany, the wistaria lamp is one of the most desirable.*

was known to have worked in the Mosaic Department. The owner confirmed my suspicions regarding its provenance, but stressed that she would never part with it as it was a family treasure. I can only hope that other members of the family are holding and caring for their glass with the same high regard – if not, contact the Haworth Art Gallery and Museum in Accrington now.

Apart from being technically brilliant, Tiffany's creations in glass somehow manage to embody the spirit of Art Nouveau in a way achieved by few of his contemporaries, apart from the notable exception of Emile Gallé. Competition in the United States came from the Steuben and Quezal glassworks, with Handel and Pairpoint chasing close behind, as table lamp manufacturers. In Europe, the Austrian glassworks of Loetz Witwe produced similar iridescent glassware to that sold by Tiffany, and in recent years several examples of this Austrian glass have been mistakenly accredited to Tiffany. I recall one occasion when the initials L.C.T. had been added with the help of a dentist's drill. The world of Art Nouveau contains its fair share of forgeries. I advise you to spend time on getting to know the subject before parting with hard-earned cash.

Tiffany and Gallé glass, and the jewellery of René Lalique, could all be purchased from the Paris shop of the German entrepreneur Samuel Bing. Bing called his gallery, which opened in 1895, Maison de l'Art Nouveau, and it was from this name that the expression Art Nouveau is taken. The term encompasses several styles.

Although the movement became popularised throughout Europe, its roots can be traced to Britain. The French actually described it as 'Le Style Anglais', accepting its origins in the earlier Aesthetic and Arts and Crafts movements. Their own version of the style, however, was based on organic and natural forms, containing elements of fantasy, eroticism and symbolism. The Italians, too, referred to the movement as 'Stile Liberty', after the London retail outlet of Arthur Lasenby Liberty, which was responsible for the promotion of a distinctly English style that had much in common with Arts and Crafts design.

Scottish and Austrian artists and designers, on the other hand, favoured severe, straight lines and a feeling of vertical movement. The Glasgow Four, comprising Charles Rennie Mackintosh, Herbert McNair and the MacDonald sisters, Frances and Margaret, were the chief exponents of Art Nouveau in Scotland. In Austria, and in particular Vienna, the members of the Secession (a breakaway movement unhappy with what they considered to be the state of the visual arts in Vienna) included Josef Hoffmann, Koloman Moser and Joseph Maria Olbrich. Hoffmann and Moser went on to found the Wiener Werkstätte (Vienna Workshops) in 1903, and in so doing helped to sow the seeds of the Modern Movement which eventually was to bear fruit in the form of the Bauhaus (see p. 100), which in turn had a very powerful influence on true Art Deco and indeed much of twentieth-century design.

A wonderfully simple and unfussy electro-plate teapot designed by Christopher Dresser.

The teapot by the English designer Christopher Dresser (above) completely fulfils the ideals of the Bauhaus, in that its construction relates to its function. It was actually made almost forty years before the Bauhaus was opened. In 1876 Dresser visited Japan, where he was heavily influenced by the simplicity of Japanese designs; they were the probable inspiration for this piece. Dresser, who had been designing silver since the 1860s, made designs for a whole range of electro-plated ware for Hukin and Heath, much of which regularly comes up for sale in the London salerooms. When this particular example turned up at a London saleroom it surprised most people, including the auctioneers, by selling for a staggering £36,000. Such a price reflects the newly appreciated importance of Dresser's contribution to late nineteenth- and early twentieth-century applied art. It's the thought that a similar teapot might just wend its way to my table at the *Antiques Roadshow* that keeps me ploughing through the cardboard boxes and carrier bags!

The work of Archibald Knox (p. 46 above) featured on our Edinburgh programme, when we were shown a delightful mantel clock of silver embellished with turquoise and peacock-blue enamel. The clock, which dated from about 1900, was originally retailed by Liberty under their own trade name of Cymric. The owner told me that she had been given it by her grandfather and that she used it as her bedside clock. In his work for Liberty, Knox also borrowed from the Celtic designs of his native Isle of Man.

Not everybody, however, was able to afford silver, and in order to meet the needs of those with tighter purse strings Liberty introduced their range of Tudric pewter. The designs followed those of the Cymric wares, and the range was a huge success; it was manufactured by the Birmingham firm of W. H. Haseler from its inception in 1903 until 1938.

German electro-plated ware and pewter were popularised by the WMF factory. The mirror on p. 45 is identical to one shown on our visit to Carlisle, and illustrates well the Continental adaptation of Art Nouveau with its flowing, curvilinear movement. Although the example shown here is genuine, complete with the ridiculously tiny WMF stamped mark, the market has been flooded with modern copies. But the reproductions shouldn't fool anyone, as there has been no attempt on the part of the manufacturers to 'age' their products. Kayserzinn, made by the German firm of Kayser, was another range of pewterware and many of their forms show a bias towards the organic, with slender stalks evolving from the sides of bowls and vases to form handles. It was after successfully retailing German art pewter that Liberty decided to launch Tudric.

The bronze figure of *Circe* (left) is the work of the Australian sculptor Sir Bertram Mackennal. I first came across her standing on the mantelpiece of a modest terrace house on the outskirts of Oxford, and she remains one of my favourite bronze studies. When *Circe* made her début at the Royal Academy in 1894, the organising committee insisted that the base was covered with red baize. On close inspection, it consists of a mêlée of male and female naked forms in a variety of impossible and meaningful positions which 'jarred upon the susceptibilities of the more old-fashioned members of the profession', to quote a contemporary review! *Circe* belongs to a group referred to today as New Sculpture because it broke the mould of historicism and romanticism so favoured during the Victorian period. Other sculptors whose work comes beneath the same banner include Alfred Lord Leighton, Onslow-Ford, Sir George Frampton and Sir Alfred Gilbert, who sculpted the famous statue of Eros in Piccadilly Circus.

It would be unthinkable not to mention Art Nouveau poster art, and in particular Alphonse Mucha. During this period poster design evolved into a highly sophisticated and individual art form. The popularity of these posters meant that even when new some of them remained up only a few hours before being removed under cover of darkness by contemporary collectors. Nothing was too mundane: cigarette papers, beer and biscuits were all grist to the poster artists' mill. Mucha, a Czech working in Paris, is probably best remembered for his many posters of the popular actress Sarah Bernhardt – whose own work as a sculptress is now considered highly desirable – and for his *Four Seasons*.

My very first *Roadshow* was in Cornwall in 1981. A Cornish farmer had brought in a pair of strange-looking chairs, and despite

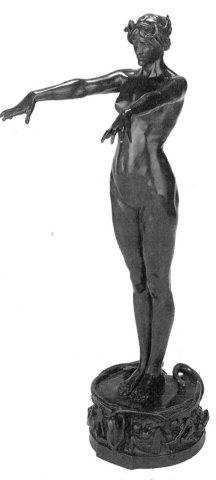

Sir Bertram Mackennal's Circe, *a bronze figure about 2 feet tall.*

A selection of colourfully glazed early twentieth-century pottery by William Moorcroft.

their bedraggled state they were immediately recognisable as the work of Carlo Bugatti (p. 52). The farmer explained that he had found them underneath the stairs and hadn't a clue where they had come from. I told him that Carlo Bugatti was a highly individual Italian furniture designer working around 1900 in a distinctive style close to Moorish. When the cameras had stopped rolling, he said: 'I was pleased to know they're worth a few hundred each', and then went on to add, 'When you were talking just then you pointed out these copper panels at the sides. Well, I must have dug

up a dozen or more in our back field – problem was they were all attached to charred wood.' The awful truth rapidly became clear. Their previous owner had put a set of Bugatti dining chairs on to the bonfire – luckily, at least, he must have forgotten about the pair left beneath the staircase.

Bugatti's work cannot be regarded as typical Art Nouveau, unlike that of the French designers Louis Majorelle, Emile Gallé or Eugène Vallin. All three belonged to the Ecole de Nancy and their work, alongside that of such Parisian designers as Georges de Feure, Edward Colonna and Paul Follot, is typified by the use of undulating, curvilinear lines. The finished products appear sculptural as well as functional. These designers treated wood as a malleable substance with little regard to grain – it would have made any cabinet-maker trained in the old traditions wince.

The Scots and Austrians took a very different approach. The inclusion of stylised shrouded females amongst the furniture and interior design work of the Glasgow Four earned them the title of 'The Spook School'. Mackintosh was fortunate in having a rich clientele, so he was able to put his full talents as both architect and designer to full stretch. His commissions included Miss Cranston's Glasgow tea rooms in 1904 and the design for the British Pavilion at the Turin Exhibition of 1902. His work is best typified by his tall-back chairs, painted or stained, with vertical splats, low seats and stretchers which almost meet the ground. Mackintosh furniture is as rare as hens' teeth, and most of his work is properly documented. If all the furniture attributed to Mackintosh were proved to be his, the poor man would still be busy in his workshop working a twenty-four-hour day!

In the ten years of the *Roadshow* we must have seen hundreds of low-value teasets in Japanese eggshell porcelain. But the Dutch Rozenburg factory in The Hague also made this type of porcelain at the turn of the century. The decoration is often influenced by batik designs from Java, imported by the Dutch East India Company, which are skilfully adapted to the vessel's shape. Rozenburg is considered by many to represent the high-water mark of Art Nouveau ceramics. The wares are clearly marked with the factory name and their trademark of a stork. Don't confuse them with the eighteenth-century products of the J. S. Lyncker factory in The Hague, which also used a stork mark.

William Moorcroft started as a designer for the Macintyre pottery during the final years of the nineteenth century and was responsible for their range of Florianware. It was quite distinctive, the coloured glazes being enclosed by slip outlines to form floral designs which rival any of the Continental creations. Moorcroft went on to open his own pottery, and over the next thirty years continued to design pieces which are recognisable at fifty paces. The factory is still in existence, so the would-be collector should read up about the earlier patterns which are now discontinued, and, if possible, concentrate on the fabulous Florianware.

This chair by the supreme individualist Carlo Bugatti turned up at a Roadshow *in Cornwall.*

Alongside Moorcroft at the top of the tree for good Art Nouveau design in pottery are those wares made by Mintons referred to as Secessionist. Influenced by the Vienna Secession, this range of pottery was mostly designed by John Wadsworth and Léon Solon. The originality of design and combination of glazes, also outlined in slip, offer tremendous scope for the collector. In my opinion they are presently under-appreciated and consequently under-valued, so if you think the price is right – but, more importantly, you like the piece – take my advice and buy it. If you don't, I might be right behind you.

Of all the media available to the craftsman, glass in particular lends itself better than any other to the demands and possibilities of Art Nouveau design. The *Roadshow* has featured glass by both Daum and Gallé on numerous occasions. Cameo glass (p. 46 below), typical of Gallé, was being made as early as the Roman period. Several colours of molten glass are gathered one upon another and then blown to form the hollow shape. After cooling, the upper layers of glass are carved or acid-etched away to the underlying layer to achieve the desired pattern. Many of these vases were industrially produced. Gallé's more celebrated early vases, however, are considered by collectors as creations with supreme sculptural qualities, formed by a craftsman who understood the technical possibilities of glass more than any of his contemporaries, with perhaps one exception – Louis Comfort Tiffany. And that is where we came in.

CARE AND REPAIR
——— ∾ ———
○ For bronze see p. 132.

ENGLISH POTTERY BEFORE 1800

HENRY SANDON

When I was younger, those of us who were interested in and collected early English pottery were thought to be a little eccentric. Pottery was regarded as the poor relation, and while the wealthy collectors would happily pay large sums for a rare piece of gold anchor Chelsea or yellow ground Worcester, they would scorn a piece of delft if it had its usual glaze chips round the rim or a piece of saltglaze or slipware full of quirky, primitive humour.

During the period that the *Roadshow* has been running, one of the most fascinating things has been to see this attitude change, to see the prices realised by fine pottery equal and even surpass those of porcelain. An example, admittedly rather extreme, may make this clearer.

For many years I had known and admired the fascinating salt-glaze pew group study of two wind players on a church bench that was in the wonderful Rous Lench Court collection of English pottery and porcelain gathered together by the late Tom Burn. One of the great joys of my life was to be allowed to handle the group, to laugh at the comical expressions of the figures as they strained to blow a note, with their long, droopy limbs, the three simulated heads carved on the bench behind them and the details picked out with manganese on the dull white saltglaze body. The group was made somewhere around 1740 in Staffordshire, and such pieces are now known to be very rare. Tom Burn had owned the piece some time and loved to tell me its history. It had been bought for £1 in a Nottingham street market, then changed hands a few times, and by the time Tom managed to track it down, in Liverpool, he had to pay £50 for it, quite a sizeable amount in those days for a piece of saltglaze.

In 1986, after Tom Burn's death, part of his collection was sold at Sotheby's to pay death duties. The pew group was knocked

Top of page Staffordshire saltglaze stoneware pew group of two wind players, modelled in about 1740.

down for £102,000, the highest price ever paid for any piece of English ceramics at auction. The Rous Lench Court auction sale was somewhat of a watershed in terms of prices, making all the experts on the *Roadshow* think again when quoting values. No one has yet brought along a pew group to a *Roadshow*, although it could happen, but we do see some amazingly rare pieces that were worthy of being in Tom Burn's collection.

Early English pottery is less plentiful than at one time, but a fascinating collection could still be built up. Roman pottery can be found that was made eighteen or nineteen hundred years ago, and one visitor to the *Roadshow* in Worthing brought in a number of examples that he had found in the ground during roadworks in London. I think he felt we should have put a higher price on the pieces, perhaps thinking that their great age made them extremely valuable. This is one lesson that we try to get over to the public: it is not necessarily age that puts the value up, but rarity, beauty and that indefinable quality of collectability.

Collectors of ceramic antiquities have to be a little cautious, as fakes abound. I will never forget the gentleman who brought in to a *Roadshow* an obviously fake Roman lamp made of modern clay; he was rather put out to be told that it was modern. 'It must be genuine,' he said. 'I bought it by the roadside in Italy, and actually saw the workman dig it up out of the mud.' It was some time before I could persuade him that the workman probably had a pocketful and would have 'found' one in the ground for the next tourist who passed by. Few *Roadshows* go by without someone bringing in a fake Roman glass bottle, made in the Middle East out of melted-down Coca-Cola bottles. Some fakes, of course, become collectable in their own right; one thinks of Billies and Charleys, those fascinating pseudo-medieval pilgrim badges and medallions

Seventeenth-century slipware dish by Thomas Toft.

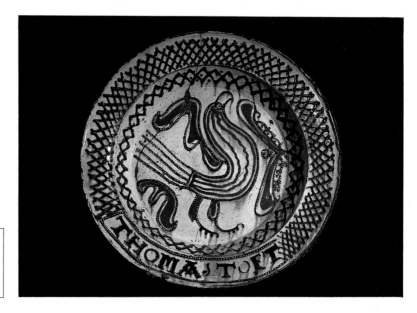

CARE AND REPAIR
———— ∾ ————
○ See pp. 64–5.

Figures like this Staffordshire saltglaze stoneware serving girl of about 1740 are among the most sought-after pieces of English ceramics.

that the two Victorian characters made to sell to keen antiquarians when the London docks were being dug. Like Samson's famous nineteenth-century porcelain reproductions, they are now quite desirable and the day cannot be far off when, as David Battie suggests, the fakers start making fakes of the fakes!

English medieval pottery is not common, as it was made for use and little has survived intact. At its finest – perhaps a wonderfully strong pitcher, thrown on a wheel with the throwing rings proudly left to give growth and vigour, with a good generous handle, and splashes of green glaze running down from the rim – you can understand why many of our present-day craftsmen potters drool over such a piece. Even damaged examples are worth a lot of money now, and they have been conspicuous by their absence at *Roadshows*. However, one may always be brought in to the next recording, so I live in hope.

The great tradition of English slipware – pots decorated with liquid clay of a contrasting colour to the rest of the pot – usually produces an example or two at every *Roadshow*. We do not often see examples of the finest and most collectable dishes, made in Staffordshire in the seventeenth century, with decoration trailed on from a slip trailer, often signed by potters such as Thomas Toft. Nor do we often see the rare pieces from Wrotham in Kent, made of a darker brown clay – such items as the multi-handled tygs or honey pots with applied studs and dots in cream slip, all under a clear lead glaze and sometimes bearing dates. The Rous Lench Court sale had a number of examples of all of these and the prices were pretty high – £46,000 for a dish signed by Thomas Toft, and £6500 for a Wrotham tyg dated 1701.

We frequently have later eighteenth-century examples of slipware brought in – large, round dishes, sometimes with milled-like edges and rounded bottoms, the red clay body trailed with snakes of slip or lines of slip 'feathered' into each other rather like the decorations you sometimes see on cake icing. The rapidly increasing prices of such pieces can quite surprise the owners and, it must be admitted, us as well. Such a piece bought for under £100 five years ago can now be worth £800–1000.

It is always especially interesting doing a *Roadshow* in one of the areas where slipware was made by the local potters. Some fascinating fragmentary pieces were shown to me in Stoke-on-Trent, dug up in the owner's garden. I recommended him to take them in to the local museum for investigation, as they could provide useful information. In Devon a wonderful harvest jug, incised with a humorous verse, was brought in. This had come down through the years to the present owner, a local farmer, and would have been made for serving cider to the farm-hands in the 1770s. It is particularly pleasurable to hold a family piece that has descended through many generations. Do not, however, think that a piece is older than it is just because it has been left to you by Grandma, who may only have acquired it this century.

One warning about slipware. There was one curious potter working at Castle Hedingham in Essex from 1865 to 1905 – Edward Bingham – who delighted in making pseudo-early slipware pots in the style of Wrotham, often with fake dates on them. These are so comically silly that no one should get caught, especially as most examples have the potter's name or the incised castle mark under the base. Perhaps these too will be collectable some day. They certainly turn up when we do a *Roadshow* in Essex, although it often surprises us when no one brings in an example of whatever is the hoped-for local speciality.

Saltglaze stoneware is often brought in to a *Roadshow*. It took a long time for England to start imitating the superb German saltglaze that had been imported from the Rhineland in the Middle Ages. The first production in this country was by John Dwight of Fulham in London in the 1670s, and we have seen examples of his amusing bellarmine jugs on many occasions.

The process of glazing stoneware by salt spread to Staffordshire and Nottingham, the latter area producing a very characteristic shiny metallic brown colour. Most saltglaze has a speckled surface like orange peel. Perhaps the finest example that I have seen at a *Roadshow* was a superb Nottingham loving cup with three handles, intended to be passed round for toasting at a wedding. It bore the original names of the owners, was dated in the 1780s and had the word 'Nottingham' on it as well. This was everything that one could hope for and the descendant who brought it in, after telling me that they had been using it as a jardiniere, was staggered to have a value of £1500 put on it. This was some years ago, and you would have to double or treble that amount now. It is worth mentioning that it was in very good condition; damage on such a piece would reduce its value somewhat.

My favourite piece of saltglaze, apart from the pew group mentioned on p. 53, was a little hollow figurine of a girl wearing a crinoline, perhaps intended to be a bell (p. 55). I remember it being thrust into my hand some years ago during one of the *Going for a Song* television programmes. I put a value of £1500 on it, a reasonable price then. At the Rous Lench Court auction in 1986 the figure came up for sale with an estimate of between £6000 and £9000, a cautious price because it had a small restoration. It was fiercely fought over and was eventually knocked down at £48,000.

Some of the most delightful examples of saltglaze are of the type called 'scratch blue', in which cobalt oxide was rubbed into a bold incised decoration. A fine example of this, a cider jug of about 1760 with a vigorous scene of a strange magical man holding a spear, went for £9500 at the Rous Lench Court sale. Nothing quite as fine as this has ever been brought in to a *Roadshow*, but we frequently see examples of undecorated white saltglaze of the late eighteenth century – perhaps a plate with an attractive modelled border in the style of silver, or pretty milk jugs with perky sparrow-beak spouts – which are not vastly expensive at present.

This seventeenth-century London delftware fuddling cup would have been made as a joke for a gentlemen's club or tavern.

Creamware coffee pot, probably made in Leeds about 1770.

Delftware is frequently seen and, although seventeenth-century examples are now rare, a large number of eighteenth-century pieces can be found. English delft, a pottery body covered with an opaque tin glaze, is a very attractive thing to collect and has a softer glaze than Dutch Delftware, with an unconscious sense of humour in the decoration, which is appealing.

One of the nicest examples of early English delft brought to a *Roadshow* was a large dish with cobalt blue dashes around the rim – known for a long time as blue dash chargers – with a humorous painting in the centre of Adam and Eve in the Garden of Eden. The snake had quite a sneering expression on his face as he proffered an apple to Eve, a buxom lass who had most of her charms covered by her long tresses and a strategically placed fig leaf, while Adam looked totally bemused. The dish was tin-glazed on the front but lead-glazed underneath, generally an indication that it would be from the late seventeenth century or just into the early years of the eighteenth. Like most English delft it had glaze chips around the rim, the fault of the very soft body and glaze; such damage is not too worrying to a collector of delft, although bad cracks or chunks missing and restored would reduce the value greatly.

I have always loved English delft and can see again the great quality of the dishes and jugs that stood on the large oak dressers in Rous Lench Court, where they looked so much at home. Some of the finest were sold in the 1986 auction, and they included an example of the vessel called a fuddling cup made in Lambeth, London, in the mid-seventeenth century (opposite). A fuddling cup consisted of a number of small pots joined together with twisted handles, and the idea was that you gave someone who had already had a bit too much to drink the challenge of drinking just one of the cups filled with strong drink. He thought he could easily do so, but as he drained one cup he did not realise that holes near the bottom of the other two fed all the drink into the one he was drinking from! This particular pot realised only £800, as there was doubt whether a date of 1644 painted on it was genuine – dates on delft were sometimes added much later in an attempt to increase their value.

Other fascinating examples of delft which we see at *Roadshows* are puzzle jugs, with holes pierced through the neck. This again was a puzzle to be solved by an inebriated drinker, who, to avoid drowning himself in beer, had to suck up the liquid through a nozzle which brought it up via the hollow handle, through the rim and into the mouth – provided he covered all the holes except the one spout. Such humour is, of course, rather robust and makes me think of Hogarthian London.

The most expensive auction price for a piece of English delft was paid for a magnificent blue dash portrait charger dated 1666, painted in colours with King Charles II standing in his coronation robes. This was sold for £78,000, and it is a sobering thought that I was once allowed to take the dish to the Birmingham television

studios to show on a programme about royal commemoratives. If you are interested in collecting delft do not be put off by such huge prices, as they only apply to very early, rare pieces, especially if they are unusual-shaped objects. Most of the delft brought in to the *Roadshow* was made in the second half of the eighteenth century, and a blue and white plate would have to be exceptional to be valued at more than £40–50, although nicely coloured ones would be more. Delft blue and white tiles are really amazingly cheap and seldom cost more than £20; coloured or printed ones are more. English tiles generally have chamfered edges and are well worth looking for.

The death-knell of delftware was rung with the development of creamware, a better-wearing body. Josiah Wedgwood made a tremendous success with creamware, calling it Queen's ware after Queen Charlotte. Creamware was made in many different parts of the country and is characterised by being very light in weight as well as creamy in colour. A later development was pearlware, which has a whiter appearance much nearer to that of the porcelain which these bodies were trying to imitate – although they are, of course, opaque pottery. Many examples are brought in to the *Roadshow*, and I am always attracted by the mugs, teapots and coffee pots, sometimes decorated in the Chinoiserie style, sometimes with rather boisterously painted flowers.

Other eighteenth-century bodies that are seen in *Roadshows* are the dry stonewares, ranging from the hard red wares of the early years of the century, that imitated the Chinese, to the basalts and jaspers of the second half of the century that were England's own development. The most famous potter in this field was Josiah Wedgwood, and there is something special about his early works. We are all hoping for one of the First Day vases, made by Wedgwood and his partner Bentley, to be brought in to a *Roadshow*, or even one of the eighteenth-century original versions of the famous Portland Vase.

For me, perhaps the most beautiful eighteenth-century pottery is that in the generic style of the Whieldon factory, either with the wonderful translucent running glazes on a plate, or the fascinating solid agate wares, with the coloured clays blended together, looking like a piece of polished agate. Sometimes we have the pleasure of seeing superb figure subjects by Ralph Wood, coloured with mottled glazes. Especially attractive are his early Toby jugs, on which the coloured glaze effects are so much more beautiful than the late eighteenth-century examples produced by painting in metallic oxides. Growing fast in appreciation are the delightful little animals, such as squirrels and swans, which have a naïve charm. Other popular animal studies are lions and elephants and, most collectable of the lot, creamware horses from Yorkshire with the decoration sponged on to the body in modernistic blotches before glazing. These figures all have vigour and humour, two words which for me sum up eighteenth-century pottery.

Above *Staffordshire model of a cat with a mouse, about 1750.*

Opposite *Diascordium was a popular cure-all in the eighteenth century, and English delft drug jars like this one were used in apothecaries' shops for advertising display.*

EIGHTEENTH-CENTURY CONTINENTAL POTTERY AND PORCELAIN

HUGO MORLEY-FLETCHER

Hugo Morley-Fletcher looks at the marks on a customer's piece of Ironstone.

Top of page Berlin gold-mounted snuff box bearing a portrait of Frederick the Great of Prussia, made in about 1765.

Of all forms of collector's piece, porcelain is the most unchanged by the passage of time. When today we pick up a piece made in Europe in the eighteenth century we see it exactly as it left the kiln and as the potter or manufacturer intended. Sadly, this does not generally apply to paintings, furniture or silver, all of which tend to change colour or wear significantly. Whether you like or dislike what was made two centuries ago, it is fascinating to have an accurate idea of what people used then and what colours and decorative styles were fashionable.

To me the ability to pick up an object is very important. In porcelain and pottery the weight of the piece is often of vital importance. The eighteenth century saw the foundation of almost fifty factories, whose wares were often unmarked. The only way one can tell where a piece comes from is by assessing all sorts of features: its weight, the exact colour of the white, the colours used in the decoration and the style of the modelling. The whole nature of the white is a key feature, for though all porcelain is white, each ware has its own particular cast. To complicate matters further, no two experts or collectors will describe the porcelain or body from a particular manufacturer in precisely the same terms: what is yellowish white to one is greenish white to another.

In almost twenty-five years of working daily with European ceramics I have never ceased to be stimulated and surprised by what was produced during the eighteenth century. From very early in the century until the French Revolution in 1789 the factories turned out a wide and varied range of wares, figures and groups. However many museums I visit, however many *Antiques Roadshows* I attend, I know that I shall never see it all and that there is always something new to discover, some shape I have never seen, some model that I do not know. Sometimes, of course, it is an object lost to the world of ceramic scholarship that one comes across. Two instances stand out particularly.

Invited one evening to look at some pottery in a Chelsea flat, I was kindly offered a drink. As I put the glass down on a small table beside my chair I noticed what looked like a Meissen snuff box. I have always been especially intrigued by porcelain snuff boxes. These portable and very personal objects are frequently the most delicate and carefully decorated things that a factory made. Because they closed and their inside was protected, the interior of the lid was a frequent site for the finest painting a manufacturer could produce. In general, painters were discouraged from signing their work, yet there are several clearly signed snuff boxes.

There was only one problem with the one in the Chelsea flat. It was larger and more richly decorated than any piece I could remember. I picked it up and found I was indeed looking at an exceptional piece (p. 62). The exterior depicted Frederick the Great of Prussia besieging a city and bombarding it with mortars – a remarkable scene. Inside the lid nymphs depicting the Arts paid homage to Prussia, whilst Arithmetic held a tablet with a sum adding up to 1741. Below this was the signature J. Wagner.

Later study was to reveal that the subject was a major event in the First Silesian War. Wagner himself was a painter recorded at Meissen from 1739, but hitherto no fully signed piece by him had been known. Just over a century before, the box had appeared in a sale at Christie's. Although described as an 'exceptional example', the fact that it was signed and dated seems to have escaped notice. It sold then for £54 12s. In 1975 the price soared to £16,000 – then the highest price ever given for a porcelain box. Today such a box could make in excess of £50,000.

Frederick the Great cropped up again in another snuff box which was shown to me during the Camberley *Roadshow*. He was proprietor as well as patron of the Berlin porcelain factory, and this time a relatively typical and deceptively simple Berlin box concealed a surprise in the form of a portrait of Frederick himself (opposite). It is now in a museum in Berlin.

Snuff boxes are the most expensive class of porcelain. However, other small objects of galanterie, such as thimbles and scent bottles, can also prove very costly. I had never seen an eighteenth-century thimble until a friend handed one to me over a restaurant table. This one had been made at Meissen around 1740. When it was eventually sold at auction in 1970 for £1575, the event made national headlines and appeared on television! In 1975 I came across a collection of some hundred and fifty thimbles, of which over a hundred were of Meissen manufacture, with others from England and France; many then passed the £1500 mark. There are probably fewer than three hundred extant Meissen thimbles. Nobody knows how many were made. The small size offered an exciting challenge to the painters, who must have used a very strong eyeglass to magnify their work: the detail is quite amazing.

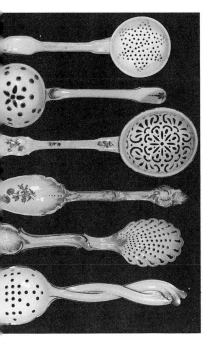

Six sifter spoons from the third quarter of the eighteenth century.

Top of page *Exterior of a Meissen snuff box of about 1741, depicting a battle scene. Inside the lid* (above) *are nymphs representing the Arts.*

Many factories made handles for cutlery as well as spoons, sugar-sifters and butter-curlers. In contrast to thimbles these can frequently be found at quite modest prices, unless of course one is dealing with a complete set with original blades and prongs. These occasionally appear, sometimes with their original fitted cases, which as well as protecting them add to their glamour.

Boxes, thimbles and table services all have one feature in common: their size and form make it difficult to mark them. So they always provide an interesting challenge for the student or expert. Since the eighteenth-century factories copied each other, this can sometimes be quite testing.

Marks can indeed be more confusing than helpful. So many people write to me describing a piece and suggesting an attribution based on a mark they have looked up. Unfortunately, most mark books do not tell you what sort of piece you can expect to find a certain mark on; indeed they do not even say whether it is to be found on pottery or porcelain, let alone whether the porcelain is of true (hard paste) or artificial (soft paste) composition. So the information painstakingly worked out proves useless. Marks are best used as supporting evidence confirming an attribution based on shape, type of ware and decoration rather than as a basis for that attribution. The Worcester factory frequently used the crossed swords of Meissen as a mark; so did Derby; whilst at Höchst, around 1760, they actually used the Meissen mark on pieces directly and precisely copied from the Meissen factory. It may indeed be that they were marking replacements for a Meissen service, but this innocent explanation is unlikely.

The crossed swords of Meissen was the most frequently copied mark during the eighteenth century. In the nineteenth and twentieth centuries it has been Sèvres that has given rise to the greatest amount of imitations. Here the situation is further complicated by the fact that large quantities of perfectly genuine eighteenth-century Sèvres porcelain were sold off undecorated around 1815 and subsequently painted up in eighteenth-century style. This is a difficult field even for the experienced and wary; there are so many dubious pieces around that, unless a piece is offered from a very reliable source, it would be best to treat it with great reserve.

Luckily the problem of redecoration is, Sèvres apart, a rare one. Most pieces of eighteenth-century porcelain have unadulterated decoration. In fact, one of the great virtues of porcelain is that it is difficult to alter – though of course it can be restored. Present-day techniques permit superficially invisible restoration to be carried out. Some of these are not detectable with ultra-violet light, a method used by many as a check. I have always preferred and relied on the naked eye backed up by a good strong light. This generally reveals all restoration on plates, cups and so on, which can be held up to the light. The nose is also useful, as porcelain and pottery have no smell at all, whilst paints and sprays do. A restored piece will tend to smell of paint even after several years, and

Four Meissen thimbles of about 1740.

particularly if it is in a lighted showcase which gets warm. On figures and groups it is sometimes very difficult to detect if necks have been repaired. Here some people like to use a pin, though the resultant scratches on the repaired surface tend to be unpopular. A pin cannot of course damage the surface of porcelain or pottery – it can only scratch restoration. On the first *Antiques Roadshow* ever broadcast, the cameras caught me using the most reliable guide I know – my teeth!

I do not like invisible restoration. If well done – so as to deceive – it is very expensive. Very often a simple repair, clean but clearly visible close to, is preferable: it certainly avoids any question of deceit. When purchasing a piece of porcelain or pottery you should always check the condition very carefully. A good dealer should tell you quite clearly what, if anything, has been done to it. In an auction – certainly in a specialised ceramics sale – the condition of each lot should be clearly described. Most auctioneers will check this for you if you ask them. Damage has a serious effect on the value of common items. On a rare and attractive piece, however, quite extensive damage may have only a peripheral effect.

Within the wide gamut of European porcelain and pottery of the eighteenth century there are great opportunities to collect, within the reach of a whole variety of budgets. Some collectors devote their attention to the products of a single factory. This is particularly frequent in porcelain-producing areas. Welsh collectors are particularly fond of the wares of Swansea and Nantgarw; in Turin they collect the porcelain of Vinovo and the faience produced by the Rossetti family; while Venetians pursue the porcelain made by the three factories of Vezzi, Hewelcke and Cozzi. In Germany, where many petty principalities and bishoprics had their own small and often shaky manufactures, there is always strong local enthusiasm for their products. Typical of this were Fulda, Würzburg and Höchst, all under the patronage of bishops with a great deal of temporal power.

Thematic collecting is also popular. A German shampoo company has assembled a whole range of porcelain groups depicting hairdressing. A collector whom I know is a great enthusiast for horses without riders, whilst others collect animals and characters from the Italian Comedy.

CARE AND REPAIR
1
- Wash in lukewarm soapy water.
- Don't use bleach.
- Stained cracks in glazed pieces respond to a solution of 2 teaspoons of biological washing powder in 1 pint of cool distilled water. After soaking for a few hours rinse in distilled water. For unglazed or biscuit porcelain, use the same solution but at half the strength.
- Use cotton buds or an artist's paintbrush to get at corners and difficult places.
- Don't immerse crazed earthenware or use it for flowers because the water will penetrate the glaze.

It would be hard to say which of these is the more keenly collected. The Italian Comedy is a theme that inspired almost every porcelain manufacturer and a few potters as well. Unfortunately, almost all Comedy figures are very expensive indeed; the most remarkable, from Nymphenburg, fetch £20,000 or more: none has so far shown up at an *Antiques Roadshow*, but I am still hoping. The animals made at the Meissen factory by the great J. J. Kändler in the 1740s include some of the most costly of European porcelain figures. Luckily for the collector of modest means, the factory also made reduced or miniature versions of several models, still to be found at reasonable prices – between £300 and £500.

In wares, collectors tend to concentrate on particular shapes or patterns, either within one factory or, where a particular idea or design was repeated in several manufactures, across the whole range. Designs in blue and white lend themselves well to this treatment, as do those wares inspired by the Kakiemon porcelains of Japan which are to be found from many of the principal European factories.

Collecting cups and saucers is a popular idea. As, however, this can be expensive (a pair of Meissen armorial cups and saucers has fetched over £30,000), another admirable solution is to collect odd cups or saucers – there is always the hope that a matching piece may turn up (in which case you may have hit the jackpot). Cups and saucers separately are much less expensive than they are together, and individual saucers are frequently just as excitingly painted as large dishes of similar type but at perhaps a fifth of the price. For a study collection, where it is essential to be able to compare different types of porcelain and learn how the colours change from one factory to another, these smaller pieces are perfect because they are easy to handle.

Pottery throughout the eighteenth century fell into two categories. Most of it consisted of tin-glazed earthenware or faience: in Germany, stonewares were extensively produced. The latter are quite easy to find and not generally expensive. The output of faience, however, was extremely widespread; it was often unmarked, and the same patterns and shapes cropped up all over the place. The result is a very challenging field for the collector.

A favourite and highly prized theme of many faience manufacturers was *trompe-l'oeil* pieces – tureens and other objects made to look like vegetables, plates of nuts and olives, and animals. You can find variations on this theme from Delft, Strasbourg, Brussels, Bassano and many German potteries. These pieces are avidly collected and their attributions are equally keenly discussed. There are many pieces in the domain of faience which will never find a precise attribution and their price is often dictated by optimism rather than certainty. In many areas, it is still possible to acquire genuine eighteenth-century pieces for less than £500. Naturally, the more important and original examples can command huge prices. As in the field of porcelain, there is wide scope for forming a

CARE AND REPAIR
—— 2 ——

○ Remove grease or oil (but not on gilded pieces) by washing in a solution of half water, half white spirit and a dash of washing-up liquid, then rinse well.

○ Don't heat any porcelain, especially if it is soft paste or cracked.

○ Don't wrap pieces in newspaper. At best it offsets black ink, at worst it attacks gilding. Acid-free tissue is best.

○ Hang plates on plastic-coated hangers only; plain wire ones can chip them. Delft, faience and maiolica are too chippable to·be hung on anything.

○ Most repairs, especially on good pieces, are best left to professionals. On lesser pieces, don't use the kind of permanent glue you would on a piece of everyday china. A water-soluble type is best.

collection on a theme that runs across the whole range of faience production, or for concentrating on the output of a single pottery.

Many pieces of pottery bearing exciting marks, dates and signatures are in fact forgeries. These were actively produced in Paris in the late nineteenth century, and the more fancy the decoration and elaborate the mark, the greater must be one's caution over the piece. Faience is the area above all in which a good working knowledge of the ware is vital.

I was once telephoned by a friend who thought he had discovered a great rarity, a niello-ed Rouen dish. Dashing round in high hopes, I discovered that it bore the unmistakable mark of Emile Samson, master imitator of early faience and porcelain. This should have been clear to the owner, but his high hopes had blinded him to the mark that was actually quite obvious. Wishful thinking is a trap to be avoided, as it can prove very expensive.

A selection of faience trompe-l'oeil *dishes.*

Right *A pair of figures of a hunter and huntress from the Fulda factory, modelled by George Ludwig Bartholomé about 1700.*

Below *Early Meissen Kakiemon tankard with silver-gilt mounts.*

Collecting is done not with a cheque book but with knowledge. Fortunately, Britain's splendid public collections enable you to study the whole range of European ceramics. There are many active and helpful members of the trade who are always delighted to explain the whys and wherefores of ceramics to an aspiring collector. Almost every week there is an auction of European ceramics somewhere, and you can go along and handle all the pieces for sale (without buying anything!). Catalogues from reputable salerooms are generally authoritative, and will give you some background information as well.

The essential thing, though, is not to rush in and buy the first thing you see because it seems a bargain. Acquire enough knowledge first to be able to spot the real bargains. Then your collecting will be an enduring pleasure.

EIGHTEENTH-CENTURY ENGLISH PORCELAIN

HENRY SANDON

England was a long time behind the Continent of Europe in discovering how to make a ceramic body that was white, translucent and had a nice ring when it was struck – the three essential elements in porcelain. When it did finally succeed, just before the mid-eighteenth century, factories sprang up like mushrooms overnight, many of them to die before the next day's dawn. While it is fair to say that no English porcelain produced in that century can compare with the finest wares of Meissen and Sevres, collecting and studying it is still fascinating.

The great European factories were often supported by kings and emperors as passions and playthings, set up to impress their rival monarchs. Enormous amounts of money were poured into the ventures, and the porcelain they made was meant to dazzle. If losses were great, the coffers of the country would be raided to make good. English factories, on the other hand, were business ventures, and if they ran at a loss would inevitably go to the wall. As a consequence their productions tend to be more ordinary, but it is this very quality of human fallibility and simplicity that appeals to so many collectors.

From the first, the English manufactories produced a soft paste, or artificial, body like many of the French factories – but unlike the Germans, who produced a hard or true porcelain from the Chinese recipe of china clay and china stone. It was not until 1768 that William Cookworthy made a hard paste porcelain at Plymouth from Cornish materials. In 1770 he moved to Bristol. After 1780 a few factories toyed with a hard paste-type formula, but the nineteenth century saw the invention of a bone china body, which quickly became England's staple porcelain.

It is not always easy to distinguish soft paste from hard paste, but the acquisition of this skill will repay a little hard work (see

Top of page Chelsea porcelain model,1745–7, of William Hogarth's dog Trump. When sold in 1986 it made the record price of £78,000 for a piece of English porcelain.

CARE AND REPAIR
∾
○ See pp. 64–5.

Glossary). It would certainly save a lot of the heartache that we see on the *Roadshow*, when the owner of what he believes to be a Chelsea gold anchor marked soft paste figure is told that what he really has is a hard paste fake made in Paris. My suggestion would be to buy some authentic examples of both bodies from a good saleroom or a knowledgeable antique dealer – if they are damaged pieces they need not cost a lot. Look carefully at these pieces and handle them, and you will learn a lot.

Soft paste porcelain is in no way inferior to hard paste. The bodies really cannot be compared in that way – they are as different as an orange is from an apple. The subtle beauty of soft paste lies in the softer glaze, which allows the colours to sink more glowingly and translucently into it, as opposed to hard paste, whose colours stand bright and glass-like upon the surface.

Most English factories had a period of experimentation, followed by a phase in which the difficulties had been overcome and better wares were made; this in turn was often followed by a decline, heralding final collapse. Up to a few years ago the middle period wares were the most expensive – the gold anchor period of Chelsea, for instance, when heavily decorated figure subjects, and vases covered with ground colours and elaborate painting and gilding, were produced. The often simple wares of the early years were relatively ignored by wealthy collectors.

Nowhere was that more true than in the case of Worcester, where I really began my porcelain pilgrimage. Pretty little pieces of the 1750s, painted disarmingly with simple birds and flowers, cost only a few pounds, whereas the elaboration of the 1760s and 1770s, with blue scale grounds, fabulous birds and elaborate gilding, fetched hundreds. The interesting thing is that nowadays the elaborate pieces can still fetch the same price, but the one-time poor relations can sell for thousands. This apparent anomaly can be explained by the rarity of the earliest pieces, and also because they possess a natural charm, while the later wares are sophisticated and slickly professional. This is not to say that they are worse than the earlier ones; in fact they are better from a technical point of view. What they have lost is that sense of accidental charm.

The following thumbnail sketches of the different factories will, I hope, make you want to learn more about them by reading some of the many excellent books that have recently been published, filled with up-to-date information gained from new research and the vitally important archaeological excavations on the original factory sites. It may sound strange to admit that we are still learning all the time about porcelain that is little more than two hundred years old – but we are. English porcelain is a subject about which there is still a lot to discover – perhaps you may find a key piece that will extend our knowledge. The factories below all produced soft paste porcelain.

Chelsea, the earliest of the porcelain factories, was founded by Nicholas Sprimont, a silversmith, and was in production by 1745.

Many of the early wares are similar in shape to silver articles of the period. The history divides up fairly accurately according to the different sequences of marks, although there is a certain amount of overlap and you should not always expect to see a mark at all.

During the incised triangle period, 1754–9, a beautiful, glassy, very translucent porcelain body was produced. Silver shapes are typical. Mainly small, ornamentally useful objects were made, such as jugs; the most famous was in the form of a goat with an applied bee – called the Goat and Bee jug. The usual mark for this period is a roughly incised △ under the base, but beware of nineteenth-century fakes of the Goat and Bee jug in a white bone china body. I have not so far seen a genuine one on the *Roadshow*.

The raised anchor period, 1749–52, saw the use of a more robust body, slightly milky white with tin in the glaze. An advertisement at the time gives an idea of what was in production: 'A variety of services for tea, coffee, chocolate, porringers, sauceboats, ewers, icepails, terrines, dishes and plates in different forms and patterns'. The decorations often imitate Kakiemon and Meissen, and the mark is an anchor on a raised pad.

The red anchor period covers the years 1752–6. Figures for table settings, such as Turks, craftsmen and Italian Comedy characters, are typical. As Horace Walpole wrote in 1753: 'Jellies, biscuits, sugar plums and creams have long given way to Harlequins, gondoliers, Turks, Chinese and Shepherdesses of Saxon china . . . by degrees, whole meadows of cattle of the same brittle materials, spread themselves over the whole table.' Covered tureens were made in the forms of animals and fish, as well as little 'toys' – scent bottles and seals – which run on into the next period. Coloured grounds were introduced. The mark is a small red anchor.

Chelsea tureen of the red anchor period, modelled to represent a bunch of asparagus.

This Bow fortune-teller of 1752 was adapted from a painting by Watteau.

A very early seaside souvenir made in 1780 at Lowestoft.

In the gold anchor period, 1757–69, figures became very gaudy, with elaborate supporting bocage. The glaze is clear, thickly applied, and tends to craze. Flat wares were fired on three supporting spurs that left scars on the base, and the Chelsea 'moons', irregular patches of white, are seen when a piece is held up to the light. The mark is a very small and unobtrusive gold anchor, but used large it was beloved of Continental fakers and at every *Roadshow* examples of these fakes are brought in. Sometimes we have the pleasure of seeing genuine pieces, and I recall one visitor who had two splendid plates identified as of the 'Hans Sloane' type, with superbly painted flowers in the centre. When David Battie told him they were worth several thousand pounds, he casually mentioned that he had a dozen more at home!

Finally we have what is known as the Chelsea Derby period. When the Chelsea factory was sold in 1769 it was run for a few years in conjunction with the Derby porcelain works. The mark is a D conjoined with an anchor, and figures have 'patch' marks under the bases, like the Derby ones.

What we now call Girl in a Swing — for lack of other information — was a mysterious factory of about the same date as red anchor period Chelsea. It most likely had some sort of connection with Chelsea — perhaps run by breakaway workmen — and while the wares are very similar they show differences in the features of the figures, the shape of the bases and the style of flower painting. The factory is named after the first identified figure. Examples are rare.

The Bow factory was at Stratford le Bow in East London, and while a patent was taken out on 6 December 1744 to use clay from South Carolina it is likely that little was made until another patent, using bone ash in the body, was introduced in 1748. Early wares are very charming, especially vases marked with an incised R and figures by the so-called 'Muses' modeller. Rose pink and opaque light blue are very characteristic colours. In the 1760s and 1770s Bow produced large quantities of middle-market blue and white in a body that frequently stains brown, rather like a tea stain, and with very small footrings. Figures with scrolled bases became very common. The body at first is a rather drab grey, heavy and not very translucent, but later on becomes creamy white and lighter. Late Bow is frequently brought in to the *Roadshow* and is not considered as highly as it may one day be.

The body of Lowestoft, which started production in 1757, is very like that of Bow — a bone ash formula — and frequently stains brown. The wares are generally ordinary, useful ones made for the market around the factory, and contain a large number of personalised named and dated pieces, such as birth tablets and the earliest tourist pieces bearing messages such as 'A Trifle from Lowestoft' — but be careful of such pieces, because many fakes were made. The factory made only blue and white until 1761, when production increased. The footrings of cups usually have a

Worcester plate of about 1770, from the service made for the Duke of Gloucester.

characteristic sloping outside and straight inner side ($\searrow$) and painters' numerals appear inside the footring. In 1771 a London warehouse was opened and the Lowestoft factory started to imitate Worcester, even using the Worcester open crescent mark on many of their patterns. The factory had ceased production by 1805, when many of the workers went to Worcester.

When we come to talk about Worcester there are three factories to be considered. A factory operating in Limehouse on the Thames in about 1745–8 was apparently continued at Bristol until 1752; then Worcester acquired the factory, lock, stock and barrel, moving production up the River Severn to that city.

No wares from Limehouse have been identified with any certainty, but they were most probably blue and white. It would be a great feather in their cap for the person who pins down the first positive example. Some few dozen marked examples of Bristol pieces are known – a figure of a Chinaman, sauceboats and creamboats – marked with the moulded name 'Bristol' or 'Bristoll', and these are highly desirable. It is likely that only blue and white was made at Bristol, but when the process was moved to Worcester, where the factory had been founded in June 1751, production was extended to coloured wares. The first year's production at Worcester used a body and glaze very similar to those at Bristol, and it is very difficult to tell the difference between the two factories. I have been fortunate in being allowed to excavate the Worcester factory site over a number of years; as a result it is one of the best documented factories of the eighteenth century.

From 1751 to about 1759 Worcester blue and white is usually marked with a symbol, probably the mark of the painter; after that date, however, it is more usual to find a crescent mark – painted on painted wares and printed on printed ones. Coloured wares generally do not have a mark except for a fretted square on wares with underglaze blue and onglaze painting, and the occasional use of crossed swords with a number 9 in the hilts. Footrings are generally triangular ($\vee$), the potting is always of a high quality, and the glaze never crazes and hardly ever stains. Very few figures were made; the factory concentrated instead on useful wares. Pieces from the 1750s have generally increased in value in the last few years, leaving a lot of the more splendidly decorated wares of the 1760s and 1770s relatively inexpensive. This is especially true of scale blue and other ground colours, although it is possible that some ground colours were applied and fired at a later date.

After 1776 the standard of production tended to decline. Bright blue printing with disguised numeral marks was introduced, and a revival is seen from 1792, the start of what is called the Flight and Barr period (see p. 79). In 1783 the factory was bought by Thomas Flight, who was joined in 1792 by Martin Barr. The simple spiral-fluted blue and gold pieces of this period are very beautiful and, in my opinion, very underpriced.

In about 1786 Robert Chamberlain started a breakaway factory in Worcester, making wares rather like those of the Flight manufactory. These, too, are underpriced.

Another breakaway from Worcester, the Caughley factory had started production by 1775 and was taken over by Coalport at the end of the century. The soapstone body is very like that of Worcester; footrings are usually square or $\cup$-shaped, and when marked have either an S or a C with a serif at the top. The wares have grown in collectability, especially the very attractive miniature or toy teawares, which were made for children and were never, as some people think, travellers' samples. At the *Roadshow* in Camborne in Cornwall, one visitor brought in an extremely rare, possibly unique, toy chamber pot, made about 1790 and with a blue painted landscape. I told her that it should be insured for something like £1250 and had the surprise of my life when she told me that she had bought it at a Sunday morning boot fair two weeks before for 25p. She would not tell me where the boot fair was held, but it is nice to know that such finds can still be made!

New Hall coffee pot of about 1790, painted in a simple pattern in the style of cheap Chinese imports.

A pair of fine-quality leopard figures made at Derby in about 1760.

The Longton Hall factory, founded in Staffordshire in 1749, produced wares in a glassy paste of somewhat uneven quality. Production ceased about 1760, but a lot of porcelain was later made and decorated at West Pans in Scotland. Some interesting figures came out of the factory; most characteristic is Littler's blue colour, very runny and blurry, looking almost as though it had been left out in the rain.

Liverpool is a very complicated city for ceramics collectors, because there were a number of porcelain manufactories close to each other, often taking over from earlier delft factories. Every now and then new discoveries switch wares from one factory to another, sometimes even removing them from Liverpool to Staffordshire, and while it is often difficult to be sure about them they offer a most interesting challenge for the collector. Here is a brief list of them. Chaffers at first made a bone ash body, then a soapstone body; the late wares bear a strong resemblance to Worcester and are very good quality. As on a lot of Liverpool wares, the footrings are frequently undercut on the inside edge and in profile look like this: ⊽ . Christian (1765–76) continued to use soapstone after Chaffers; the blue has a pale grey tint and the glaze is often a duck egg blue-green. Pennington (1769–99), one of the poorer Liverpool factories, used bone ash; the blue varies from grey-blue to almost black, and the glaze pools in the footrings form a 'thunder-cloud' effect. Gilbody (?1754–61) is the rarest and

Large vase of hard paste porcelain with typical Continental-style painting, made at Bristol in 1772 under the direction of William Cookworthy.

most collectable of the Liverpool factories. Reid comprises a small group of wares now linked with a recently excavated factory on the site of the Pomona Inn in Newcastle-under-Lyme. Ball (?1755–69) made some of the best Liverpool wares; the colour has a 'sticky blue' look. Woolfe (1795–1800), with partners Miles Mason and John Lucock, is now thought to be Staffordshire.

Derby produced some of the finest English porcelain figures. At first, from the 1750s, concentration was focused on the ornamental rather than the useful, since the early wares did not withstand hot liquids. Early figures were fired on stilts, but on later ones the characteristic patch marks are found under the base – rough, round, dark marks where the figure rested on pads of clay during firing. Arthur Negus, in his inimitable way, used to call these marks 'thumb prints'. He also used to point out that no eighteenth-century English figures are found with blue eyes. Watch has to be kept for the many later French fakes of Derby figures, always in a hard paste body, unlike the genuine soft paste. In the later eighteenth century the factory produced some of the best hand painting and gilding seen in this country, and sometimes wonderful pieces are brought in to a *Roadshow*.

While the factories listed above produced soft paste porcelain, Plymouth and Bristol made hard paste. Plymouth took advantage of the abundant china clay and china stone from Cornwall. The factory only lasted from 1768 to 1770 before being transferred to Bristol, but in that short time William Cookworthy manufactured some interesting porcelain. Splendid figure subjects were made, and the factory also produced useful wares, often decorated in blue in the style of Worcester. The blue, however, is usually of a very grey tint, and thrown vessels frequently exhibit the characteristic 'wreathing', a spiralling twist in the body. The mark is the alchemical mark for tin, a 2 and a 4 conjoined.

Production went on until 1780 at Bristol, where the improved hard paste body enabled a lot of fine useful wares to be made. The mark is a small onglaze blue cross.

The hard paste porcelain formula was continued in Staffordshire by New Hall, although it appears that firing sequences produced a body and glaze less hard and glassy than those from Bristol. A similar body was produced by a number of other factories, such as Chamberlain in Worcester and Coalport. Look out for all these wares.

In the last years of the eighteenth century the surviving factories went one of two ways: either up-market, like Worcester and Derby, making fine wares for the wealthy; or, like New Hall, Coalport and other prolific factories, catering for the middle classes. These simpler wares offer scope when you are looking for relatively inexpensive porcelain, and as well as giving pleasure stand a good chance of becoming collectable. My personal choice, however, will always be the wares of the 1750s – sometimes quite primitive, and always disarmingly honest.

Nineteenth-Century British and Irish Pottery and Porcelain

David Battie

If I had to pick one piece to sum up British ceramics from the nineteenth century it would have to be a blue transfer-printed earthenware plate. Untold millions were fired in the bottle kilns of Stoke-on-Trent (Smoke-on-Trent would have been more appropriate), to be shipped by the boatload all over the world.

The most common design is the old favourite, the Willow Pattern, which was introduced at the end of the eighteenth century. Not a copy of a Chinese design, it is an English concept using Chinese elements. There is no truth, by the way, in the story that a piece can be dated by the number of figures on the bridge. Prices can vary from a pound or two to over £100 for a rare marked example. English landscapes, some identifiable and copied from engravings in books, were popular and remain so. A large meat dish depicting a cathedral could fetch £300–400. A few very rare pieces are printed with prize cattle – a meat dish with a bull can make over £1000. Most common – and Spode's Italian pattern is the commonest – are Continental ruins, particularly in Italy.

In 1813 the Mason factory introduced a new earthenware body called Ironstone, which summed up its qualities of strength and durability. It was heat- and chip-resistant and would stand up to rough handling in the kitchens of the day. The early designs were transfer-printed in black and hand-coloured with Oriental figures in gardens, flowers or copies of Imari. Bold, decorative tableware, it is now much collected; an early plate can fetch £100, but most can be bought for £20–40. Devotees of Mason will spend £500–1000 on a soup tureen, cover and stand. The Mason's Ironstone mark is now the property of G. L. Ashworth of Hanley. Confusingly, it is still used on an earthenware body in pieces cast from early moulds and in the same colouring. Be warned! (A helpful tip in dating most English ceramics is the presence of the

Above *Transfer-printed blue and white Staffordshire pottery meat dish.*

Top of page *Mason's Ironstone sauce tureen and dinner plate of about 1820, based on an eighteenth-century Chinese original.*

word 'England' on the base of pieces made after 1891, and 'Made in England' on those made after 1902.) Numerous Staffordshire potters copied Mason's discovery and applied similar coats-of-arms marks; these too are now fetching respectable prices.

There is a long history in Britain of making plates to commemorate important events. In the nineteenth century, knowledge was more widely disseminated through newspapers than it had been earlier, so the public were much more aware of political changes, success in battle or the death or coronation of a monarch. Transfer-printing meant fast production, and by the 1840s the new railways could spread the wares rapidly through the country. Those living in the first two decades of the nineteenth century had a great deal more to feed their appetite for gossip than does the reader of a tabloid today. First they had a king, George III, who was by all accounts barking mad, although his condition has since been diagnosed as porphyria. His son, who therefore became Prince Regent, was a spendthrift and a womaniser but a fanatical enthusiast of the arts and architecture. His excesses were depicted in the political cartoons of the time and his disgraceful treatment of his wife, Queen Caroline, who, when she tried to attend his coronation in 1820, was refused admission on the grounds that she had no ticket, also featured on pottery. She is portrayed wearing a characteristic large hat set with the three ostrich feathers of the Prince of Wales. Small plates and jugs with this decoration can now fetch a couple of hundred pounds.

Queen Victoria's 1837 coronation mug is very desirable, and examples will make over £500. Various teasets of her and Albert, usually in bright pinkish red, are common, costing £20–30 for a cup and saucer. The coming of the railways, far more of a marvel then the landing on the moon this century, was commemorated with mugs crudely transfer-printed and blobbed with colour.

Apart from commemorative wares, figures were also made in large numbers. Many early portrait figures of such heroes as Nelson, Napoleon, and Victoria and Albert were made of porcelain, simply coloured in underglaze blue, enamelled and gilt and with gilt script titles. The collector usually sticks to a theme, be it military, religious or theatrical, and prices depend on rarity and the number of collectors competing for the same pieces. Small variations such as mis-spelling crept in through illiteracy or tiredness, but unlike postage stamps this does not make them more valuable. Occasionally a major change was made, usually to simplify production, and this can have a dramatic effect. A mounted Sir Robert Peel is known with hand either down or outstretched. Today's prices are £400–600 and £2000-plus respectively.

Pot lids were the first serious form of advertising packaging. Brightly coloured topical pictures were transfer-printed in Staffordshire by a number of makers including Pratt of Fenton, the largest. The lids attracted the eye away from the fact that, despite a large pot, the amount of hair pomade, meat or shrimp paste

Staffordshire pottery plate of about 1820, printed with a portrait of Queen Caroline.

CARE AND REPAIR
⚬ See pp. 64–5.

Pot lid, 'The Second Appeal', by Pratt of Fenton.

contained within them was quite small. The earliest examples date from the middle of the century, continuing in production from increasingly worn plates until the 1920s, by which time there was a flourishing collectors' market. The rarest can now fetch over £1000, the most common £20–30, and collectors have the benefit of a price guide which lists every known lid so that, as with stamps, one can fill gaps in a collection.

Interest in colour was a very Victorian preoccupation and coincided with the first serious study of earlier works of art on a historical basis. By 1850 large books of decorations, masterpieces of ceramics, glass, metalwork and so on, illustrated in colour by chromolithography, were published at enormous cost and became source material for the Stoke-on-Trent potters. One fascination was with Italian maiolica of the sixteenth and seventeenth centuries. The Victorians spelt it majolica, which usefully differentiates the English wares from the Italian. Experiments with different glazes led to colours similar to those of Renaissance Italy, or so the Victorians thought, hence the borrowing of the name. Actually they bear little resemblance, apart from their lead composition, being brighter altogether. The earliest pieces date from the 1850s and 1860s and, though technically competent, were simply copies of Continental originals. Before long, however, Victorian exuberance took over and an ever-growing range of completely dotty objects poured off the production lines.

Majolica camel by George Jones, 1878.

Minton's masterpiece of majolica at the 1862 Exhibition in London was the St George Fountain, about 40 feet high and surmounted by a life-size saint and dragon. After the exhibition was over it was bought by the Victoria and Albert Museum and erected at Bethnal Green Museum, where it slowly fell apart and was removed by the Council in 1926. One is loath to speculate as to its value today – £150,000 upwards, I suppose.

Valuing majolica is something of a hit-and-miss affair as there are a few very wealthy American buyers who will pay very high prices. Unfortunately, once they have an example of a particular model they stop buying it, with the result that the kind of piece that makes £5000 in one sale may make no more than £1000 in the next. Very irritating! As an example of prices in general, when I wrote *The Price Guide to 19th and 20th Century British Pottery* in 1979, illustrated on the jacket was the George Jones camel (left) which I estimated at £200–350. The companion figure – of a much less interesting donkey – recently fetched £3000.

We have visited Scotland many times with the *Roadshow* and the occasional Scottish pot appears. The most entertaining come from the Wemyss factory. In 1882 a ceramics decorator from Hungary, Karel Nekola, was appointed chief painter at the Fife Pottery, where he developed a bold freehand style which rapidly became popular. It was taken up by the major London retailer Thomas Goode, who had a flourishing trade with the landed gentry, and before long it became the 'in thing' to have in the guest bedroom a Wemyss washing set. Bedroom sets were not the sole production of this factory. It also made an amusing series of pigs in several sizes decorated either with shamrocks or, that most popular of all Wemyss motifs, a full-blown pink cabbage rose. Honey pots, tea wares, candlesticks and vases also appear. There are many collectors of Wemyss ware, the most famous of whom is Her Majesty Queen Elizabeth the Queen Mother, who has a large collection. It is particularly favoured by actors and ballet dancers, who like its bold theatricality. Wemyss is not common, and this fact, combined with strong demand, leads to high prices. A small jug with roses might fetch £40, a small pig £500, a large one £2600. A very large and rare carp sold for a record price of £3300.

Wemyss is a soft and fragile pottery and should be treated with great care, as indeed should all ceramics. My heart jumps every time I spot someone in the queue swinging a jug by the handle. We never pick up pots by the handle, but always by putting our hands round the body or inside. An incident at a *Roadshow* will act as an awful warning. Henry Sandon had a Minton copy of a Sèvres tureen and, knowing my interest in copies, called me over. He had the piece in his lap and in taking it from him I inadvertently pressed one of the handles quite gently. It broke off. Shock, horror all round! Examination showed that the casting of the handle was faulty and it also had a firing flaw. Several cups of tea later the

Wemyss pottery pig painted with Scottish thistles.

*One of a pair of Flight, Barr &
Barr Worcester candlesticks,
dating from about 1810.*

owners departed with an amicably agreed insurance claim.

We will move swiftly from pottery to porcelain, and the transition from flamboyant Wemyss to fine Regency porcelain is something of a culture shock. From the late eighteenth century and for the first forty years of the nineteenth the famous Worcester factory went through a number of changes in title, namely: Flight; Barr and Flight & Barr; Barr, Flight & Barr; and Flight, Barr & Barr. I can never remember them in the right order, nor recall the dates. Whenever I have recorded a piece on the programme I have either looked it up first (well, it's only a little cheat – we can't remember everything!) or asked Henry Sandon, who seems to have filed away every date in connection with the factory. We constantly refer to Geoffrey Godden's *Encyclopaedia of British Pottery and Porcelain Marks*, which is the bible for collectors of English ceramics – so much so that the author's name is flippantly shortened to 'God'. The queue is frequently puzzled by one expert shouting to the next table: 'Lend me God a minute!'

James Hadley is famous for the figures of Oriental types which he modelled for Royal Worcester. This, one of a set of six, is of Shaban, the gold brocade maker, and was made in 1887.

The dessert wares and vases of this period had a rich coloured ground or simulated marble around panels painted with breath-taking accuracy and in minute detail with feathers, shells and birds. Landscape scenes and buildings also appear, and are usually identified on the underside along with the beautifully painted script mark and address. The quality of the burnished honey gilding has never been surpassed. Honey gilding was the original technique of getting the gold on to porcelain. Yes, it is gold and almost pure, a higher standard than used in most jewellery. Reduced to a powder and ground with honey, it is painted on and fired. It comes out of the kiln matt and can be left, but is more usually burnished with an agate stone for full brilliance. Some modern Continental porcelain bears proudly on its backside the legend: 'Guaranteed 22 carat gold'. True, it is; but if you scraped all the gold from a million plates it would hardly buy you a cup of British Rail tea, so little is used. By the 1880s mercury gilding had appeared. Heating mercury in a kiln gives off poisonous fumes, which killed off the workers at alarming speed. The gilding also had an unpleasant brassy quality.

From the 1840s to the 1870s Worcester went through a bad patch, but picked up when James Hadley became principal modeller. He produced a large number of excellent figures after Kate Greenaway children, classical nymphs, Eastern water-carriers and personifications of the British racial types. These now have a wide following and have risen rapidly in value.

We can always guarantee to see a lot of Goss on the *Roadshow*. This Stoke-on-Trent factory made a range of porcelain of generally little interest until William Henry Goss, an amateur archaeologist, spotted a gap in the market in the form of the bicycle saddle-bag. The cycling craze hit Britain in a major way when the safety bicycle appeared, and trainloads of enthusiasts set off to some unspoiled part of the country to pedal round it. Goss realised that what was needed was a small, cheap souvenir which could be taken home to prove where they had been. He produced a range of miniature vases based on relics in local museums and bearing the appropriate coats-of-arms. Historical information was found on the base along with his crest, a goshawk. These tiny pots can be found crowding the shelves of antique shops for a few pounds apiece. More attractive are his range of houses representing dwellings of the famous, such as Dr Johnson, Shakespeare and Wordsworth. These are a much more serious matter and range from £30–40 for Shakespeare's house to £1300 for Hop Kiln.

Goss also made parian ware, but it is very uncommon. The study of Greek and Roman sculpture set off a vogue for marble and the potters introduced a new material which imitated the famous parian original. It was a white, or slightly off-white, porcelain which cast well and was not prone to misfiring. Original carvings were reduced on a pantograph and then moulded to cast as many copies as necessary. At a time when prudery about the human body was so strong that it was common to drape table legs and refer to them as 'unmentionables', it may seem surprising that naked ladies figured so largely. They seem to have escaped condemnation by being labelled 'Art'. Naked ladies on panthers, on rocks, in chains – no drawing room was complete without one. It is only in the last few years that they have been accorded the serious consideration they deserve, but they are still not expensive. A 14-inch figure would be £200–300.

Parian was also used to make jugs. In Victorian times you went out with a jug to have milk measured into it by the milkman and the children were sent with one to the alehouse for beer. It was a vital part of any household, and worthy of considerable artistic attention. Indeed Sir Henry Cole, a major mid-century figure, looked on cheap ceramics, well produced and designed, as a means of making the public aware of the high ideals of art. These jugs, often with appropriate moulded decoration such as hops and vines, biblical subjects (for the teetotal), commemorative designs or reflecting the fashionable Gothic taste, can still be had for £15–20, and to my mind are amongst the best buys in ceramics today.

I now launch a new theory as my contribution to original research in this book. I believe the Victorians had a hole fetish. Making holes in porcelain has a long history stretching back to the Chinese in the seventeenth century; it got under way again in Regency England, when dessert services appeared which looked as if a hungry caterpillar had been at the rim. The high priest of the holephiles was a Worcester knife-wizard named George Owen (p. 82). He took a cast vase that was still leather-hard and behind locked doors, to keep his mystery from prying eyes, set to work with a razor-sharp blade. He is supposed to have started cutting without any preliminary guidelines and to have worked with amazing speed. Certainly the latter must be true, given the number of surviving holes attributed to him. Even so, pieces would have been worked on for several weeks or even months, being kept the entire time in a box under a wet towel so that they would not get too dry and hard to work on. One poor wretch was set to work to count the holes in a particular large vase: there were 5350.

For fifty years and more such examples of Victorian artistry were derided by the Modern Movement, but the cult has undergone a resurrection and Owen's works are once more avidly collected. Some unsigned pieces, possibly because they were not (w)holly successful, make £150 upwards, but the same piece signed is three to five times the price, with major examples fetching several thousand.

We have visited England and Scotland; finally we turn to Ireland. The Belleek factory in County Fermanagh, founded in 1863, is still in production and famous for its eggshell-thin porcelain. The wares are usually influenced by nearby marine life such as sea urchins, shells and seaweed. Colour is used sparingly – just a thin

Parian model of Venus by Robinson and Leadbeater from the last quarter of the nineteenth century.

Right *Pierced Worcester vase by the incomparable George Owen.*

Below *Belleek spider's web cake plate, about 1900.*

wash of pink or green on the nacreous, or shell-iridescent, glaze. The factory also produced baskets by weaving threads of rolled clay. It is a miracle that any of these extremely fragile productions have survived, with not only the basket itself intact but also the hundreds of hand-modelled petals forming the flowers with which they are encrusted. Devotees will pay thousands for good examples. The rarest of the rare are cake plates in the form of spiders' webs and almost as fine. One of these recently sold for £1800. The same designs are still being made today, but collectors opt for early pieces made between 1863 and 1890. The mark was then changed to include 'Co. Fermanagh, Ireland'. Most major pieces return to Ireland or cross the Atlantic to the many Americans of Irish descent. It is this constant crossing and recrossing of international boundaries that makes the study of ceramics so endlessly fascinating. No matter where we take the *Roadshow* we can be sure of finding pots from every quarter of the globe, imported for both decorative and functional use and now resting, often unrecognised as masterpieces, in houses ranging from miners' cottages to country mansions.

NINETEENTH-CENTURY CONTINENTAL POTTERY AND PORCELAIN

DAVID
BATTIE

David Battie and a Roadshow *customer discuss her ceramic cockerel.*

I never fail to be amazed by the patience of the British queuer. General theory has it that we grew used to queuing for everything during the last war, but then so did the French and the Germans, and they have not adopted it as a national pastime. After an hour or two in the porcelain queue (always the longest), very many packages reveal no more than the same sort of object: either Japanese eggshell porcelain (see p. 130) or, more likely, Continental biscuit porcelain figures. These must have been made and imported by the million, and frankly we know next to nothing about them. The poor owner, I am afraid, is likely to get: 'Biscuit porcelain, made in France or Germany at the turn of the century. Very common. £10–15.' This is not boredom or rudeness on our part. It is only that, apart from explaining that the term 'biscuit' indicates that the piece has been fired once only and the coloured details painted straight on to the body and fired without a glaze, giving an icing sugar effect, nothing more can be added.

The bulk of the nineteenth-century Continental porcelain that we see on the *Roadshow* was influenced by products of the previous century. In the eighteenth century France (Sèvres) and Germany (Meissen) were the patterns that other countries and factories copied. It may be a little hard to swallow, but the hallowed names of Chelsea, Derby and Worcester were all making reproductions of their Continental rivals – and in many cases copying the marks as well, so as to complete the deception. In the second half of the eighteenth century England began to stir with the Industrial Revolution, and technology was applied to everything from textiles to ceramics. We had developed transfer printing on pottery in the middle of the century, and several factories were using it in underglaze blue to produce designs more rapidly than could be done by hand painting.

Top of page A *pair of Meissen candelabra figures.*

A pair of fairly common French biscuit porcelain figures. These are rather better than many we see on the Roadshow.

By the end of the eighteenth century Meissen was a pale shadow of its former self, making poor-quality porcelain – at least in comparison with earlier periods – in a style which was no longer fashionable. The painting, mainly of flowers, had not changed for thirty years and the strict quality control over the body itself had deteriorated. Nevertheless, it is not unattractive and is fairly plentiful. A collector with limited funds could well build up a collection of turn-of-the-century Meissen in good condition for relatively little. A coffee service, perhaps incomplete but decorative, could be bought for, say, £200. The marks at this time, apart from the usual crossed swords in underglaze blue, have either a dot between the hilts (1763–74) or a star (1774–1814).

The factory pulled itself up when a new director, Carl Wilhelm von Oppel, was appointed in 1814. New models were introduced, but invariably and confusingly in eighteenth-century style and in eighteenth-century clothes, and some old models were reused. The result can be very muddling to the inexperienced, but there are clues to the difference between the eighteenth- and nineteenth-century figures. The earlier figures usually have a flat unglazed bottom and the mark, if there is one, is small and on the side of the base at the rear. The flat base often warped in the firing, and in the nineteenth century the hollow glazed base was developed, which enabled the piece to be fired on the rim only. The mark was relocated in the hollow and was accompanied by incised (scratched into the wet clay) and impressed marks. The former was the mould number, such as C.32, and a pair would have consecutive numbers. The impressed mark was that of the 'repairer', the term used for the man who assembled the still damp limbs, dogs, leaves and so on which were needed to make the group. Occasionally there will also be a painted decorator's mark. While there are endless copies and interpretations of Meissen throughout the nineteenth century, usually with a more or less accurate attempt at the mark, the presence of all three – swords, impressed and incised marks – is a sure indication of genuine nineteenth-century Meissen.

By the middle of the century the quality was as good as ever, and no factory could touch Meissen for paste, painting and gilding. Rejects had the mark cut through; they were then sold and decorated outside the factory, but the market seems unaffected by this. There was obviously a ready market for these decorative and colourful figures that evoked a bygone age, and large numbers can be found in England. The factory, now behind the Iron Curtain, is still in production, still making the same figures from the same moulds and with the same high quality.

In France in the early years of the century Napoleon's influence was paramount: his military successes were all echoed in porcelain. The Egyptian campaign of 1799, on which Napoleon took a number of archaeologists with him to record the antiquities, started a great vogue for sphinx heads, pseudo-hieroglyphics and supposedly Egyptianesque forms. Napoleon equated himself with the Roman Emperors, and vases based on Roman and Greek amphorae were produced, based on the Neo-Classical forms of the last twenty years of the eighteenth century. The famous Sèvres factory, which had been the personal property of King Louis XV, had been appropriated by the state after the Revolution in 1789 and, like many state-run enterprises, was soon at a point of total financial collapse.

A new director, Alexandre Brongniart, was appointed in 1800, and he immediately set about improving cashflow by putting on the market vast quantities of reject stock, mostly undecorated. This was snapped up by both Paris and, even more eagerly, Staffordshire manufacturers. The decorators set to work to enamel and gild these blanks in old Sèvres style, using genuine pieces to guide them and, where possible, copying the marks as well. There was a ready market for these copies, as Sèvres had always been a popular factory in England, where its soft paste was greatly in sympathy with the products of our own factories such as Chelsea and Worcester. The last sale of blanks took place in 1840, and certainly a great many of the so-called 'clobbered' pieces seem to date from then up until the 1880s.

How do we tell them from the genuine article? Well, until a few years ago we couldn't. Even now a great deal is being sold, in my opinion, as right when it is not. There are clues. The sale of vast quantities of blank rejects is in itself significant – it suggests rigid quality control, which would fit in with what we know of Louis XV's and Louis XVI's attitude to the factory. They would be unlikely to countenance anything but the very highest standard. We can, therefore, doubt a piece with anything but the most minor flaws. Almost incredibly, the records of the factory have survived, and there is a record of most of the major pieces – who painted them, when they were fired, how they came out of the kiln, how much was charged for them, and who bought them. Certain painters specialised in certain subjects, and not infrequently the faker has got his painters muddled or his dates wrong. The Sèvres factory used a date code system from 1753, and we know the dates when the various painters worked at the factory. If the piece bears a date before a certain painter joined or after he left, then it is clearly wrong. Their styles were distinctive – after all, they were painting birds or flowers or figures because they had proved themselves good at it – and many pieces can be exposed on the grounds of bad painting.

Perhaps the most reliable clue is of a technical nature. When fired and left undecorated, soft paste porcelain reabsorbs moisture from the air. If, after more than a few weeks, it is decorated and fired again this moisture, now under the glaze, is rapidly driven off. Most, and sometimes all, escapes where it entered through the unglazed footring, but often it is forced through the glaze, frequently round the foot, leaving behind tiny black pinheads, some-

Eighteenth-century Sèvres dish decorated later, in about 1840 and probably in Staffordshire, in Sèvres style.

One of a pair of Jacob Petit candlesticks made about 1840.

times called 'spit-back'. There may be only a few (and they should not be confused with glaze flaws), or the whole back can become a grey haze. Presence of this disfiguration is a very strong warning sign indeed. The famous turquoise blue ground developed by Sèvres was a popular colour for the Victorians to add to blanks. Look on the back of the plate for 'bleed', where spots of blue have spattered from a plate nearby. Finally, named portraits of the court of Louis XV, particularly when within jewelled paste borders, can be discounted.

It may seem strange to spend so long on a group of fake porcelain, but large quantities do appear on the *Roadshow* and they are by no means without value. A plate painted with sprays of flowers makes around £60–80, a jewelled cup and saucer £200–500, and a large tray with a battle scene could bring £1000. Genuine Sèvres porcelain from the nineteenth century, when they were making only hard paste, is exceedingly rare. I cannot recollect having seeing more than a couple of pieces on the entire series. It is also extremely expensive: single finely painted dinner plates can make £1000 each.

Sèvres was not the only factory around Paris; a large number of others made useful and decorative wares in all ranges of quality. Frequently they were unmarked, and we cannot always attribute a piece with certainty. One factory which did mark, and whose products we see in fair numbers, is Jacob Petit. The mark is, conveniently, JP. They made a wide range of wares over thirty years, and one common characteristic feature is the strong and brilliant use of coloured enamels and gilding. These were applied with skill to vigorously modelled clock cases, with which Jacob Petit is particularly associated, tea wares and vases. Many suffer from a rather heavy appearance, but at its best Jacob Petit will stand comparison with many better-known names. In decoration the exotic East predominates, and mounted Arabs leap over the tops of clocks to fetch around £600–1500. Another famous, or maybe notorious, Paris factory is that of Emile Samson, established in 1845 and specialising in reproductions of earlier ceramics, glass and enamels from England, the Continent and the Near and Far East. Samson seems not to have been a forger. He advertised widely that he was making reproductions and most, if not all, of his works bear his own mark in addition to that of the original. In many cases it was all too easy to erase his mark and pass the piece off as genuine. The most obvious defect in Samson's operation was the fact that he was often obliged to make hard paste copies of soft paste originals, as he did not have the latter material available. Indeed, some of his copies of the early French factories, such as St Cloud, were made in a cream-glazed earthenware. We can now spot most Samson copies from the other side of the room, but up until the 1930s the market was fooled. Certainly there were other manufacturers up to the same tricks – Herend in Hungary for one. Samson's products were well made and decorative and

Sèvres plate from the Chateaubriand service, 1823.

they now have a following in their own right, particularly in Paris. A Samson copy of a Chinese armorial plate of the 1740s will fetch £100 today, while the original is still only £300; something wrong there, I think.

In the minds of many people, French porcelain means Limoges. At the mere mention of the word they see flashing lights, pound signs and the friendly tinkle of the jackpot. I think this is a folk memory left from the early years of this century when Limoges enamels – a different thing altogether – were making quite unbelievable sums. The Limoges area of France was the rough equivalent of our Stoke-on-Trent, with a number of factories producing quantities of useful wares, though nothing of any great merit, and preferring, quite rightly, to remain anonymous. There is little we

Copy by Emile Samson of a Chinese armorial plate.

can attribute until the end of the century, when the designs of the Art Nouveau movement trickled through to Limoges and numbers of services for fish, dinner and dessert were made with debased Art Nouveau borders, all in faded pastel pink, apricot and yellow in pale imitation of Royal Worcester. Most of the decoration has been transfer printed or tinted on a printed outline. It is all perfectly dreadful and deservedly does not fetch much. Plates can be had from £1.

Another factory which influenced nineteenth-century porcelain was the Imperial Manufactory at Vienna, one of the earliest in Europe to make hard paste porcelain. It went through several crises of management in the first half of the nineteenth century, and it appears that early blanks which bear a three-figure date code may well have been decorated at a much later period. The only guide is quality and style. Their main speciality was spectacularly rich hand painting on vases and dishes, usually of classical subjects such as nymphs. Vases have a claret or deep blue ground with complex borders in other enamels and relief gilding. Similar borders appear on plates – a well-painted example will make £200 for a classical subject, and up to double that for a pretty girl. A pair of small vases with covers and on the usual high square base cost about £200 and can make £8000 upwards when really large and decorative.

Towards the end of the century, vast numbers of mass-produced wares in similar style but with the 'painting' transfer printed flooded the market. Sometimes signatures were added by hand, or more often incorporated as part of the printed decoration, so cannot be used as a guide to the technique used. Favourite spurious signatures include those of Fragonard, Boucher and Angelica Kauffmann. At this date the image was formed of numerous small dots, much like the colour reproduction in a magazine, and close scrutiny will reveal this. Similar wares are still being produced by the factory today, mostly with a rich burgundy ground and very brassy gilding.

The Vienna mark is a shield in underglaze blue or occasionally impressed, often referred to as the beehive mark, which it resembles if turned upside-down. Like those of many major factories, the mark was copied by unscrupulous potters. There were decorators working in Vienna on plaques made both there and in Berlin and Dresden.

In pre-electricity days making a light at night was a fiddly job. The alternative, leaving a candle burning throughout the night, produced too bright a light, so various tricks were adopted to reduce the glare. One was a night light in the form of a castle or cottage in which the candle inside shone through the windows. Around the 1830s lithophanes were developed. These were mostly of German origin, although they were also made in France, Britain, Bohemia and even America. The technique called for great modelling skill and was done by coating a glass sheet with a layer

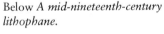
Above *Limoges plate printed and painted with a fish, about 1900.*

Below *A mid-nineteenth-century lithophane.*

of wax. With a light shining from behind, the sculptor scraped away and built up layers to form a picture, usually a genre scene, religious or portrait, often copied from a popular painting. From this, moulds were taken which were used to cast thin sheets of porcelain. Looked at under ordinary light, they offer a meaningless, badly moulded negative of a design, but held up to a light, as intended, they are magically transformed into a brilliant picture in a full range of tones. Lithophanes were used to form shades to lamps and are occasionally found in strange shapes, made to fit a particular shade. Few people collect them, as display is so difficult; nevertheless good examples from the Berlin factory (the best) can make £100 upwards.

The idea of using a slab of porcelain much as an oil painter might use a canvas had been around since Sèvres examples were used as insets in furniture. In the nineteenth century Berlin, Vienna, Dresden and Meissen all produced blanks that were bought by independent decorators to work on. Very little that they produced was actually original: almost all were copies of old masters or of popular contemporary paintings hanging in galleries across Europe. Many are very skilfully reproduced, and they have a brilliant, smooth finish which appeals to many people. Saleability depends on many factors, the most important of which is subject matter. An attractive young girl, particularly if barely clad, is tops, followed by large crowd scenes or a few naked girls being carried off. Slave scenes are also very desirable. Reproductions of detailed old masters such as Dutch seventeenth-century interiors are popular. Religious scenes are bottom, particularly the New Testament

CARE AND REPAIR

∞

○ See pp. 64–5.

(the Old Testament is supported by Jewish collectors). The only buyers of the New Testament seem to come, weirdly, from Japan. The Japanese are in fact the major buyers of these plaques and large sums can be paid. A very large example can make over £10,000, but an attractive girl on a 10×6-inch plaque will still make £1000. Apart from size, another vital consideration is the factory. For some inexplicable reason Berlin examples are worth more than plaques from other factories, although the quality of the painting varies as much as on any other. The other odd thing is that the £1000 girl would be worth £300 painted just as well on canvas.

The earthenwares of France during the nineteenth century mostly comprised useful jugs, dishes, pots and covers and are of little interest. As they compared unfavourably with British products they were neither imported nor even brought back by tourists. However, what did grow for the tourist trade was a flourishing business in reproduction eighteenth-century faience. Rouen suffered most from these pastiches, certainly in terms of numbers, although many of them were well made, large and decorative. A 24-inch dish recently sold for £400, but the smaller candlesticks, shoes, boxes, inkwells and so on can be had for £10 or so.

At the beginning of the century, minor factories in eastern France were continuing the tradition of the genuine eighteenth-century faience plates (see p. 64), decorated with birds, flowers or figures which have a robust charm. Not well painted, but brightly coloured, they go well with pine and are accordingly bought by interior decorators for £40 upwards. Condition here is not all-important – most have chips along the rim, as the tin glaze is very fragile, and even a hair crack is acceptable.

At the end of the century the art pottery movement got under way, and the Bordeaux area produced a range of small, brilliantly enamelled vases, dishes and bowls in designs mostly influenced by Japan, China and the Middle East. They are still relatively inexpensive and examples can be bought for only a few pounds – my hot tip for the future.

In Paris, Théodore Deck founded a factory which was to have great impact in the field, winning major prizes at international exhibitions. Mostly these were for very large dishes painted with portraits in classical style, *japonais* subjects or, later, Art Nouveau designs. In a way, they were simply ceramic blanks on which a skilled painter had chosen to work, much as Berlin plaques were – although Deck's were original works of art whereas the others were simply copies from one medium to another. Deck is highly rated, particularly in France, and prices range from a few hundred to several thousand pounds.

By 1900, apart from mass-produced wares from centres such as Vienna, Bohemia and Limoges, most factories had taken the spirit of Art Nouveau on board. A new and very different century had begun.

Bohemian porcelain plaque made by Lippert and Hass, Schlaggenwald, and painted by Johann Quast, 1843.

TWENTIETH-CENTURY ENGLISH POTTERY AND PORCELAIN

HENRY SANDON

Henry Sandon examines a pottery dish brought in to the Roadshow.

Although ceramics of the twentieth century are not of any great age, they can be highly attractive and desirable. Age does not of itself make craftsmanship great – it is the quality of the work that counts. It is worth remembering that a Chelsea figure was new when it was first made.

I have always been especially interested in the wares of our own century, finding in them so many reminders of my own upbringing. Perhaps only music can evoke the atmosphere of a period better than a pot. Since twentieth-century wares are so much closer to us in time it is possible to know much more about many of the craftsmen involved, and I believe that this adds greatly to our understanding and enjoyment.

Many of the great English porcelain factories continued into the present century, producing fine-quality wares. But not all that they made is valuable or collectable at present, especially mass-produced wares. Even though a piece may have been made by Doulton, Wedgwood or Royal Worcester, it is not a valuable antique if it belongs to one of the cheaper ranges of tea wares, transfer printed or decorated with a lithographic print. Lithography really came into its own in the twentieth century and can be of superb quality, despite the fact that it was mass produced by screen and photographic processes. Many collectors and owners are surprised at having a colourfully decorated vase or plate, hitherto thought to be of great value, identified as a cheap printed item. 'But you can *feel* the colour,' they plead, 'and it *is* signed'! To be able to feel the colour does not make it a painting, nor does the existence of a signature make it special, for there may be a hundred thousand printed examples, all the same as the next.

To tell whether a piece is printed, take a strong magnifying glass to it. If it is a lithograph, the subject should blow up into a mass of

Top of page Royal Doulton jug in the form of a red-haired clown.

91

Royal Lancastrian goblet made at the Pilkington factory in 1908.

regular dots, rather like a photograph in a newspaper. If it is an etching, you should be able to see masses of straight bits that make up the broad outline of the scene, which would then be painted over by hand. While that can be quite skilful work, it does not compare with fine hand painting throughout. At the Worcester factory many of the painters would not sign their real names to such etching and overpainting, but used false signatures. I learned this when I saw a plate with a scene of a castle painted over an etching signed H. Sivad. I could find no trace of such a painter, so I asked the great artist Harry Davis if he knew who it might be. 'Why, that's me!' said Harry. 'It's Davis spelt backwards, to show that it was not all my own work.'

The ease with which fine colour lithography can be produced has led to the great number of printed 'limited edition' items, especially plates, made in recent years. Hardly a Sunday supplement is published without an advertisement for a set of floral thimbles or the latest in an unending series of Christmas plates. These are produced in what are termed limited editions, implying a carefully controlled issue of a small number of pieces. In fact they are not really limited at all. The dealers, who are often not even the manufacturers, use phrases such as 'hand-crafted' and 'master-pieces of great investment potential'. In reality they can be mass produced from a quickly applied lithograph, at a unit cost which is a small fraction of the sale price. If you try to sell them you would be unlikely to get back anything near their original cost. The best advice is that you should buy such things if you like them and wish to keep them. Certainly they can look splendid and can give a lot of pleasure, as long as you do not expect to make a fast profit.

The finest wares of our great factories can be very collectable and are always a joy to see at a *Roadshow*. Just thinking of some of the items that have given me particular pleasure over the years makes my heart beat quickly again, in the way it does when a piece is unwrapped and we wonder if something superb will emerge.

One of them was a Royal Crown Derby vase beautifully gilded by Désiré Leroy, the gilder who was trained at the great French factory of Sèvres. Unfortunately the piece was badly damaged, which naturally reduced its value a lot, but the work was so beautiful that you could forgive it anything. Never let damage put you off buying a lovely piece that you like. It can give you great pleasure, as long as you realise that it isn't always easy to resell a damaged piece; and don't be persuaded to pay for a damaged piece what you would give for a perfect one.

Some fine Wedgwood is brought in, and especially fascinating are the strange pieces designed by Daisy Makeig-Jones. Particularly collectable are the fairyland lustres, full of the magical imagery of fairies and goblins. The vases can be very beautiful, but the large plaques are particularly valuable. Generally speaking, a plaque is worth more than a vase or a plate, perhaps because it is the nearest thing in ceramics to a framed painting (p. 95).

Doulton figures and character jugs are brought in to most *Roadshows*. These have been made in huge numbers by Doulton in Burslem and many are still in production. To be worth a lot of money the piece must have been made for only a short while and be no longer in production. This information can be found in 'bibles' listing all the items, and their publication contributed a great deal to the collectability of the pieces. There is no doubt that the publication of a major book, in which collectors can find full information about a specific subject, plays a major part in generating interest, and leads to an escalation in values. A collectors' club can play a big part in increasing values, as can specialised auction sales. All these factors have led to prices for some Doulton character jugs going through the roof. When they are brought in to a *Roadshow* we have to see whether the jug depicting a clown, say, has got red hair or white, and then hope that the value we suggest, based on the figure that the last one sold for at auction, is right. Sometimes we need to be clairvoyant to get it right, since the rarest figures make £5000 or more. Valuations for collectors' items are always subject to whim and fashion.

I am always pleased to see Royal Worcester at a *Roadshow*. It is especially delightful to be able to tell the owner some personal facts about the painter, gilder or modeller, many of whom I had the honour of knowing personally. The human-angle stories about them are the things that people remember. I have seen several

Thistle vase by Hans Coper in matt-glazed stoneware.

examples of the work of John Stinton, the extraordinary painter born in 1854 who lived into his 102nd year, painted Highland cattle for such a long time that his fellow craftsmen said he grew to look like them, and yet had never been to Scotland in his life. He had never seen real-life Highland cattle, and did all his superb work from postcards that his friends sent him. One particular characteristic was that he always buried the feet of the cattle in heather or water, so that they were not visible. Fakes have poorly painted animals with their feet clearly showing. It is sad to realise that there are fakes of pieces as recent as those painted by Stinton, but once things become collectable someone will always make fakes. A fine large vase or plaque, costing at the most £100 not so many years ago, can be worth a few thousand now.

Perhaps the most exciting single piece of Worcester ever brought in was a vase superbly hand-pierced by the incomparable George Owen. (See p. 82 and the description of Owen's work by David Battie on p. 81.) The owner had been told it was worth £80, but on that day I put a value of £1250 on it. Even that would now

Three large Royal Worcester vases, painted between 1913 and 1920 by Harry Davis (sheep), Walter Sedgley (roses) and John Stinton (Highland cattle).

Fairyland lustre wall plaque designed by Daisy Makeig-Jones in about 1920.

be below its present value, so if the owner reads this book I suggest a revaluation, as also of the eighty other fine Worcester vases he said he had at home. Then there were the seven plates from a dessert service made by Worcester for Ranjitsinhji, the Maharajah of Nawanagar, who was a famous cricketer. This service had been painted with scenes of the Maharajah's Indian palaces by Harry Davis, whom I regard as the finest ceramic artist of this century. I well remember Harry telling me what a joy it had been to paint this fine service in the 1920s. He frequently described to me the scenes depicting these incredible buildings shimmering under the fierce sun and glowing in soft moonlight, but I had never seen any examples. Then suddenly out of the blue these seven plates were on a table in front of me, and heaven opened up. So many people mentioned the joy they felt at seeing the plates brought via the television screen into their living rooms that it gave me great personal satisfaction to be the medium between owner and viewer.

Another beautiful service that I remember with great pleasure was a Royal Worcester dessert service painted with still-life subjects in the Dutch style by William Hawkins, the foreman painter before Harry Davis. The service comprised the full eighteen pieces – twelve plates and six dishes. It is always nice to see a service that has not been split up among different members of a family.

Other interesting factories whose wares I enjoy seeing are those that continued the art pottery movement of the late nineteenth century, such smallish firms as Ruskin, Royal Lancastrian, Della Robbia, Brannam, Moorcroft, Poole, Bernard Moore and the Martin Brothers, many of whom made fascinating experimental glazes. These perhaps come more under the aegis of Eric Knowles and his interest in Art Nouveau (see p. 45) and Art Deco (see p. 98), but since he pinched from me at one *Roadshow* a Royal Worcester vase painted with a Harry Davis scene of Tynemouth

Royal Worcester sculpture of white doves modelled by Ronald van Ruyckevelt, made in a limited edition of twenty-five for the Silver Wedding of HM The Queen and Prince Philip in 1972.

Martinware model of a grotesque bird, signed and dated 1900.

Priory and enthused about it, I will do the same about some of his favourites! Particularly attractive to me are the high-fired reduction experiments of Ruskin; the flambé effects of Bernard Moore; and the lustre decoration of Pilkington's Royal Lancastrian factory. I am sure that these are under-appreciated at present.

One range of ceramics that is seldom brought in to the *Roadshow* is that of the modern craftsman potter, the work of an individual working on his or her own or with only an assistant or pupil. This movement started at St Ives with the work of Bernard Leach, the father of English craftsmen potters. While a mass of ordinary things like coffee beakers are turned out, the best of the modern potters are producing some of the most exciting ceramics of all time. Values at auction do not necessarily indicate quality, of course, but it is perhaps an indication of the growing interest of collectors in such things when you can find a vase by Bernard Leach fetching £1000 or more, or a majestic, modernistic stoneware sculpture by Hans Coper being knocked down for £35,000.

A really fine piece of modern ceramics, made of stoneware, earthenware or a porcelain body, can be a delightful thing, giving great pleasure to handle, use or just to look at, and will undoubtedly be the antique of the future. The potter and pot that you like will obviously be a very personal decision, and it is wrong for someone else to put their thoughts into the mind of another. My own favourite craftsmen potters of the twentieth century would have to include Bernard Leach, his son David and wife Janet, Michael Cardew, Lucie Rie, Hans Coper, Alan Caiger-Smith, William Staite Murray, Geoffrey Whiting and Raymond Finch. One of the fascinating things about collecting the work of modern potters is that you can go to the pottery, perhaps meet the potter and buy the piece that attracts you, often for a relatively small sum. I once had the idea of asking some of the potters whose work I most admired if I might buy a pot that they particularly liked. These pieces, highly regarded by the potters themselves, have given me great enjoyment over the years.

Forget the age of a piece. Forget, if you can, whether the factory or potter is highly regarded and collected. Buy it if you like it, and I am sure you will never be sorry. There ought to be a law preventing people from buying a pot that they do not really like but are buying purely for investment! Perhaps a society should be formed to save such pots from the wrong purchaser – a sort of RSPCP.

If I was allowed to take only one pot with me to a desert island I have often pondered which I would choose. I think it would be one of the magnificently comic birds that the Martin Brothers made around 1900, each one a completely different character, looking sly or crafty, shy or wicked. A great friend of mine in America collects them because they remind him of his friends or enemies. To visit his house and meet the people beside the Martinware birds that they resemble, without their being aware of the connection, shows just one of the infinite forms that collecting can take.

CARE AND REPAIR
∘ See pp. 64–5.

ART DECO

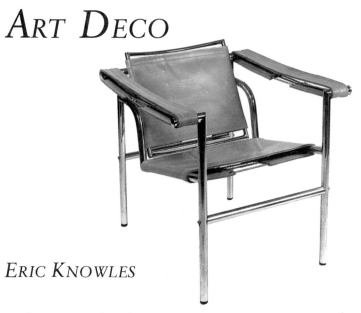

ERIC KNOWLES

Back in 1981, when the *Antiques Roadshow* visited Lancaster, the weather was living up to the north-west's midsummer expectations – it was raining. But the length of the queues hardly reflected the weather, and as usual we had been rushed off our feet since the doors had opened at 10 a.m.

During the early afternoon I had placed before me a rather weary-looking thirties' chalk figure, in the form of a scantily attired young woman being dragged at speed by two sleek greyhounds whose leashes she held in her outstretched hand. The poor girl's situation was made even worse by the fact that each dog had only three legs, and the group looked totally absurd. The owner explained that the dogs had been casualties of the Blitz, which somehow made them more endearing but regrettably didn't help in making the group worth more than a few pounds.

Before my next contestant was able to take the hot seat I heard an unmistakable voice from behind me say: 'I really feel sorry for the likes of you, having to deal with modern stuff. Do you know that the last time I gazed upon a figure such as that I was at a fairground looking down the barrel of an air-rifle and trying hard to blow it to pieces for a coconut!' Arthur Negus had not been impressed, and to be honest few people would have been. It is an unfortunate fact that for many years such objects have mistakenly been considered as 'typical' Art Deco, when in fact nothing could be further from the truth. I sincerely hope that if you read on you will understand why.

The term Art Deco is derived from the Exposition Internationale des Arts Décoratifs et Industriels Modernes, held in Paris in 1925. It was originally planned to take place in 1915, but the outbreak of the First World War meant an indefinite postponement. After the Armistice the Exhibition was re-scheduled to take

Top of page *Chromium-plated tubular steel armchair designed by Le Corbusier.*

CARE AND REPAIR
◇∽◇

- ○ For bronze see p. 132.
- ○ For ivory see p. 137.
- ○ For silver see p. 29.

place in 1922; however, because many basic raw materials were in short supply it did not finally open until June 1925. The main criterion for all entries was that of being 'modern'. In the minds of the organisers, the Exhibition was to be a celebration of the future.

The Exhibition site was in the very centre of Paris, on opposite banks of the River Seine. The records and photographs reveal it to have been a huge and fascinating event covering 30,000 square metres of landscaped grounds and including such fine buildings as the Grand Palais. The firm of Citroën installed some two hundred thousand electric light bulbs to cover the entire Eiffel Tower. At the flick of a switch, the tower was transformed into the world's largest advertising display. The multi-coloured bulbs were arranged to offer nine alternating displays, which included stars, comets, flames, animated signs of the zodiac and the name 'Citroën' in gigantic letters. The idea was 'brilliant' in every sense.

So what are the characteristics an item must possess to qualify as Art Deco? At this point I must stress that the term can often prove baffling, since it is regarded by many people as an umbrella heading for a number of styles which had begun to emerge about 1910. Briefly, I group these styles under two distinct headings, Traditionalist and Modernist.

'Bacchantes', produced in opalescent glass by René Lalique during the late 1920s.

'The Starfish Girl', a bronze and ivory figure by Dimitri Chiparus, 1933.

The Traditionalists would include such French furniture designers as Emile Jacques Ruhlmann and André Groult, whereas the Modernists would include Ludwig Mies van der Rohe and Marcel Breuer. The Traditionalists, as the name implies, were quite prepared to adopt simplified eighteenth-century forms and to incorporate into their designs rich and expensive materials such as macassar ebony and ivory. The Modernists, however, were quick to reject both the materials and philosophy of their contemporaries, whose products they saw as being affordable only by the rich élite of society.

For the Modernists, the twentieth century was to be a brave new world of steel, concrete and glass. Regarded by many as a guiding light for the movement, the architect and designer Le Corbusier went so far as to announce that 'a house is a machine for living in'. To him the movement represented the rationalisation of Cubism, the semi-abstract style of painting adopted by artists such as Braque and Picasso as a reaction to Impressionism. In Germany the Modern Movement found a focal point in the Bauhaus, which opened in 1919 primarily as a school of design under the leadership of Walter Gropius. Its principal aim was to bring together architects, engineers, designers and artists with the purpose of producing objects whose design and construction related to their function. Gropius was succeeded as director in 1928 by Mies van der Rohe, who remained until the school was closed by the Nazis in 1933. Hitler obviously considered its ideals too avant-garde.

Both the Modernists and the Bauhaus placed emphasis on geometrical design; in china, this is particularly evident in the work of Clarice Cliff. Other influences included the vivid colours employed in the costume designs of Léon Bakst for the Ballets Russes, Aztec art and, more significantly, Egyptian art. The discovery of Tutankhamun's tomb in 1923 caused a flood of Egyptian-inspired furniture, pottery and jewellery. West African tribal art, 'discovered' by the Cubist painters, suddenly became chic; the talented interior designer Eileen Gray would often use tribal artefacts in her interiors to help give emphasis to the modern elements.

Above all else it must be remembered that, after the upheavals of the First World War, the very structure of Continental and British society had altered irrevocably. The horror of those years, coupled with renewed optimism for a brighter tomorrow, meant that many people were only too willing to forget the past and accept the modern world with open arms. This was the Jazz Age, when women cut their hair and shortened their skirts. Cars were getting faster, ocean liners bigger and even more luxurious, buildings kept getting taller and Lindbergh was making the first solo transatlantic crossing by air. The twenties continued to roar until the Wall Street crash of 1929 brought the whole party to an abrupt end and shook the economic structures of both the USA and Europe to their foundations.

Phoebe Stabler's silver figure was symbolic of the speed and improved communications of the inter-war years.

Fortunately for me, most people who attend the *Antiques Roadshow* do not take the word 'antique' too literally – strictly speaking, it only covers items at least a hundred years old. As a result I have been able to see and handle many Art Deco objects. Our day in Edinburgh turned up trumps when out of the proverbial bundle of newspaper (the *Roadshow* and the nation's fish and chip shops are probably equally dependent upon the stuff) appeared a fascinating glass car mascot designed by the French master glassmaker René Lalique. It was in fact just one of a range of twenty-seven individual glass car mascots designed and produced by Lalique. Originally retailed in about 1930 under the evocative title of 'The Spirit of the Wind' or sometimes 'Victoire', the mascot took the form of a young woman's head with highly stylised, swept-back hair. The mascot could be illuminated, which probably made night-time driving both sensational and possibly hazardous – I'm quite sure that I would have become totally mesmerised by that glass sculpture glowing on the bonnet. The casualty rate from stone chippings or small boys armed with catapults (remember, the thirties was also the age of *Just William*) must have been alarmingly high. Such is their scarcity today that, whereas in 1930 you would have paid £7 17s 6d for an illuminated example, those offered at auction today have recently sold for prices in excess of £4000, especially if the clear glass has been given an amethyst tint.

All Lalique's mascots could be fitted to any make of vehicle, although 'The Spirit of the Wind' is often erroneously referred to as being specifically for use on Rolls-Royces. Such a suggestion would probably have been most upsetting to Charles Sykes, the designer of the bronze mascot used by Rolls-Royce which bears a similar title, 'The Spirit of Ecstasy'. One Lalique glass car mascot which did end up on the bonnet of a Rolls-Royce took the form of a peacock's head. The proud lady owner had it installed on her vehicle back in the thirties in the firm belief that Lalique had designed the mascot for her sole use. Regrettably the peacock head was a stock design made in both clear and 'electric' blue glass. But I think, under the circumstances, the lady might be forgiven for her apparently unshakeable convictions – her name was Miss Peacock. The car and its mascot became separated a few years ago when another owner sold the vehicle for around £4000 but decided to keep the mascot. It was recently entrusted to me for sale and made £9500 at auction.

Imitation is the sincerest form of flattery, and there was no shortage of French glassmakers prepared to produce wares like those of Lalique. Opalescent glass, pioneered and used to perfection by Lalique, was soon to become a staple product of glassmakers such as Sabino and Verlys, together with a host of smaller glassworks making similar moulded glassware. Pâte de verre glassware enjoyed a growing popularity, especially those works produced by Almeric Walter and Argy-Rousseau. The technique

'The Spirit of the Wind', a glass car mascot by Lalique.

Rug designed by Edward McKnight Kauffer, inspired by Cubism and woven by the Axminster carpet factory during the late twenties and early thirties.

of making pâte de verre glass involved crushing the glass into a powder, mixing it with water and an adhesive, and then adding it in thin layers to a mould until the desired thickness was achieved. The mould would be fired in a kiln to make the paste fuse. If the object survived the hazardous firing process it emerged as a semi-opaque material with a slightly waxy surface. The process was known and used by the ancient Egyptians, and then revived during the nineteenth century by the Frenchman Henri Cros. An example made by Almeric Walter at his glassworks in Nancy and designed by Henri Bergé made an unexpected appearance at the Scarborough *Roadshow*. It took the form of a small tortoise which had been made for use as a paperweight (pâte de verre glass is a dense material and deceptively heavy).

Bronzes, and in particular chryselephantine or bronze and ivory figures, have featured on the *Roadshow* on at least a couple of occasions. Our day in Watford brought a real gem out of the attic when a lady showed us a figure by Ferdinand Preiss. The sheer quality of his work never ceases to amaze me, and this figure, known as 'Con Brio', was no exception. Wearing shorts and a bikini top, the young woman possessed a pair of legs that made Betty Grable look knock-kneed. Preiss's figures, however, tend to concentrate on Germanic Aryan ideals of fitness and health, and given the choice (not to mention the few thousand pounds required), I would probably be more inclined to collect the figures of Dimitri Chiparus. 'The Starfish Girl' (p. 100) is a perfect example of his style. Chiparus's women are attired in beaded or studded catsuits or similar exotic costume, and their heads are often adorned with close-fitting caps or futuristic helmets. All his creations could quite happily have had walk-on parts in Fritz Lang's *Metropolis* or a *Flash Gordon* episode, and all, given the current prices paid, are to be considered expensive women.

Be on your guard for the fake bronze and ivory figures now being produced – the latter are actually bronze-coloured metal and plastic. Try to familiarise yourself with the real thing, and think twice about buying what appears to be a real bargain.

Over the past few series there has been no shortage of Art Nouveau silver (see pp. 46 and 48), but good Art Deco silver seems in general to have eluded me. The chances of finding a good French teaset by Puiforcat or a Bauhaus example by Marianne Brandt are always going to be slim, and though an Art Deco teaset by the Danish silversmith Georg Jensen was once featured on the programme, it was many moons ago.

The work of the silversmith Omar Ramsden always manages to combine craftsmanship with good design, yet his work is really more influenced by the Arts and Crafts style of the later nineteenth century than by the Modern Movement of the late 1920s. Unlike the jewellers of the period, the silversmiths appeared to treat Art Deco design with a certain amount of caution, and this probably accounts for so few items being brought along to the *Roadshow*.

The trophy designed by Phoebe Stabler (p. 101) is quite a dramatic example of the type of work that was being achieved during the 1930s.

Of all the pottery produced during the 1920s and 1930s it seems ironic that probably the best known and most collectable was retailed by Woolworth's for very modest sums. What would Clarice Cliff think today of some of the prices paid for her work? Produced by Wilkinson & Co. at their Staffordshire pottery during the thirties, Clarice Cliff designs are instantly recognisable for their bold use of contrasting primary colours and the geometric shapes of her teawares. The pattern names of Fantasque and Bizarre are highly appropriate. Her 'Age of Jazz' figures are prob-

'Age of Jazz' group, designed by Clarice Cliff.

During the 1930s the Viennese factory of Goldscheider made a number of fashion figures such as this dancer.

ably the most sought after of her designs; the two couples shown are a single object despite the optical illusion of two, one behind the other.

A contemporary of Miss Cliff was Susie Cooper, whose designs were first produced by Messrs A. E. Gray & Co. Ltd until she set up her own pottery in about 1932. In relation to the prices commanded by Clarice Cliff, Susie Cooper is vastly undervalued.

Remarkable though it may seem, the *Roadshow* has yet to produce what I would consider a fine piece of Art Deco furniture. During the inter-war years, the British who could afford fine-quality modern furnishings tended to buy from such makers as Heal's and Gordon Russell. These firms might be regarded as the Conran and Habitat of their day. Members of the chic Knightsbridge set could content themselves with the presently hugely under-rated furniture designs of Betty Joel. The same designers, alongside Hille & Co., produced fine dining room and bedroom furniture, usually in light woods such as sycamore or bird's-eye maple. The problem with much of this type of furniture is that it is often difficult to sell at auction, because of its large size and the fact that most people nowadays live in more modest houses or flats than those for which the pieces were originally intended.

Another exciting development was the use of laminated furniture by the British-based company Isokon. Similar furniture was being produced by the architect and designer Alvar Aalto at his Helsinki company, which traded under the name Finmar, from about 1931.

Chromium-plated tubular steel furniture was introduced during the same period, and pieces to designs by both Marcel Breuer and Mies van der Rohe are still being produced today. The Barcelona chair is an example, a testimonial to the 'timeless' look they created. The leading British manufacturer was known as Practical Equipment Ltd or PEL, and a good number of years ago I came across a workman's skip piled high with PEL stacking chairs. When I approached the foreman with a view to buying them I was told in no uncertain terms that there was no chance. When asked why, he explained: 'They're Art Deco, mate! Don't you know the Victoria and Albert Museum have a couple on display?' The world, it seems, is full of experts – it must be the *Antiques Roadshow*!

In 1929 Waring and Gillow, that bastion of fine-quality furniture manufacture, set up a department of modern French furniture under the directorship of Paul Follot and Serge Chermayeff. Follot had initially worked in the Art Nouveau style before making a transition towards Deco, and is now regarded as one of the progenitors of Art Deco. After 1925 his creations followed public taste by adopting Cubist and geometrical shapes. By the end of the decade he was working in the Modernist style. Serge Chermayeff was, as his name suggests, born in Russia, but he was educated in

Sideboard by Gordon Russell. Such pieces are still not expensive, perhaps because they were designed for larger homes than many people live in today.

Britain before studying art and architecture on the Continent. His furniture was quite distinctive in its use of contrasting veneers, and examples of his work can be viewed in Brighton Museum. That museum, incidentally, houses one of the country's most comprehensive collections of both Art Nouveau and Art Deco, and is well worth a visit.

Sir Gordon Russell established his Russell Workshops in Broadway, Worcestershire, and concentrated during the early twenties on traditional English furniture such as ladder-back chairs, using local woods such as oak and yew. Then, as today, traditional English furniture was probably the real breadwinner for many a furniture manufacturer. His adoption of a distinctive linear style during the early thirties was to have quite a profound influence on young British furniture designers working in the 1950s and 1960s.

I couldn't resist including the Art Deco rug (p. 102). I found it on the floor of a very smart Belgravia apartment which also contained various items of good-quality French Art Deco furniture. When I informed the owner, a retired army major, that the rug was designed by and signed with the initials of Edward McKnight Kauffer, he gave a wry smile. 'I bought it from the man himself back in 1930. He was a Yank, do you know?'

I suppose that that sort of situation, in which you can get a direct link with the original designer, is one of the reasons why dealing with twentieth-century decorative arts is so interesting. Looked at another way, what are the chances of John Bly meeting an acquaintance of Thomas Chippendale, or Hugo Morley-Fletcher having lunch with a business associate of Josiah Wedgwood?

TWO CENTURIES OF EUROPEAN GLASS

ANTHONY J. LESTER

'I'd like to buy this rummer, please.' It seems strange that I still remember such a simple phrase, uttered some twenty-five years ago, but it proved to have a very significant impact on my life.

When I left school I hired a stall at a market, where I offered for sale a wide range of secondhand items under the optimistic heading of 'Antiques'. Amongst the bric-à-brac was a large, heavy glass, which I had priced at two shillings. This proved to be my first sale of the day, and for that reason alone it is memorable. However, it was the word 'rummer' used by the purchaser that had made such a positive impact. What was a rummer? To me it was just a glass. My enthusiasm to learn led me the next day to the local library, where I diligently studied a book devoted to antique glassware.

What I had sold was an early nineteenth-century glass, used primarily for beer and ale, and which was, I suspect, a standard drinking vessel in many a pub at the time it was made. Reading the book opened my eyes to a subject of which I had previously been ignorant. Visits to museums ensued, simply to look at glass, and I soon became totally captivated. From then on I started to collect glass, and over the years have spent a great deal of time trying to solve some of its many unanswered mysteries.

Who discovered how to make glass? It is said 'that some mariners who had a cargo of natron [soda] on board, having landed on the banks of the river Belus, a small stream at the base of Mount Carmel in Palestine, and finding no stones to rest their pots on, placed under them some masses of nitrum, which being fused by the heat with the sand of the river, produced a liquid and transparent stream'. This famous story comes from the pen of the Roman historian Pliny the Elder. It is a nice tale, but certainly a complete fabrication; perhaps Pliny had partaken of a little too much grape

Top of page *A selection of inexpensive but collectable glass, including a slag glass jar (far left), a cloud glass vase (fourth from right), a Mary Gregory ruby tumbler (second from right) and a carnival glass jug (far right).*

This nineteenth-century Viennese enamelled Ranftbecher *sold for over £4000 in 1986.*

English enamelled glass is rarer than Continental. This superb piece by William Beilby, commemorating the birth of the Prince of Wales in 1762, went at auction for over £52,000 in 1985.

juice when he wrote it! The intense heat required to melt the sand would have resulted in cremated food, to say the least. The more probable explanation is that glass was developed accidentally in a pottery kiln. But this is all speculation; the only thing that can be positively established is that there is evidence of glassmaking 3500 years ago.

The first great name of English glassmaking was George Ravenscroft (1632–83), the inventor of 'flint glass', now commonly known as lead crystal. By introducing lead oxide into the compound he produced 'a particular sort of crystalline glass resembling rock crystal', for which he applied for a patent in March 1674. The following month Ravenscroft submitted samples of his new glass to the Glass Sellers' Company, the body of manufacturers and importers who represented the trade. They were so impressed that they established him in a glasshouse at Henley-on-Thames in Oxfordshire. Here he was able to continue manufacture and pursue further research away from the eyes of his London competitors. Yes, there was industrial espionage even in those days!

Whilst Ravenscroft's early products had a tendency to crizzle (a fine crazing and deterioration of the surface of glass), by 1676 he seems to have rectified this problem sufficiently for the Glass Sellers' Company to offer his products with the guarantee 'no crizzling or money returned'. The great advantage of using lead oxide was that it resulted in a glass of increased durability and transparency, whiter in colour and with greater refractive properties than the soda glass which it largely superseded.

Glass that can be attributed to Ravenscroft is now extremely rare and expensive, although a goblet was brought into one of the *Roadshows* which was almost certainly made at Ravenscroft's glasshouse. Arthur Negus often told the story of how, as a young man, he inadvertently sold a Ravenscroft dish for thirty shillings. Perhaps there are yet other pieces awaiting discovery. I keep on looking!

In the eighteenth century it became the height of fashion to serve, after the main course, a selection of nuts, French figs, preserved fruits, raisins and marshmallows in specially designed glasses. But by far the largest number of glass objects that have survived from the eighteenth and nineteenth centuries are drinking vessels. Whilst the lower classes frequented the many taverns, the gentry visited their clubs, where gentlemen's lunch parties would often continue late into the night. It was the custom to drink many toasts, and toastmasters were an important part of the proceedings. Special glasses were designed to contain only small amounts of wine for use by the toastmaster, in the probably vain hope that he would remain sober. It is on record that many still became inebriated, so much so that a replacement would have to be summoned. Other glasses with especially sturdy construction were known as firing glasses. These were thumped on the table in praise

A group of eighteenth-century drinking glasses.

of toasts or speeches, when they would give the effect of gunfire.

The main criterion for dating eighteenth-century English drinking glasses is the shape and formation of the stem. They passed through many changes of fashion, and the various styles overlap considerably.

Baluster stems were popular from around 1690 to 1725. 'Baluster' is an architectural term used to describe a short pillar that is slender above and pear-shaped below. This was also the shape of the baluster stem glass, either the right way up or, more commonly, inverted. To prevent the foot of a glass being damaged, glassmakers invariably turned the footrim under, creating what is known as a folded foot. This feature is common on glasses made before 1750; after that date it becomes a rarity. From 1725 to 1760 balustroid stems were made. This group of glasses is a lighter development of the baluster glass, usually with a longer stem, and with simpler knopping. The knops are the decorative knobs of glass on the stem.

Light baluster stems, in vogue from around 1735 to 1765, are without doubt the most elegant and beautiful of all eighteenth-century glasses. Once more the knop forms are similar to those of the baluster group, but the combinations are normally more complex, sometimes incorporating as many as five different knops. The glasses are tall – generally $6\frac{1}{2}$–$8\frac{1}{2}$ inches – and slender, with bowls of large capacity. Many of the best-quality glasses are finely engraved with features such as coats of arms, figures, scrollwork and inscriptions. It has always been assumed that these glasses were manufactured in Newcastle-upon-Tyne and exported to Holland to be engraved. However, new research has revealed that they were actually made and engraved in Holland, and some were then exported to England for the wealthier drinkers of the day. I would go one step further and predict that in time research will prove that other glasses, now believed to be English, are of Continental manufacture – and vice versa.

Plain-stemmed glasses were produced in the period 1740–75 to meet the needs of all levels of society. For this reason, their quality varies enormously; many are badly proportioned and the stems are lopsided.

Of all the eighteenth-century glasses opaque white twist stems, made from about 1755 to 1780, must be the most easily recognisable, even by those with little knowledge of antiques. They were formed by arranging rods of opaque white enamel glass (made by adding arsenic and antimony to the basic raw materials) upright in a circular mould; clear molten glass was then poured in. When set, the block was removed from the mould. This mass was then reheated, drawn out and at the same time twisted, the resulting intricate patterns being determined by the arrangement of the canes in the mould. The stems would then be cut to an appropriate length and a bowl and foot added.

By 1750 England had become one of the world's major glass manufacturing centres. There were, for instance, over twenty large glassworks in London, plus dozens of cottage industry works. Glassware was being exported to many countries, including America, China, Japan and India. The Continent, too, supported a thriving glass industry. Whilst English glass was mostly subdued in style, its Continental counterpart was generally flamboyant; heavy enamelling and engraving were popular. However, the greatest exponent of hand-painted coloured enamels on glass was William Beilby (1740–1819), who worked in Newcastle (p. 107).

The value of eighteenth-century glasses depends on condition, quality and rarity of form, such as an unusual bowl shape. Forgeries do exist, but several characteristics distinguish the genuine article. Over the years manufacturing techniques improved and glass became whiter. Items made this century are very clear and of a brilliant colour, whereas eighteenth-century glass is quite dark. Grey-green, smoky blue, red and yellow tints all appear in glass throughout that period. Wear marks normally take the form of very fine, haphazard lines and pitting around the extreme outer edge of the foot, and to a lesser degree on the rim of the bowl. Beware of parallel scratches, which are artificially produced. Seeds are impurities, often minute, which are frequently found in antique glass; small bubbles are another common feature.

Fine old cut glass, sparkling and lustrous beneath flickering candlelight, has a magic to which we can all warm. Cutting in the true sense of the word had a wide vogue on the Continent long before the craft was established in England. Records show that cutters were operating in this country as early as the reign of Queen Anne, although few examples survive of earlier date than the mid-eighteenth century.

CARE AND REPAIR

- Wash in warm soapy water.
- Never hold a glass by the stem while washing or drying the bowl (or vice versa), for the glass may break.
- Dry decanters well after washing and store with the stoppers off.
- Never force a stuck stopper. To free, wipe a mixture of meths and cooking oil over the area where the stopper enters the neck and leave for a couple of days, when it should come out.
- Don't leave port, sherry or wine in decanters for long periods or they will go cloudy on the inside. To remove cloudiness use spirit vinegar or tablets for cleaning dentures, but don't leave decanters soaking for too long.
- Don't wrap glass in newspaper, which attracts moisture and can cause bloom. Use acid-free tissue.
- For all repairs consult an expert. Chips can sometimes be ground down, and breaks refired.

ANTHONY J. LESTER

In many eighteenth-century pieces, where lines were intended to be cut horizontally they are undulating and far from parallel, there are wavy rifts in the glass, and the edges are not of uniform thickness – all adding, I believe, great charm and character. These irregularities were in no way due to bad workmanship, for in those days they had only a thin cutting-wheel, operated either by pedal power or by an assistant turning a driving-wheel, connected by a leather belt to a pulley fixed on the cutting-wheel spindle. The uneven speed made uniformity impossible.

In 1745 the Government placed a tax on the raw materials for glass, and raised it again in 1777. This, coupled with other changes in the law, drove many English cutters to set up workshops in Ireland, where there was no such tax. Until about 1825, the year in which the Irish themselves imposed a tax on their glass, vast quantities of high-quality Irish cut glass were imported into England. Contrary to popular belief, it is not generally possible to distinguish Irish glass from English, but many dealers still label most cut glassware of this period as Irish – 'English or Irish' is the correct terminology.

A group of 1850s' bells known as 'friggers' – end-of-day pieces which glassblowers were allowed to keep or sell for themselves.

Claret jugs and vases made in the 1880s in cameo glass, a Roman technique. Layers of different-coloured glass were etched or carved away to create a pattern.

The Industrial Revolution took its toll: from about 1830 large batches of machine-made pressed glass were produced, putting attractive glass within the reach of millions but forcing many cutting firms out of business. Luckily for today's collectors, the wealthy still demanded the real article, so a number of glass cutters managed to survive. They produced high-quality jugs, vases, dishes, tumblers, candlesticks and, of course, the ever-popular decanter. One small tip when buying a decanter: because stoppers break easily they have often been replaced. Always examine the stopper carefully to ensure that it is of the same cutting and colour as the base, and that it fits snugly into the neck of the decanter.

English cut glass, particularly Victorian and Edwardian, is one of the few bargains left for the astute buyer. Take a look at new cut glass, then go around the antique shops and have a look at older examples – its greyness is one indication of age. Look at the price labels: I think you may be surprised to find that these pieces often cost no more than the modern equivalent.

The technique of press-moulding had been developed in America during the 1820s. The process was simple: the worker poured molten glass into a mould, and then brought down a plunger which squeezed the glass into every crevice. When the glass had cooled and solidified the mould was opened and the article removed. By the 1880s pressed glass had become the major product of many British glassworks – one Gateshead factory alone was producing 150 tons of finished glass per week. The variety and quantity grew in leaps and bounds: the firm of Sowerby had over two hundred different sugar bowls listed in their 1885 catalogue. Much of this material is available to the modern collector at quite modest prices.

This Baccarat pansy paperweight sold for £8640 in 1986.

Collectable glasses, some antique and some modern, all bought during 1987. The middle one is Chinese, the rest English, and none cost more than £4.

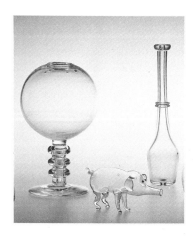

Left to right: a lacemaker's globe, a hollow pig which probably once held perfumed water, and a toddy lifter of about 1815. The globe, filled with water and put near a candle, concentrated the light on to the lace pillow. The toddy lifter worked like a pipette in transferring toddy from a bowl to a glass.

Among other types of Victorian and early twentieth-century glass to look out for are slag glass, made in the Midlands and North of England during the second half of the nineteenth century. The characteristic streaky effect was achieved by adding to the molten glass waste slag from blast furnaces. Attractive coloured glassware painted in white enamels, usually with scenes of children, is known as Mary Gregory. The genuine article was made from about 1870 to 1900 in Britain, the USA and Bohemia, but modern reproductions are made in Czechoslovakia – be warned! Pressed carnival glass, with its metallic iridescence, was first made in the USA in 1908 and became an immensely popular product of factories all over the world. Cloud glass, a favourite of the 1920s and 1930s, was made in several different colours and is now very collectable.

It has taken glass a long time to begin to attract the popularity enjoyed by other antiques, and for this reason I suspect that there are still many important glass items lying forgotten in cupboards and lofts. Two years ago, whilst carrying out a valuation of pictures in a house, I noticed a splendid paperweight on a window sill. It was a rare French Baccarat weight, and the owner, who considered it of little value, was both shocked and highly delighted when it eventually sold for £8200. The finest paperweights were made about 1845–60 and the very rarest now fetch prices in excess of £50,000, which seems remarkable for such small works of art. There are, not surprisingly, many forgeries, but they tend to be much lighter in weight and lack the brilliance and workmanship of the older weights.

Glassware today is attracting a growing number of collectors, and many items that were dismissed a few years ago are being sought with alacrity. Some twentieth-century glass can now be worth more than early pieces, so my advice is always to seek a professional opinion – perhaps when the *Roadshow* visits a town near you!

Papier Mâché

John Bly

In 1853, an issue of *The Illustrated London News* showed a picture of ten cottages and a ten-room villa made entirely of papier mâché! Under the headline 'Papier Mâché Village', the magazine explained that it was made by the firm of Bielfeld for export to Australia. At the same time advertisements were appearing for boats, ships and even bridges made of the same material – the same material, indeed, of which at least one example is brought in to every *Roadshow*. I recall one lady who had a collection of fans, which she prized most highly and kept in an old box. It transpired that none of the fans was anywhere near the value of that papier mâché box.

In the 1850s papier mâché had been around in England for nearly a hundred years, and its early uses were not confined to small pieces. We know, for instance, that in the 1780s Queen Charlotte had a sedan chair made of papier mâché panels, whose light weight made it possible for the chairmen to travel at a far greater speed than before. More ordinary chairs and tables were by no means uncommon, and other pieces of furniture such as pianos and even beds were made in this material.

Papier mâché is really interwoven with japanning, that art of the East which we have been trying to imitate in England since the late seventeenth century (see p. 136). The Orientals could use wood as a base for their lacquer, as their natural gum dried hard. Britain had no natural gum for lacquer, and the substitute had to be oven-baked, which of course warped the wood. So in the eighteenth century tinware was adopted as a base, and paperware came along as an alternative.

Over the years the term papier mâché has been used to describe three distinct methods of manufacturing reconstituted materials. The earliest came to England from France prior to the 1750s, and

Top of page *A set of graduated trays with Chinese decoration incorporating pearl inlay, made in about 1830.*

consisted of reducing rag paper to a pulp and mixing it with chalk, fine sand and glue. This was then pressed into oiled boxwood moulds and, when dry, stoved and japanned. In 1786 one Obadiah Westwood patented an improvement and made tea trays, boxes, caddies, bottle stands, ink stands and frames for pictures and mirrors. The next type stems from a patent developed in 1772 by Henry Clay, who placed sheets of porous paper saturated with flour and glue over a pre-formed mould. Clay first referred to this as paperware, but it became known as papier mâché during the 1830s. Finally, the type used for furniture after 1836 was made from substantial panels and blanks of rolled rag pulp, which could be treated almost like wood before japanning.

I think it must have been this last sort of papier mâché that caused so much hilarity in a country auction one day. A Victorian bed with a japanned foot and headboard and with a half canopy over the top came up for sale. 'And now, ladies and gentlemen,' announced the auctioneer, 'the lot you have all been waiting for – the half tester bed', at which point a dealer, no doubt wishing to deflate the moment, said, 'How do you half test a bed, sir?' and the whole room collapsed with laughter. I never see a piece of papier mâché – or, for that matter, a half tester bed – without thinking of that wonderful moment.

From 1772 Clay was the prime producer of papier mâché, with tea trays – or paper trays, as they were known – his most popular product. Even Dr Johnson acquired one when he visited the factory in Birmingham in 1774, and Clay was appointed 'Japanner in Ordinary to George III and the Prince of Wales'. Competitors were inevitable, and in 1780 a firm with the delightful name of Small & Son, Guest, Chopping and Bill were making papier mâché panels and presumably tea trays. In 1802 Clay retired, having made his fortune, and sold out to his competitors. In 1816 the new firm was in turn taken over, by Aaron Jennens and T. H. Bettridge, and so began the truly great age of the innovative decoration of papier mâché. By the 1830s Birmingham and nearby Wolverhampton supported more than twenty companies, and the wares they produced were unquestionably the finest in the world.

Both Clay's firm and Jennens and Bettridge stamped their wares, and such a name on the underside of a piece will enhance its interest and value. If genuine – and there are copies around, so beware – the quality of decoration will be superb, but lack of a name or stamp does not automatically mean an inferior piece.

Early decoration on trays and boxes was of an all-over type, usually floral, but by the beginning of the nineteenth century the outer edges and borders only were covered, to leave the centre panel clear. At this time the most popular shape for a tray was a plain rectangle with slightly rounded corners and a plain edge set at an angle. The most desirable are those in sets of three graduating in size and topped with a matching bread basket.

Paper rack of about 1840 with pearl decoration and a flower spray, and a slightly later spectacle case.

A pair of fans by Jennens and Bettridge, painted with scenes of Osborne House and Ryde, Isle of Wight.

The normal colour for papier mâché during its 120-odd years of manufacture was black. However, red, yellow, green and blue were also used: such pieces are extremely attractive and very valuable, as collectors seek them avidly. Until the 1820s the materials used for decoration were basically enamel, and bronze, silver or gold in powder or leaf form. The powder gave a filmy, wispy effect and the metal leaf provided the solid lines.

In 1825, however, George Souter, who worked for Jennens and Bettridge, introduced mother of pearl inlay – at least, that is what we call it. In fact it is thin flakes of either an oyster-like shell which has a green tinge, or the giant seasnail or 'aurora', which is pinkish. Because of its deep translucence it appears to be inlaid, but actually a thin sliver somewhere between $\frac{1}{100}$ and $\frac{1}{40}$ of an inch thick is merely stuck on to the surface. Pearl inlay was most popularly used in panels of flowers, but in architectural scenes – with, for example, one of the sides of a tower pink and the other green – it could create a most dramatic effect.

The mid-1820s saw a profusion of different designs. Wellington's successful campaigns against Napoleon had left the British with justifiably patriotic tastes, and scenes and emblems of war and victory were often incorporated. It is easy to forget the extent to which people were concerned over the imminent invasion by the

Mid-Victorian black and gilt tray with a romantic scene.

French. One of Jennens and Bettridge's foremen recounted that, when he was a boy, he remembered his mother being so afraid of Napoleon Bonaparte's arrival in Wolverhampton that she buried her best bonnet in the garden for safety; presumably it was dug up every Sunday before she went to church!

At the same time we had a revival of the Gothic style that had reappeared in the late eighteenth century, and 'Old French' was also emerging, made up of heavy foliate scrolls, carving and other decoration typical of Louis XIV, XV and XVI. For this reason it gained the name 'Tous les Louis' as well as 'Rococo' and 'Baroque'. To complicate the issue further, our third Chinoiserie was in full swing, and the novels of Sir Walter Scott were heightening the imaginations of the young with idyllic romance in the age of chivalry. All had features which were displayed in decorative form on papier mâché, but Chinoiserie was to have the greatest single effect as demand for the style led to an increase in the import of Chinese lacquer. Of the huge range of items that started to appear, the most attractive were undoubtedly the workboxes and worktables with plush-fitted interiors, bright-coloured silks and every conceivable device and instrument to assist a young lady with her needlework.

In answer to the imports, the English papier mâché factories produced even more caskets, teapoys, hand screens and panels decorated in the Chinese style. The English and Chinese products can easily be confused, but the basic construction is a guide to the difference. This type of Chinese lacquerware is usually on a wood base, whereas the English version is papier mâché. The base material will clearly show through on rubbed corners, and any break will immediately reveal either the brown, grey-green flaky papier mâché or the white splinters of wood.

The chief exponent of the Oriental style in England was another employee of Jennens and Bettridge, Joseph Booth, who is best known for the type of Anglo-Oriental designs which were also popular on contemporary Staffordshire china. Another Booth, well known for his delicate gold work in the Indian style, was Edwin, who went on to become the famous tragic actor and father of J. Wilkes Booth, who assassinated President Lincoln. From the time of Henry Clay, some of the best papier mâché was decorated by prominent artists, and here the quality of the painting must be your guide. But beware. Prior to the Registration of Designs Act in 1842, contemporary paintings could be copied without question, and there were many artists quite capable of reproducing the work of a master to such good effect as to pass for the real thing. So if you find a table top apparently painted with a Birket Foster, a Cipriani or a Morland, have it checked out before you book that world cruise!

Scenic decoration remained fairly exclusive, but the idea was so popular that a cheaper means of creating it had to be found, certainly for smaller items. From 1845 engravings were applied by

Blotter case decorated with the lilies of the valley popularised by William Jackson in the 1840s.

transfer on to box lids and small panels, usually with a cream ground, and after 1860 the print itself was pasted on to the surface.

One of the most important guides to dating comes from the style of flower painting, a theme which had remained popular since Henry Clay's time. His painting had an all-over design with large flower heads, but by the 1830s, after a period of plain centre panels within a formal border, naturalistic sprays in strong colours became the most sought after. This style was introduced by George Neville, yet another Jennens and Bettridge man, and looked all the more striking because he had developed a background of jet black which would not fade or corrode into a muddy green as the earlier black had tended to do. It is important to remember that even these naturalistic sprays should always be finely painted: splashy, loose flowers indicate a date after 1850.

Papier mâché of this type can be a botanist's dream, for many an artist became expert at depicting certain plants. James Grimes was best known for hawthorn blossom and snowdrops; William Jackson specialised in lilies of the valley; William Borne in verbena; but probably the best known, or the most easily recognised, is David Sargent, for his sprays of fern leaves. Sargent worked from 1832 to 1850, but his designs were much copied. Here again the superb quality of the original is the guide to genuine 'Sargent's ferns'.

After 1850, marbling and graining in imitation of woods such as walnut, maple and rosewood became popular. The most striking of all these simulations were made after 1862, when a pair of gates decorated with vibrant green malachite came across from Russia as part of the International Exhibition of that year. They so intrigued a decorator named George Harper that he developed a technique for copying this material, and a whole range of items, particularly desk sets, blotters, stationery cabinets and inkstands, were produced in simulated malachite. This is eagerly sought after today.

Another good clue to dating papier mâché is the large-scale appearance of aluminium powder in the 1860s. This added a further wistful quality to the romantic historical scenes that were so popular at this time.

Just a couple more names and dates are necessary to complete the picture. In 1847 a patent was issued on the application of what we now call gem inlay. Basically, a panel was cut away to receive real and imitation gemstones, enamels, ivory and tortoiseshell, to be overlaid with glass. The effect was dazzling and automatically indicates the work of Jennens and Bettridge, for no one else adopted this process. The second date is 1851, the year of the Great Exhibition. England was on the way out of an economic trough and the Crystal Palace provided an immense boost to trade and industry, with some fifteen thousand exhibitors participating from all over the world. Nothing was ever the same again in the history of the decorative arts, because firms were encouraged to create and display the finest work possible. Ironically it was to this

Mid-Victorian davenport decorated with mother of pearl.

Mid-Victorian brush with (left to right) a writing slope, table bureau and tea caddy.

end that the papier mâché industry was forced to set in motion its own demise.

The problem was that by 1850 production and decoration of papier mâché were already as fine as they could be. The only way to improve was to over-embellish, and this was done to such a degree that it had an adverse effect on the market. At first the novelties were intriguing, and although only a few of the leading manufacturers actually exhibited at the Crystal Palace, the amount they displayed was astounding in quantity and ingenuity of production. One piece, a vast antique-style vase similar to the Warwick Vase, was 4 feet 6 inches high and 2 feet across the mouth.

But spectacular decoration and huge items could not halt the decline in demand. Papier mâché had been over-exposed and over-decorated, and in order to keep up with innovations and remain commercially viable cheap and shoddy work crept in. The result was that people refused to pay the price for the better-quality work and despised the poor-quality. As an instance of this deterioration, during the 1870s a set of three trays could be made and sold for about 35p; just a hundred years earlier Henry Clay was making £3 profit out of each tray. Some craftsmen tried to restore precision and quality with mosaic and other symmetrical designs, but it was too late. Workshops closed down and highly skilled men and artists were unemployed. The last shop, that of McCallum and Hodson, closed in 1920, and with it went the last of the papier mâché industry for today's collector. But we mustn't be too gloomy: it had a wonderful run and created some of the most ingenious, attractive and useful items for today's collectors.

CHINESE PORCELAIN

GORDON LANG

Gordon Lang looks at a piece of Chinese blue and white porcelain.

Top of page *Late Ming box and cover, decorated in the Wucai palette, with the mark of the Emperor Wanli (reigned 1573–1619).*

For many people the word 'Ming' is synonymous with delicate Chinese porcelain of eggshell thinness, although few have anything but the vaguest idea of what it looks like or what it is made from. People are confused about the terms 'porcelain' and 'china', and the view I so often hear is that the former is superior to the latter. 'China' they regard as mere earthenware, with a printed 'willow pattern', probably made in Staffordshire. This confusion is not just a modern problem, and a few guidelines will help those who are uncertain of the difference.

In the sixteenth century Chinese porcelain was called 'purcellyn', 'porcelayne' or even 'purseland'. By the seventeenth century it was also given the names 'Indian ware', 'Cini', 'Cheney' and finally 'China'. These pieces came from the dimly perceived Orient, and labels such as 'China' or 'Indian' were applied indiscriminately to all porcelain, whether it hailed from China, Japan or even Korea. By the eighteenth century virtually all Oriental porcelain was called 'China'. To emphasise this point it is worth quoting from the patent taken out by the proprietors of the Bow factory in 1744, in which they stated their intention of making a ware which would prove 'equal to, if not exceeding in goodness and beauty, China or Porcelain ware imported from abroad'. Authorities today accept that both terms refer to the same material, be it hard paste (true porcelain) or soft paste (artificial or hybrid porcelain).

Porcelain was invented in China during the T'ang dynasty (618–906) or perhaps even a little earlier. It is generally understood to be fine and semi-translucent, and to produce a sonorous ring when struck gently. This is the accepted formula, but there are many examples of true or hard paste porcelain which do not conform to these criteria. The exceptions are sometimes heavily potted and opaque and give only a dull 'clonk' when tapped.

Blue and white bottle dated 1557 and bearing a Portuguese inscription, a sign of the new trade with the West at this time.

Two primary ingredients, both with Chinese names, go into the making of porcelain. Kaolin is a clay formed by the weathering or decay of felspathic rock; it is found quite naturally in valleys near hills or mountains composed of this kind of geological material. The second ingredient is petuntse, or white stone, from the same felspathic rock, but undecayed. Petuntse is pulverised and mixed with kaolin to form what the Chinese themselves have called the 'flesh and bones' of porcelain.

In Europe our acquaintance with this fascinating material is a relatively recent phenomenon. Marco Polo, the celebrated Venetian traveller, was the first European to describe this material as 'porcelaine' or 'porcellana' in the account of his travels to and sojourn in China in the late thirteenth century. In England the earliest reference to porcelain is in a letter at the beginning of the sixteenth century from the surveyor of customs at Southampton, one Henry Hutoft, to Thomas Cromwell, secretary to King Henry VIII, informing him of the arrival of gifts for the newly crowned king. Included in the schedule are 'three pieces of earthe paynted called Porseland, Hobeit the merchant saith before they shall be presented, there shall be to every one of these things certain preparations, such as chains of gold and silver, with colours and other things for the furniture of the same'. The fact that these pieces were to be embellished in this way gives some indication of the rarity and esteem in which porcelain was held at the time. In fact, the very few pieces of porcelain that arrived in Europe before the sixteenth century were to be found only in royal or very grand collections such as those of the Duc de Normandie or the Duc de Berry.

In 1498 Vasco da Gama, the great Portuguese navigator, rounded the Cape of Good Hope and reached India, opening up the sea passage to the Far East and its countless treasures and commercial opportunities. The prime target for the Portuguese was the lucrative spice trade, hitherto monopolised in the Mediterranean by Venetian merchants, who themselves had to deal with the Orient through overland Arab traders.

By the second decade of the sixteenth century the Portuguese had established themselves in China and had begun trading. From the middle of the century porcelain, some specially commissioned but none the less ancillary to the spice cargo, began arriving in Lisbon aboard enormous vessels called carracks. The Portuguese enjoyed unfettered trade for some fifty years until the Dutch and English conflicts with Spain and her satellite Portugal dealt a fatal blow to their operation. The capture of two carracks, in 1602 and 1604, was a major event in the expansion into northern Europe of the rich China trade, now based on tea, spices, silk and porcelain. On board these vessels were nearly two hundred thousand pieces of porcelain, which were subsequently sold at auction in Amsterdam and Middleburg. These sales were a sensation – paralleled only by the 1986 auction by Christie's in Amsterdam of the load

CARE AND REPAIR

∽

○ See pp. 64–5.

from the *Geldermalsen*, a Dutch East Indiaman sunk nearly 250 years ago – and royalty were among the purchasers. Henry IV of France bought a suite of porcelain, and James I of England 'acquired a great quantity of rare objects that the Dutch had seized on board a Portuguese cargo ship'. The acquisitions of these two monarchs probably accounted for only a tiny fraction of the load, and the bulk must have been sold to European aristocrats and the expanding merchant classes. From this time can be traced the beginnings of 'chinamania', which by the reign of Charles II some sixty years later had reached epidemic proportions among the fashionable classes.

At the end of the seventeenth century the Chinese began to produce armorial services, commissioned by noble European families. A drawing of the coat-of-arms would be sent out to China and copied – not always accurately – as part of the decoration. These services were to become immensely popular in the eighteenth century.

Pair of Yuan dynasty temple vases from the Percival David Foundation. Painted in underglaze cobalt blue, they are dated 1351.

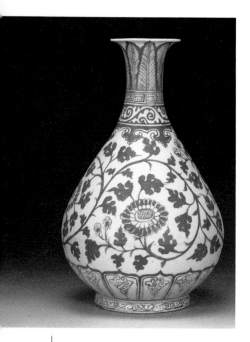

Late fourteenth-century bottle decorated in underglaze copper red.

In his *Tour through the Whole Island of Great Britain* of 1724–7 Daniel Defoe wrote of this passion for collecting china and laid the blame at the door of Queen Mary, wife of William of Orange.

. . . the Queen brought in [from Holland] the custom or humour, as I may call it, of furnishing houses with chinaware which increased to a strange degree afterwards, piling their china upon the tops of cabinets, scrutores [escritoires or writing bureaux] and every chimneypiece to the tops of the ceilings and even setting up shelves for their chinaware where they wanted such places till it became a grievance in the expense of it and even injurious to their families and estates.

Defoe was almost certainly referring to blue and white porcelain, since the coloured (that is, enamelled or polychrome) wares did not arrive in northern Europe in significant quantity until about 1700. These polychrome porcelains included, from Japan, the bold brocaded Imari type and the beautiful, sparingly decorated Kakiemon group, and, from China, the Wucai – which literally translates as five colours, though in practice is often more or fewer – followed by the brilliant famille verte and a little later the famille rose groups.

Just as the Portuguese had dominated export trade in the sixteenth century, and the Dutch in most of the following century, so did the British East India Company for most of the eighteenth century. But imports were severely reduced in the 1790s by the officers of the Company, who found that much of the demand for tableware was now being catered for by domestically produced ceramics, especially the recently developed creamware. Chinese porcelain, however, was the most universal, the most revered and the most respected throughout the civilised world. As with the Stradivarius violin, no one has since achieved a quality to compare with the finest porcelain produced by the Chinese. Their mastery of the medium for six hundred years remains unsurpassed.

What Marco Polo saw in the late thirteenth century could only have been the monochrome wares produced in the Song (960–1279) and Yuan (1279–1368) dynasties. These included the green-coloured celadons and the bluish white *qingbai* ware, this latter group neatly fitting his description of 'bowls . . . the colour of azure'. Both types were decorated by either carving or moulding or even a combination of the two techniques, and were not seen in the West before the twentieth century. The *qingbai* group and the closely-related *shufu* wares have many of the physical characteristics of early underglaze decorated porcelain.

Painting in cobalt blue or copper red under a clear glaze was introduced in the first half of the fourteenth century, perhaps shortly after 1323. Mastery of this technique was attained relatively quickly, as the pair of large vases in the Percival David Foundation collection in London (p. 121) show. These vases, essential to our understanding of the development of early blue

Fifteenth-century wine cup decorated in doucai *colours. It bears the mark of the Emperor Chenghua (reigned 1465–87).*

and white, are painted with great skill. Since they are also the earliest dated specimens of blue and white, it is worth spending a little time looking at the content and layout of their design. The form, incidentally, is taken from that of an ancient bronze vessel, a common practice among both Song and Yuan potters. The decoration is composed of eight horizontal zones; one, the main central area painted with dragons among clouds, is sandwiched between lesser bands enclosing stylised scrolling flowers, stiff leaves, phoenixes and Buddhist emblems. The entire arrangement is subordinate to the actual form of the vessel.

In the fifteenth century the design became the dominant feature of the vessel or dish. The Emperor Yongle (1403–24) not only established Peking (Beijing) as his capital but also elevated the kilns at Jingdezhên in Jiangzi province to imperial status. From his reign until the collapse of the Ming dynasty in the seventeenth century the kilns enjoyed imperial patronage with implicit quality control. It is from this period that reign marks first appear on Chinese porcelain, the earliest ones usually being scratched into the surface of the porcelain before the object was glazed. Such marks are frequently executed in an archaic script, very lightly incised and difficult to see on casual inspection.

The wares of the early fifteenth century are orderly, spacious and well balanced, in contrast to the somewhat bolder and more crowded style of the fourteenth century. The characteristic glaze of this period is thickly applied, greenish or bluish in colour, and when closely examined in a slanting light has a surface texture like orange peel, though more finely grained. The cobalt blue used under the glaze at this time varies enormously from a greyish blue to a rich ultramarine, but whatever tone is used almost every piece is suffused with small areas of black pigment, probably caused by the over-generous loading of the painter's brush. The effect produced, called 'heaped and piled', is typical of the early fifteenth century.

Following an unsettled period in the mid-fifteenth century the Emperor Chenghua ascended the dragon throne in 1465. While some pieces made in this period are difficult to distinguish from

Early Ming blue and white bowl with the mark of the Emperor Xuande (reigned 1426–35).

Blue and white dish inscribed in Arabic and bearing the mark of the Emperor Zhêngde (reigned 1506–22), whose court was run by Muslim eunuchs.

earlier ones, a number of types are quite distinctive. The legendary palace bowls are elegantly painted in an almost feminine manner with flowers or fruit in soft underglaze blue. An outline-and-wash technique is utilised, contrasting strongly with the broader and more painterly brushwork of previous periods. The glaze of this reign is one of the most readily recognisable: it is smooth, with no suggestion of the 'heaped and piled' effect, and has a rather smoky ivory appearance, unlike that of any other period.

Another very rare and equally celebrated group is that painted in polychrome or coloured enamels, termed by the Chinese *doucai* (*tou ts'ai*) or 'clashing or contending colours'. These invariably small objects are finely painted in underglaze blue with overglaze coloured enamels, including red, yellow, green and a soft manganese or aubergine. Among the best-known items are tiny wine cups painted with cockerels and hens – called, not surprisingly, chicken cups. Both the palace bowls and the chicken cups are made in exquisite porcelain which demands handling and close inspection in order to appreciate fully the virtuosity of the potter and painter. In my opinion these pieces are as wonderful as a portrait miniature, a Battersea enamel snuff box or a Fabergé hardstone carving.

In the early years of the sixteenth century decoration became crowded, a style which typifies most of that century. Although the decoration is closely packed, it is carried out in a lighter, more fussy manner using outline-and-wash, and is not to be confused with the strong painting of the fourteenth century. The reign of the Emperor Zhêngde (1506–22) is remarkable for a small group of blue and white porcelain bearing inscriptions in either Persian or Arabic with quotations from the Koran. These pieces were ordered by the Muslim eunuchs who controlled the palace bureaucracy, and are mostly objects designed for the writing desk, such as pen-boxes and brush-rests. The underglaze blue of this period is clear but slightly greyish, and is covered in a thick glaze with a decidedly bluish or greenish cast.

The succeeding Emperor, Jiajing (1522–66), was an ardent Taoist, intolerant of other beliefs, and he immediately removed the corrupt and sybaritic Muslim eunuchs from the court. The dominance of Taoism is evident from the number of pieces of porcelain decorated with peach trees, whose branches are twisted to form the word *shou* which symbolises longevity, a subject central to that religion. Other common Taoist themes of this period are the pine, the dappled deer, the crane and the Eight Immortals, frequently executed in a rich and runny purplish cobalt blue. This cobalt is termed 'Mohammedan blue', probably because the best ore was imported from Persia.

The beginning of trade with the West at this time gave more impetus to the already declining standards in porcelain manufacture. Already the signs of mass production could be seen: improperly refined materials, poor brushwork and the use of conventionalised and repeating motifs. The designs are broken down into

Ming blue and white double-gourd bottle with the mark of the Emperor Jiajing (reigned 1522–66).

Late Ming kraakporselein *dish from the first half of the seventeenth century. The name probably derives from the Portuguese carracks in which the porcelain was imported to Holland.*

a number of simple elements, loosely combined and with little coherence. A good example is the blue and white bottle with a Portuguese inscription dated 1557 from the Victoria and Albert Museum (p. 120).

Towards the end of the sixteenth century there was a further development in mass production: the design, particularly of flatware, was broken down into linear compartments. A plate would have a central theme, usually birds and flowers, which would be surrounded by a wide border of small panels or compartments, each enclosing a flower or precious object. This technique required little skill on the part of the painter, as each element of the design had become so simplified that it could have been done by a small child. Not only was porcelain crudely painted, but it was also poorly finished. A typical base would be thinly glazed, revealing the circular and radial lines made by the potter. The dish would be supported on a footring spattered with kiln grit and roughly trimmed with a knife. This type is called *kraakporselein* by the Dutch, and it is logical to suppose that they did so because it originally arrived on board the Portuguese carracks. *Kraakporselein* was imported in huge quantities until the 1640s, when internal problems in China cut off the supply from the porcelain manufacturing town of Jingdezhen to Western traders.

The story of Chinese porcelain in the latter part of the Ming dynasty is not entirely that of a tradition in decline. The outstanding exception is a distinctive group of mainly hollow wares made from about 1630 until the mid-1640s. This group has been called transitional porcelain, as it was made during the period covered by the fall of the Ming dynasty and the succession of the Qing or Manchu dynasty. The term is not entirely satisfactory, because it only applies to a relatively small proportion of the total export trade made at the time, of which *kraakporselein* makes up the greatest part. The best traditional porcelain is characterised by a fine white paste (i.e. body), a smooth bluish or greenish glaze and highly proficient brushwork. A number of new forms appear, probably to Dutch demands, and these include tall cylindrical vases (rollwagons), vases with bulging sides, globular bottles with tall necks and a whole series of vessels based on contemporary European metal, stoneware or glass originals. Many are painted with narrative subjects drawn from Chinese printed books, the figures set in idyllic rocky landscapes with plantains and bamboos surrounded by swirling clouds.

During the civil war which accompanied the demise of the Ming dynasty in 1644, the kilns at Jingdezhen were destroyed. This event gave the new porcelain manufactories at Arita in Japan a chance to gain a commercial foothold in the West, and certainly they were remarkably successful for a while until the Chinese recovered. In the 1670s the Jingdezhen kilns were rebuilt and in 1683 they were placed under the jurisdiction of a director answerable to the Emperor. Ts'ang Ying-hsüan was responsible

Pair of famille verte vases, export ware made in the reign of the Emperor Kangxi (1662–1722).

for the reorganisation and output of the kilns; he made a number of innovations, including copper red and green glazes and the famille verte palette.

The porcelain made in the reign of Kangxi (1662–1722) is very good technically, but the painting lacks a little spontaneity. The cobalt is pure and is married perfectly to the dead-white paste under a thin, very clean glaze. The following reigns, those of Yongzheng (1723–35) and Qianlong (1736–95), saw the arrival of the famille rose palette and several original glazes, some contriving to simulate other materials such as hardstones, bronze, lacquer and wood. Interest was also revived in the classical wares of the Song dynasty, and reproductions of earlier *ge*, *guan* and *ruyao* wares appear in the second quarter of the century. Towards the end of Qianlong's reign, however, there was an increased tendency towards over-elaboration and decadence in the porcelain produced for domestic consumption. Likewise the export ware became somewhat mechanical, vaguely following the European Neo-Classical style.

The nineteenth century witnessed a serious decline in the quality

Right *Famille rose nine peach vase with the seal mark of the Emperor Qianlong (reigned 1736–95).*

Below *Although this blue and white bottle bears the seal mark of the Emperor Qianlong it is painted in early Ming style and the shape is one that was popular in the even older Song dynasty (960–1279).*

of both imperial and export porcelain, and in the latter category one has only to look at the repetitious, overcrowded wares emanating from Canton throughout this period to realise the truth of this statement. Apart from 'Canton' china, little or no innovation took place; only copies of earlier periods were produced. The vast bulk of what we see today is of this date or even later, and only hints at the sublime accomplishment of the classical wares of the fifteenth century.

The story of Chinese porcelain continues not only through the archaeological excavations in China but also by other means in Britain. It is my experience that a great deal has been contributed to our understanding in recent years by the rediscovery of hitherto neglected material, including documentary evidence. This has been unearthed not just in our institutions and museums, but in our stately homes and more modest dwellings as well.

In my world, that of the auction house, many doors are opened which are not normally accessible to enthusiasts. Occasionally such moments prove to be as exciting to me as it must have been to Aladdin when he entered the cave of the Forty Thieves!

JAPANESE CERAMICS AND WORKS OF ART

DAVID BATTIE

My love of Japanese works of art has taken not only a long time to develop but has been arrived at by a tortuous route. I started life in the world of antiques as a book porter at Sotheby's twenty years ago. Various early jobs included guarding the lots on view, dealing with ballet dresses (the less said about that the better) and numbering sales. When transferred to porcelain I hated it for six months and then became an addict. Chinese and Japanese pots can give me the same sort of excitement that other people get hang gliding or listening to Mozart.

Chinese blue and white porcelain of the late fifteenth century (see p. 119) is somewhat outside my price range, so I content myself with Japanese Satsuma. This very fine earthenware was named after the area in Japan from which it came. Fairly heavily potted, of a creamy colour and with a minute overall crazing of the glaze, it was produced in quantity from the mid-nineteenth century. When I began cataloguing Japanese objects I recorded all the marks, usually of the potter or decorator and sometimes where he lived. Now and again, with great excitement, I found a dated piece. Any documentary object is of great importance as it helps to build up a picture of how techniques and styles have changed, enabling us to put a date on other, undated, examples. These Satsuma pots were all in similar style with strong, thick enamelling – particularly in a deep, rich blue – and gilding. The date was fixed by a *nengo*, a name arbitrarily chosen and applied for a year or more; most were from Bunka (1804–16) or Bunsei (1818–29), but it now seems that these dates are not to be relied upon.

The richly coloured and gilded ewer on p. 132 was sold in 1974 for £260, and an almost identical example appeared on the *Roadshow* some years ago. I would probably take this with me as my luxury if I was ever stranded on a desert island. The dragon

Top of page *Late nineteenth-century bronze by Genryusai Seiya, depicting a fight between a tiger and crocodile.*

writhes round the pot, forming the handle and spout, in a most lifelike way. In the East dragons are symbols of good fortune, and I would expect this one to bring me rapid rescue from my island. Meanwhile coconut milk could not but taste like nectar poured from its mouth.

At the beginning of the twentieth century the Japanese skill at miniaturisation, not yet at work on cameras and microprocessors, was evident on Satsuma. Finely enamelled and gilt plates, vases and *koro* (incense burners) were made, decorated with detailed scenes of Japanese life: rice planting and harvesting, spring blossom, festivals, and animals, birds and flowers. There are three important decorators, Yabu Meizan, Sobei Kinkozan and Ryozan, all of whose work has appeared on the *Roadshow* at one time or another. Small dishes by one of these will make from several hundred to several thousand pounds, and a good vase £10,000. Nevertheless work by other good but not major artists can be bought for £40 or so.

Japanese porcelain appears in larger quantities than pottery, and a great deal of it is Imari. Made at Arita since the seventeenth century, it was exported through the port of Imari and the name stuck. The characteristic colours are underglaze blue, iron red and gilding, sometimes with additional enamels. Baskets of flowers, dragons, *ho-o* (phoenix) and trees are the main elements in the design; figures rarely occur. Early dishes have spur marks on which the piece stood when it was fired. Later this was abandoned and it rested on the footring. Pairs of covered vases range in size from a few inches at £30–40 up to 5 feet at £3000–5000. A dinner-size plate is £30, and a 12-inch dish about £100. Imari was never signed and rarely marked until the very end of the nineteenth century, when a new development was to stencil the blue design to speed up production. Although the glaze softens the inevitable dotted effect, it is usually still apparent and the design has the broken lines characteristic of stencilled work.

Another region producing quantities of porcelain for export was Kaga and the kilns at Kutani. Incense burners, vases and tea wares abound, varying in quality and ranging in price from a pound or two to several hundred.

So low had Japanese production sunk in quality to meet demand from the West that a factory was founded calling on the best talent available to restore standards. This was Fukagawa (the name means 'deep river'). The clean blue-white porcelain was used to make a range of new shapes and designs, many influenced by Chinese as well as earlier Japanese wares. It is quite rightly now sought after, and prices for good examples are rising rapidly. A large dish can make much the same as an Imari example, and double if it is a really good piece.

Among the most commonly found pieces that are readily identifiable are those from Noritake. The factory, still in business today, seems to have started at the end of the nineteenth century

Iron vase by Komai inlaid in gold and silver, late nineteenth-century.

Large late nineteenth-century cloisonné dish.

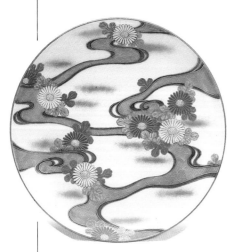

Fukagawa plate of the late nineteenth century.

and made mass-produced wares to European designs. Tea services were a staple line, with bands of hand-painted flowers between coloured borders garishly embellished with relief gilding. Vases are also common and many have scenes of rural England with nothing in the shape, colouring or subject which would lead one to suspect they were Japanese. Most are marked with a curious, spider-like symbol that seems to have escaped from a video game. Later the word 'Noritake' appears, or simply 'Foreign'. Junk shops countrywide have examples from a pound or two.

At the bottom of mass-produced Japanese porcelain are egg-shell services. The tea ceremony held an important place in Japanese life, and great honour could be bestowed by inviting a guest to drink from an ancient teabowl. Any samurai worthy of the name would commit *seppuku* (ritual suicide) rather than be caught drinking tea from an eggshell teacup! They are among the very few objects we see on the *Roadshow* which, arguably, have no merit whatsoever. Although the china itself is the thinnest ever made, the cups do not retain the heat and are really too fragile for use. Many of the forty or fifty pieces we see on every *Roadshow* are hand-coloured over a transfer-printed outline, despite the proud claim on the base that it is 'Guaranteed Genuine Hand-Painted Samurai China'. The Trades Descriptions Act would weed them out rapidly today. Occasionally an example will demonstrate the Japanese flair for design, with a few stylised chrysanthemums, and these are not unattractive. Since all eggshell porcelain is lumped together in antique shops from £2 to £5 a piece, it is possible to build up an interesting collection of pieces for a very small outlay.

The Japanese ability to manipulate minuscule bits and pieces is nowhere better displayed than on cloisonné ware. The technique is ancient and may well have reached China from the West, an unusual direction of influence, and then travelled to Japan. Little is identifiable there until the mid-nineteenth century, and early pieces display definite Chinese characteristics.

Making a piece starts with hammering the vessel from sheet metal to make what is known as a blank, and drawing the design on to it. Thin wires of copper, brass, silver or, very occasionally, gold are fixed in place following the drawn pattern. The cells thus formed are filled with enamel paste and the piece is fired in a kiln, producing an unrecognisable mess of fused colour. The lengthy process then begins. Highly skilled polishers set to work smoothing the surface until the wires reappear. This took anything up to a year for a major piece. Individual makers specialised in designs which ranged from simple patterns to complex diapers, birds and flowers. The human figure very rarely appears. A later development was known as wireless cloisonné, not because you could pick up Radio 2 on it but because the wires, having served their purpose, were dissolved away in acid so that the colours could flow together. Some of the major makers signed their pieces, engraving either into the base or on to a metal pad.

The quality ranges from the worst possible rubbish to quite breathtaking examples. The former can be had for a few pounds, whereas a signed vase of the same size by Namikawa Sosuke could fetch £10,000. Other important names are Ando Jubei, Namikawa Yasuyuki and Hayashi Kodenji. Fortunately there are not too many makers' names to learn in cloisonné, and identification is fairly easy. Collectors are more neurotic about condition than in any other field; each piece is minutely examined for flaws, cracks or pinholes. Unlike porcelain, cloisonné cannot

Yabu Meizan earthenware vase.

Satsuma dragon ewer by Seiuntei Kozan from the third quarter of the nineteenth century.

CARE AND REPAIR
❧

○ Avoid touching *shibuichi* or *shakudo* inlays, whose patination (and value) are easily destroyed by the acid in skin.
○ For the same reason never touch bronze, apart from gentle dusting.
○ For ceramics, see pp. 64–5.
○ For cloisonné enamel, see p. 34.
○ For weapons, see p. 162.

be satisfactorily restored. Brilliant colours, attractive designs and superb craftsmanship make cloisonné highly desirable for the interior decorator, and the larger pieces (and some vases can be 5 feet high) can make very high prices. While a pair of 18-inch vases could sell for up to £2500, a 5-foot pair would be £10,000–20,000. Forgeries are unlikely, as the technique is too labour-intensive to undertake today. However, common or garden vases have been seen with signatures of major artists added recently.

Silver has always been an expensive metal in Japan, and its use was restricted to inlay until the late nineteenth century. It then became more readily available and pieces, particularly bowls, were made for export. Typically they have a fluted body with repoussé flowers – usually chrysanthemums, the national flower. As the relief was high they were made double-walled with a smooth second skin on the interior. Engraved signatures sometimes appear, and most are stamped *jun gin*, meaning pure silver. The standard of purity of the silver is higher than in Britain, and the metal is therefore softer. Over-enthusiastic polishing means that many pieces have worn through, making a hole in the price as well as the piece. Japanese silver is not too expensive at present, as the melt value is low, and small bowls, ideal for peanuts at a cocktail party, can be bought for £20–50. A large, heavy example could make the upper hundreds. I can't recall ever having discussed any Japanese silver on the *Roadshow*, although it is not uncommon. I suspect that the silver table corners it before I do.

Although their silver is attractive, the Japanese skill with base metal is even more remarkable. They have been producing swords of unsurpassed hardness and sharpness for a thousand years, some blades taking years to complete. Armourers were used to making helmets, sword guards (*tsuba*) and mounts (*fuchi kashira*). The sword or, for the samurai, two swords was a prime symbol of status and manhood, and the family blade was venerated. The coming of the barbarians, as the Westerners were called, in the mid-nineteenth century was in fact a mixed blessing to previously insular Japan. On the one hand the old way of life vanished: an edict was proclaimed banning the wearing of swords, for instance, which must have been a severe shock to the traditional Japanese and of no little concern to the metal workers who had lost their livelihoods. On the other a vast market opened up in the rest of the world for those who could adapt; and adapt most did, using their skills to produce vases, jardinieres and sculpture.

Constant experiment had developed a range of alloys unknown to the West, combining gold, silver, tin, copper, iron and steel which was then engraved, textured and surface-finished by heating and with chemicals. In response to demand the simple designs of the first half of the century became more complex, with inlays of gold and *shibuichi*, an alloy of silver and copper, and *shakudo*, which was copper and gold with other metals laid into bronze or iron in designs of figures, fish, birds, flowers and monkeys. Origi-

*Late nineteenth-century gilt
bronze group by Miyao.*

nal patination is all-important: these pieces must not be cleaned under any circumstances. Inexperience can reduce the value of, say, a box by Komai, famous for his designs in gold on iron, from £1000 to £100. Rumour has it that there are Japanese who can repatinate so that detection is impossible. Perhaps. In any case the cost would be exorbitant.

At the other end of the size spectrum, the Japanese were undaunted by the large-scale objects demanded by the international exhibitions at which they showed. They had, after all, cast the largest bronze sculpture in the world, the Buddha at Nara, which was over 53 feet tall. Vases 8 feet high were shipped to the West to impress exhibition visitors and later to be sold there. No piece as large as this has appeared on a *Roadshow*, but at Bognor in 1980 a lady appeared with a samurai archer by Hoko. He was the best example I had seen, and I have rarely seen better since. At the time I valued it at £5000; now, with the interest from the Japanese themselves in good-quality bronzes illustrating their illustrious past, he would probably make £15,000 at auction. Superbly animated tigers with polished stripes, lions and other wild animals were also made. The quality varies, but those by Seiya are among the best and several have appeared on the *Roadshow*. Most measure between 9 and 30 inches, but I recently saw a tiger over 6 feet from nose to tail. He would fetch about £20,000, but smaller casts can be had from £150.

A word of warning: some of these bronzes are suspect. I have seen them reproduced in so-called cold-cast bronze, actually a mixture of bronze powder and resin, and also in bronze, brand-new from Japan. They are of high quality and detection is not easy. The underside, as with so many works of art, can provide a clue. The originals are smooth where they have been stood, usually on their original wooden base, and movement over the years has produced a fine network of hair-like scratches which is impossible to fake. Modern pieces are often badly finished on the base, sometimes with saw marks and no genuine wear. The wood base is worth examining closely – faking a patina on wood is a lot more difficult than it is on a bronze.

The greatest of the Japanese bronze sculptors is Miyao, pronounced Me-ya-oh, not – as some do – like a cat's miaow. His was a large studio specialising in slightly stylised figures of warriors, peasants and fishermen, often with gold or gilt inlay. The naturalistic figures which echo the Tokyo School ivories (see p. 141) leave, as their Western counterparts did, the original modelling marks in the clay or wax from which they were cast. I find bronze one of the least sympathetic of materials, and Renaissance bronzes of the sixteenth century, which have most inhabitants of the art world fainting in ecstasy, leave me quite unmoved. However, there are some Japanese bronzes which I could happily live with, particularly the peasants and children which provide a window on a long-lost Japan.

ORIENTAL IVORIES, JAPANESE LACQUER AND FURNITURE

DAVID BATTIE

Before every *Antiques Roadshow* we all meet for dinner, at which I regularly predict the size of the crowd we will have next day and the type and quality of objects brought for us to examine. There is an extraordinary consistency to my predictions: they are always wrong. One pattern, however, has emerged, for a visit to a port or nearby town will provide a large number of Oriental works of art. From the time of Elizabeth I, the British were one of the leading nations of the world, and by Victoria's reign they dominated a large part of it. We travelled the globe as sailors, merchants, tea and rubber planters, missionaries and administrators; we bought local artifacts and we brought them home as souvenirs. The result of all this scavenging is still very much in evidence in Britain, and a *Roadshow* held in any other country would be much less likely to turn up the treasures that we see regularly.

We have been trading with China directly or indirectly from the second half of the seventeenth century and amongst the porcelain, tea, silks and so on were ivories. By the late eighteenth century a wide range of objects was being produced, and the volume increased throughout the nineteenth century. Chinese ivories are quite different from Japanese. The former display a dedication to minuteness of carving on such objects as pierced balls, one inside another. Sometimes there are as many as twenty which are believed (though not by me) to have taken up to a year to carve. Small ones are an inexpensive £10, whereas a really spectacular example might cost £1000. In a similar vein are the baskets and covers constructed of a thin sheet of ivory finely pierced with lines and holes. Most of these have been damaged over the years, as they are extremely fragile, or have warped. When they survive intact, however, they can bring £300 upwards.

The Japanese are supposed to have invented the folding fan, but

Top of page Japanese ivory eighteenth-century netsuke carved by Gechu, which sold in 1987 for the world record price of £110,000.

King and queen from a Madras ivory chess set of about 1820.

the Chinese examples are better known. Their guards are carved with scrolling flowers or figures, and the leaf part of the fan is a tracery of pierced lines or stars, often with a shield into which the owners' initials could be carved. Again they are fragile and damage can reduce values fivefold, but in a good state £60–400 is the usual range to be expected.

In the days when calling on one's neighbour was a vital ingredient in the social cement, the visiting card played a significant role. These were larger than today's business cards, and their ivory cases were carved with figures in gardens, birds, dragons – even Napoleon's tomb. Most date from the 1830s onwards, and *very* occasionally a dated example appears and makes £400–500. For ordinary examples £30 will buy a poor one, and Boney's tomb starts at £250.

Chess pieces were made in large numbers in both Canton and Macao; many of the former have figures set on pierced balls. Size and quality vary widely, and accordingly so does the price. A miserable set may be only £20, whereas a large, well-carved one with 10-inch kings might make £8000. Chess sets, along with Immortals (religious figures), are now being carved in Hong Kong in vast numbers. Heaven knows how many elephants are being illegally killed to support this trade. I can only urge you not to buy. The standard of craftsmanship is generally poor and the figures are artificially aged by heat and smoke. Many bear spurious reign marks of the Ming and Qing dynasties, so treat all these figures with caution.

India also produced ivories, mainly for the British Raj. Groups of figures such as maharajahs carried in litters or on the backs of elephants in howdahs, and accompanied by foot soldiers, were popular; so were bullock carts and snake charmers. Chess sets were made in various locations, those of Delhi and Madras being widely different in style. Early nineteenth-century examples of the former are quite wonderful – the pieces are turned and petalled and fluted and stained green, red or brown. Madras examples represent opposing armies in a riot of colours and gilding. Because of their decorative appeal they can be fiendishly expensive – between £1000 and £8000! Odd pieces, which can be found for a few pounds in antique shops, are a good way of obtaining a cross-section of different styles and periods.

In both China and Japan the influence of Westerners was restricted to control their vigorous attempts at preaching and converting, which only led to discontent. Foreigners could, for instance, only trade from certain Chinese ports. In Japan this isolation was taken to extremes, and the country remained closed to any progress in the industrial sense until Commander Perry of the US Navy sailed into Yokohama harbour in 1853. The impact was dramatic in both directions. The Japanese discovered technology and new markets; the West was given a view of the world from a different perspective. Japanese goods were shown at the

Chinese ivory pierced ball and stand, mid-nineteenth-century. Not only is this a very large example but the ball contained at least twenty smaller spheres.

London International Exhibition of 1862, and by the end of the century stores such as Liberty's were stocking Japanese goods in quantity. It is believed that the first woodblock prints to reach this country did so as wrapping paper round other goods. Whatever the truth of that, the asymmetrical, perspectiveless, pattern-making style of Japanese art was to affect painters, textile designers and furniture makers throughout Europe. As a nation whose backbone was the Industrial Revolution, the British immediately appreciated the extraordinary craftsmanship. Although made almost entirely by hand, with immense labour and dedication, the finished results had the precision, meticulous attention to detail and polish of machine work.

Amongst the earliest imports was lacquer, of which there are several different kinds. Lacquer produced in Europe in the eighteenth century is not strictly lacquer at all. Japanese lacquer is true lacquer, produced from the sap of a species of *rhus* tree which is tapped in much the same way as rubber. The sap is extremely poisonous, and the workers who boiled and treated the raw material often died after a few years. Once strained and ready for use, the sap is applied with a brush on to a thin framework, which is usually wood but can be fabric. Layer after layer is applied and allowed to dry between coats. The drying process is attractively eccentric in that it will only work in wet conditions. Special rooms were constructed with water running down the walls to create the right atmosphere. If allowed to dry in dry conditions, the surface hardens but not the underneath, which remains wet. Major pieces would receive up to one hundred extremely thin coats, each differing, to produce the design. The last few layers could contain small pieces of gold leaf – squares arranged irregularly, in a pattern, or as tiny flecks known as *nashiji*.

The earliest pieces made use of the mirror-black ground as an element of the design, in contrast with the gold lacquer which might be partly raised in low relief. Generally, the later in the century the piece, the less ground is visible and the more gold is in evidence. Some of the late pieces are of quite spectacular quality and we have seen some on the *Roadshow*. On one occasion I was discussing a table, of which more later, when a lady came up with a *kodansu* (p. 139), which is a small, rectangular box of three drawers enclosed by a hinged door. The whole piece was brilliantly decorated in lacquer with flowers and birds but, like much that we see, not in good condition. The wood used in the construction was light and very soft, and a knock will easily dent it. To the collector these dents are a major drawback and make a great deal of difference to the value, although they can be skilfully repaired and restored – but only in Japan.

It comes as something of a shock to realise that the Japanese eat almost exclusively off something which starts out as a deadly poison. But by the time lacquer is processed, it is quite harmless. Impervious to boiling liquids, acid and alcohol, it is both light and, when made for domestic use, very strong. It is still being made in Japan, although whether it is true lacquer I know not. Bowls and serving dishes, salad servers and so on in mirror-black, a brilliant sealing-wax red and gold are not expensive – a tip for the antique of tomorrow.

The traditional Japanese house was constructed largely of paper, with thin wood supports. There were two reasons: one was that such a building was likely to survive the regular earthquakes that shake the country, and the other was that the densely packed buildings caught fire with monotonous regularity, and to rebuild

Late nineteenth-century Japanese lacquer screen signed by Komei and inlaid with ivory, mother of pearl and coral.

CARE AND REPAIR
————— ❧ —————
- Keep ivory away from sunlight and radiators or it will crack.
- Ivory likes some humidity and is best stored in a closed cabinet with a glass of water. Open the cabinet from time to time to prevent mould forming.
- Dust with a brush.
- Don't wet ivory with anything but alcohol or meths on a cotton bud. The resultant dry white surface can be restored to its former state by rubbing with your hands.
- Store ivory in acid-free tissue, and not cotton wool.
- For lacquer see p. 116.

137

Japanese ivory okimono of an ama (fisher girl) coming to grips with an octopus. About 4 inches high, the piece dates from about 1900.

them with such basic materials was a matter of a few days. Paper walls make poor supports for shelves or hanging pictures, with the result that there weren't any. Life was conducted in one room, which could be divided up with sliding screens, and as there was no furniture everything took place at floor level on the *tatami*, a mat of fixed size. A building was measured by the number of mats it could contain. This lack of display space meant that a family might, at best, have an alcove where the wife would hang a scroll above a vase of carefully arranged flowers. As the season or mood changed, so did the scroll and vase, but the idea of having several vases on view at the same time would have struck the Japanese as bizarre in the extreme.

Furniture was limited to boxes – boxes in which clothes were kept, boxes for scrolls, boxes for writing equipment, boxes for games – all in different shapes, sizes and designs. Many found their way to the West when they became redundant after the Japanese adopted a more Western way of life and storage. They also took to making, both for domestic use and export, a range of shelves and cabinets in all qualities from appalling to wonderful. They display the skilfully balanced asymmetry that was the Japanese contribution to world design and which, once it arrived in Europe in the 1870s, influenced Impressionism and Art Nouveau.

The display pieces, usually about 3 feet 6 inches to 4 feet in height, and with perhaps three shelves and a small cupboard in gold lacquer, its hinges and brackets of chased silver, can make £10,000 or more when of the best quality. Larger cabinets have a carved wood framework of leaves, birds and flowers and panels of lacquer inlaid in mother of pearl and ivory in a technique known as Shibayama. There is more than a suspicion that many of these were carved and constructed elsewhere in the East, perhaps in Malaysia, but incorporating Japanese panels. The quality and balance are not quite right for Japan. The price, since no one is sure, is unaffected.

Chairs, settees, desks, bookcases and even beds, all carved in a heavy, rosewood-like timber which I have never heard anyone identify with total conviction, are well known and appear regularly on the *Roadshow*. They are rather bulky for today's taste, with sinuous dragons crawling over their backs, ball and claw feet borrowed from eighteenth-century England, and the flapping, long-tailed *ho-o* bird. The more I see of them the less sure I am that they are Japanese at all. Again, somewhere south-east of China is my bet – and made, of course, to European commission.

Until the adoption of Western dress in the 1870s the Japanese were at a major social disadvantage – they had no pockets. The kimono was worn by both sexes and small objects were contained in the inro, a little nest of boxes hung from a cord at the waist. The cord was threaded through holes in the netsuke, a toggle of wood or ivory, and pushed under the obi or sash. Early netsuke were no more than twigs, but in the seventeenth century the fashion for

Nineteenth-century Japanese lacquer kodansu.

carving figures or animals began. It was in the late eighteenth and early nineteenth centuries that the best pieces were made, and extraordinary time and skill were expended on these miniature sculptures. A man might own several, selecting which to use during the day much as we might a tie. Over the years the netsuke received a certain amount of wear, and this is acceptable – indeed it is one of the points used to detect a copy from the real thing, as wear is impossible to fake convincingly.

The netsuke is a functional object and must not have protruding parts which would snag clothing. It must be the right size and weight (although large ones were made for wrestlers and small ones for children), and most are roughly triangular in form, as this is how the tusk was cut and supplied to the carver. How he has created a work of art given these limitations is one of the criteria used to judge a good netsuke, along with the carver himself and his reputation. Identification is not easy, as early netsuke were rarely signed. The carver might change his name several times in his life and there are both contemporary and later copies. Given these complications, it is hardly surprising that prices can range from £20 to the world record price of £110,000 paid in 1987 (p. 134).

There is an added problem – plastic copies. It might be thought that anyone could spot plastic, but the moulds are made of flexible rubber which pick up every tiny crack and hole and even the grain of the original. The weight and colour are also right. There are two reliable methods of detection. One is to hold a red-hot pin in a pair of pliers and stick it in somewhere unobtrusive. There will be a puff of smoke and a smell of burning plastic if the piece is a forgery, but ivory will barely mark or smell. A better method still, once one has got the hang of it, is touch alone. Ivory conducts heat from the hand rapidly and thus feels cold; plastic does not, and therefore feels warm. Subject areas for modern forgeries are always widen-

Nineteenth-century Japanese inlaid fruitwood display cabinet inlaid with ivory, lacquer and mother of pearl.

Japanese lacquer four-case inro, nineteenth-century.

ing and now include scrimshaw, the handles of corkscrews, umbrellas and sunshades, paper knives and also chess sets – so beware.

Back to the real thing. Western dress meant no more work for the netsuke carver, but his carvings and those of his predecessors were snapped up by traders and shipped to Europe by the barrelful. Never a nation to sit and bemoan its bad luck, the Japanese carvers turned their nimble hands at first to carving more netsuke, but of lower quality, in Western taste. This meant more detail, and preferably with figures illustrating a story. No longer hidebound by the necessity of small size, the netsuke grew and grew. The holes atrophied, then disappeared, and the netsuke turned into an okimono, roughly translating as a standing object. These were sometimes carved from a single piece, but more often, as they became more complex and enlarged, an oval of ivory was set with figures, animals and birds illustrating Japanese domestic life. The quality of carving, as always, varies, but the very best display movement, expression, conviction and often humour. Some of the most spectacular groups were carved using different materials such as wood for the body and ivory for the head, hands and feet; inlays such as stained ivory, horn, mother of pearl (haliotis shell), coral and even silver and gold were also used. The price range is great, from £10 for a poor group made from left-over scraps of ivory or bone to thousands of pounds for the best.

So great was the market that by the end of the century the standard of carving had deteriorated appallingly. A netsuke carver named Ishikawa Komei started a revival of lapsed skills and these carvings, usually over 10 inches in size, are wonders of sculpture. Certain guidelines were adhered to by the members of the Tokyo School of carving: with rare exceptions the figure was carved from a single piece of ivory without the help of assistants; the chisel marks were left and not polished away, although they are never obtrusive; and the base had the raw ivory exposed. On the whole the Japanese are not great admirers of their ivories, but pieces showing nobles, samurai, sumo wrestlers and so on are sought by the Japanese themselves if of sufficient quality. The subject is all-important. On one occasion I telephoned a Japanese dealer in great excitement telling him we had a very fine carving for him to see. Of a fisherman about to cast his net, it was by Homei, another major artist. When he arrived the dealer's only comment was, 'Oh no. No good. Dirty old peasant.' The expression has gone down in the Japanese Department folklore and is regularly trotted out when discussing the values of a collection of ivories.

The banning of the wearing of swords in Japan led to large numbers of blades being sold to Europeans. Quick off the mark as ever, the Japanese then started to make swords for export, but it was clear that ignorant Westerners could not tell a good blade from a bad one and that it was the scabbard that interested them. Lacquer was rather a subtle material, whereas ivory had an exotic quality and made immediate impact. So for the first time ivory sheaths were produced, carved with flowers, dragons, diaper patterns, monkeys, fish, figure subjects and so on. Some of them are of marvellous quality; a large scabbard could make £3000, one for a dagger £1500, but these are top prices and there are plenty to be had for £80 upwards. Be very careful when being sold ivory. Many cheap, nasty scabbards are of bone, bound in brass and stamped with the Tokugawa *mon* or badge. The natural curve of a tusk fits perfectly with the curve of a sword blade, but bone comes straight and has to be cut in short lengths – hence the brass bands. Bone is a 'live' material fed by blood vessels, which, however it is carved, will always show as tiny brown or black holes or lines. Such scabbards should cost no more than £30.

Despite hot lights, seemingly endless crowds of people, a dry throat and the prospect of a five-hour drive home at the end of a recording, I rarely wish for a sharp Japanese blade to take the honourable way out. There is always the knowledge that the very next package to be opened may set the pulse racing and the adrenalin flowing, and have a bewildered owner relieved of his property and booked in for a recording session an hour or two hence. Not this time? Never mind: where are we off to next?

This superb Tokyo School ivory falconer signed by Ishikawa Komei sold in 1986 for £19,000.

OILS, WATERCOLOURS AND REPRODUCTIONS

ANTHONY J. LESTER

Anthony Lester (left) talks about a picture to its owner.

Top of page This Victorian oil painting of a terrier sold at auction in 1987 for £1800, but such popular subjects can easily go higher.

I have always considered myself very privileged to have had, from the age of five, an instinctive love of art and antiques – a passion that has grown unabated. How well I remember, as a schoolboy, going with my father to an auction sale of the contents of a house. Having viewed the better items, I wandered into the garage, which housed the usual outside effects. Among the garden sundries were three pictures catalogued as prints. Imagine my excitement when I found that one was by an artist I had actually heard of and, what is more, it was not a print but an original watercolour! I duly marked my catalogue, but had to wait impatiently for several hours for 'my' lot to come up.

'Well, what am I bid for these three prints? The frames are quite good. . . . Somebody say two shillings.' (Those were the days!)

'Yes!' I shouted enthusiastically, having not yet learnt the more discreet twitching-of-the-eyebrow technique of bidding.

The price slowly crept up, my heartbeat increasing with each bid.

'At twenty-five shillings . . . sold, to the young gentleman.' The auctioneer's hammer fell. I had made my first purchase at auction – it cost me six weeks' pocket money!

It was, however, well worth the sacrifice, for it established my enduring interest in watercolours, an art form that has given me so much pleasure, both visually and mentally. Despite the fact that the past decade has witnessed a reappraisal of watercolours, and prices have risen dramatically, to many people watercolour is still an inferior medium to oil. I find this attitude strange, for the creation of a quality watercolour requires tremendous skill. In oil painting, when a tone is unsatisfactory or a mistake is made it can be simply wiped out or painted over. Not so with watercolour: once the brush touches the paper it has left its impression – an error means a fresh start.

The name Tom Keating, that lovable rogue of a forger, still sends shivers down the spines of many a collector and dealer. Whilst I have not seen any Keatings at a *Roadshow* (at least I hope not), I have seen many fakes and forgeries. I recall some twenty years ago viewing a picture sale in one of the London auction rooms when the distinguished artist Sir William Russell Flint walked in, having been told that one of his pictures was included. Pausing before a picture of a typical Russell Flint scantily clad lady, he suddenly exclaimed, 'I never painted this picture.' As the general hubbub of the saleroom turned to a deathly hush, a flustered head of department was summoned and, after his whispered conversation with Sir William, the offending picture was hastily withdrawn. Now that Russell Flint is dead I suspect that this picture has once more come out of the closet and now forms part of somebody's prized collection. This and many similar anecdotes keep me on my guard when examining any picture – but, of course, we are all fallible!

When first confronted with a picture, we instinctively look for a signature. To many people it is the most important feature, but the fact is that signatures are of the very least value in assessing a picture. Some years ago I bought a wonderful-quality oil painting

Lilian Stannard (1877–1944), Late Autumn. Another watercolour on a currently fashionable theme.

William McTaggart (1835–1910), In Charge. My first purchase at auction, this picture still gives me pleasure and has also increased considerably in value.

CARE AND REPAIR
——— 1 ———

○ Frames protect pictures and preserve their value, so it is worth paying for the best workmanship and modern, acid-free materials. Old frames may need renovation or replacement.

○ Frame watercolours and prints with a mount to stop them touching the glass. Chalk, pastel and charcoal are very delicate and may need extra-deep mounts.

○ Hang watercolours away from sunlight, which fades them.

○ Hang all pictures from nylon cord. Wire and chain can corrode and break, and string rots.

See also p. 149.

of an old woman walking in a wood. The picture, signed and dated by a minor nineteenth-century artist, had a pre-Raphaelite feel about it and was reminiscent of the work of Sir John Everett Millais (most noted for his charming study, *Bubbles*). I must confess that, had it not been signed, I would have guardedly attributed it to this great nineteenth-century artist.

I soon sold the picture for a modest sum. You can imagine my horror when about a year later, walking past the window of a well-known London gallery, I saw my picture of the old lady. I stood there transfixed, not by the picture but by the label below it: 'Sir John Everett Millais'. Dusting myself down, I entered the gallery and enquired about the picture. 'Oh yes, sir, a stunning example by Millais, signed and dated,' enthused the smart assistant. The painting was removed from the window for me to examine it at close quarters. The original signature had been removed, and in its place was a spurious Millais monogram and, in keeping with its new-found glory, a five-figure price tag. Apparently they had bought the picture privately in good faith, the monogram being the decisive factor in purchasing – they had been well and truly caught.

It must be said, however, that only a small minority of wrongly attributed pictures are deliberate forgeries. Many of the leading eighteenth- and nineteenth-century watercolourists supplemented their income by teaching, and hundreds of their pupils made copies of their masters' work. Often pupils' watercolours were doctored by later 'gentlemen', who found that simply by adding a fraudulent signature of a well-known artist they could make a comfortable living out of the gullible.

The attractive watercolour of a Yorkshire woman drying her washing (p. 146) was sold several years ago at a provincial saleroom. It was catalogued as being the work of one of the great nineteenth-century watercolourists, Peter de Wint (it bears a false signature 'P. de Wint'), and commanded a price of over £500. However, it is the work not of de Wint but of one of his most talented pupils, Mary Anne Roundell (born about 1800). As part of her training she was required to make copies of finished drawings by de Wint, and in some of her watercolours she received the assistance of de Wint himself. He would perhaps, by way of instruction, paint in some trees or add a figure. Remember, a genuine work by a well-known artist is 'signed' in every brushstroke – a signature is superfluous to an unimpeachable drawing, and it can add nothing to a drawing that is not 'right'. It is also a fallacy to assume that a prestigious name implies quality. Even the most talented of artists have their uninspired days. The art of recognising excellence cannot be taught. It is something you acquire through continued exposure to good-quality works of art. Visits to art galleries, museums and salerooms will help in developing a good eye. Study each picture for several minutes. Is everything within the composition in proportion? Does the colouring harmonise? Does the composition itself work – or is it perhaps too cluttered or too one-sided?

Exhibition and dealers' printed trade labels can be of great help in establishing a picture's history and authenticity. The label of the dealers Thomas Agnew and Sons Ltd is a good example. Over the years their trading name and address changed as follows: Zanetti and Agnew 1817–28, Agnew and Zanetti 1828–35, Thomas Agnew 1835–50, Thomas Agnew and Sons 1851–1932 and Thomas Agnew and Sons Ltd from 1932 to the present. In addition, from about 1900 Agnew's labels have had a stock number, which runs consecutively. No. 10,000 was reached in September 1939, while no. 26,370 passed through their gallery in 1965.

The label of Dicksee and Co. of St James's, London, could indicate that the picture was exhibited at a major exhibition. The firm was the official agent for the collection and delivery of pictures to most of the international art exhibitions during the late nineteenth century. The labels of other nineteenth-century galleries which held regular exhibitions and had a worthy reputation for dealing in quality pictures can be similarly traced. Remember that a picture's provenance can influence its value, so if you ever have a picture reframed always make sure you retain any labels.

George Faulkner Wetherbee (1851–1920), Knucklebones.

ANTHONY J. LESTER

Opposite *A typical nineteenth-century amateur watercolour – the figure is out of scale and the trees resemble green cotton wool. We see a lot worse on the* Roadshow!

Mary Anne Roundell (b. about 1800), Wash Day. *Once attributed to the famous watercolourist Peter de Wint, it is now known to be by one of his pupils.*

Many of the leading London auction rooms use a small oblong sticky label to record the property reference number. Since 1873 Christie's have stencilled a code in inch-high black letters and numbers (before that they used a painted number) on the back of every framed picture accepted for sale or examined by them. The first stencil was 1A, then 2A and so on. When 1000A had been reached, 1B began, until 1900 when, having used all the letters of the alphabet, they began a two-letter system. Since 1978 the letters have preceded the numbers. Although Christie's was bombed during the Second World War, they had had the great good sense to remove all their archive material to the country for safety. They are thus able to trace marks, which will give such information as the vendor's name and, if the picture has been sold by them, the date, price and purchaser.

For canvases, too, help is sometimes at hand in the form of a retailer's or manufacturer's name and address, usually in black on the reverse. Any canvas bearing the famous name of Winsor and Newton must date from after 1832, the year of their foundation. Until 1859 their address is stencilled '38 Rathbone Place, London', but in about 1860 the district letter W was added. In 1888 they extended their premises to 42 Rathbone Place (now renumbered 51). George Rowney and Co. were established in 1789. Between 1844 and 1848 they traded as Rowney, Dillon and Rowney. Their address '52 Rathbone Place and 29 Oxford Street' indicates a date between 1862 and 1881. Reeves and Sons were founded in 1777. Between 1829 and 1845 the address is '150 Cheapside'. 'Reeves and Sons Ltd' indicates a date after 1890.

Within the complex world of art nothing is straightforward and these imprints, though dating the canvas, do not necessarily reveal the date when the picture was painted. Consideration has to be given to how long a shop or artist kept the canvas before it was sold or used.

The other pitfall occurs when artists of another generation paint over an old painting. In his early days, one well-known artist of my acquaintance could not afford new canvases, so a visit to the local rag-and-bone man often proved worthwhile. For a few shillings he could buy a stack of unwanted family portraits or unfashionable still-life subjects. I often wonder if he painted over a work of art which could now be worth thousands of pounds!

Like canvas, watercolour paper can sometimes give you a visual means of dating. Manufacturers' watermarks are clearly discernible when the paper is held up to the light. The most frequently found mark is J. Whatman, used from the late eighteenth century onwards. Just below this mark the year of manufacture will occasionally be found. You must remember, however, that the paper may have been lying around for years before it was used. A client brought me one day for valuation a drawing which purported to be by Thomas Rowlandson, the remarkable caricaturist whose works have always been eagerly sought by collectors. For this reason fakes abound, and I was instantly suspicious, for the drawing lacked the vigour of line so characteristic of Rowlandson's work. I removed the picture from its frame and, as luck would have it, the paper was watermarked with the date 1835. This was definitely not one of Rowlandson's best years. After all, he had been dead since 1827!

Before we pass from originals on to prints and reproductions, a word or two about current fashions in paintings. 'A good commercial picture' is how most art dealers would describe George Faulkner Wetherbee's delightful watercolour *Knucklebones* (p. 145). It is in good condition, of wonderful quality and painted by an eminent artist. But above all it is a very saleable item, because of its subject. Apart from children, other popular themes are old English thatched cottage scenes; marine subjects (calm seas being preferred to violent waves); flower studies, whether in a garden or in a vase; attractive female nudes – much favoured by Japanese collectors; anything of a sporting nature, particularly horse-racing, hunting and the rare subject of polo; animals and birds; and good topographical views, especially colonial scenes. Taboo subjects are anything of a religious or biblical nature, including church interiors; dead birds and animals; creatures fighting, such as two dogs in vicious combat; and run-of-the-mill family portraits, unless of a pretty female. There are, of course, exceptions to the above: a religious painting by one of the old masters would still be of considerable value.

By far the greatest number of prints brought to the *Roadshow* are steel engravings, which were produced from about 1830. These engravings, often taken from books, are the familiar hand-coloured prints now seen in so many antique shops. With the aid of a magnifying glass you will see that the picture is composed of numerous fine lines. There will also be a print mark – an indentation all round the print where the paper was applied to the printing block. Fashions today are the same as for paintings.

Etching by Harry Morley, RA (1881–1943). Notice the plate mark and the inscription on the bottom of the etching.

To Dorothea Selous.   Harry Morley

CARE AND REPAIR
2

- Glue a thin sliver of wine bottle cork to each bottom corner of the backs of frames. They keep the picture away from the wall and prevent damp building up.
- Dust oil paintings with a soft brush.
- Cleaning and restoration of oil paintings are for experts. Canvas tears should be treated as soon as possible.
- Brown spots (foxing) on prints and watercolours are removable, but should be dealt with only by a specialist restorer.
- Vertical or horizontal brown lines on watercolours or prints are caused by split backing boards which have let air enter and 'burn' the paper. In very bad cases the paper splits. Brown lines can sometimes be rectified, but only by a specialist.

For expert advice contact the Association of British Picture Restorers, Station Avenue, Kew, TW9 3QA

See also p. 144.

It's always sad when I have to disillusion someone who thinks mistakenly that their picture is an original oil. Every *Antiques Roadshow* brings forth quite a number of pictures of this kind. They are, in fact, photographs which have been overpainted. Usually small in size, their give-away is that though the clothes and background are covered in oil paint, the faces, hands and feet are left unpainted; the photographic process is easily seen in these areas. Because of the nature of the paper, the oil paint often flakes. These pictures, which have little value, generally date from around the 1880s.

'Pen and ink' drawings too are not always what they seem — most of those I see at a *Roadshow* are etchings. This process uses a resin-coated metal plate, through which lines and strokes are made by means of a needle. Acid is applied, which eats into the metal where the cuts are made. The plate is then cleaned and inked and the paper is laid on it under a press. Clues to identifying etchings are that the design will feel slightly raised if you run your fingers across it, and as with engravings there is a slight indentation all round the edge of the print where the paper was applied to the plate. Various pencil inscriptions are usually found on the lower plate margin; they may include the engraver's signature, the title of the picture and possibly a dedication. Other markings may include two numbers separated by an oblique line, for example 75/100. This would indicate that the etching is number 75 from a total of 100 impressions made before the plate was destroyed. With each impression the plate wears just a little, so the first ten or so will always be the crispest. A very few etchings are worth thousands of pounds, so don't be afraid to seek advice.

Modern photographic reproductions abound, and some can be quite valuable. At one *Roadshow* in the North of England a gentleman brought in a Russell Flint reproduction and related with pride how he had framed it. 'I was given this print unframed five years ago. Luckily I found a frame in a secondhand shop for £1 and it was just the right size. I had to cut all the white margin off the print so it would fit, but who wants that anyway?' I asked him if there had been a signature on the lower margin. 'Oh, yes, and some printing along the top margin.' What a shame. He had saved himself about £15 on framing, but by cutting off the signed margin he had devalued the print by hundreds of pounds. Never cut the margin off any signed print. Think of the surround of a print like the perforations on a rare stamp — cut them off and no collector will ever be interested. This particular gentleman went away perfectly happy because, he said, 'Its value is unimportant – I would never dream of selling it, whatever it's worth.'

The strongest recommendation that I can give today's collector of modest means is to concentrate on twentieth-century watercolours, with their rich diversity of styles. Apart from the often used clichés of quality, condition and buying what pleases you, my advice is: be a trend-setter rather than a name-dropper.

CLOCKS AND WATCHES

SIMON BULL

Simon Bull (right) delves into the workings of a handsome clock brought in to the Roadshow.

Top of page *Late nineteenth-century French gilt and spelter garniture de cheminée.*

Opposite *Enamelled gold and diamond-set watch, 2 inches in diameter, made by Jehan Cremsdorff in Paris about 1650. To date the world's most expensive watch, it sold recently for nearly £750,000.*

Judging by the number of people who struggle into the hall at every *Roadshow*, red-faced and breathing hard, black 'marble' clocks are still to be found in many British homes. They were produced in enormous numbers from the latter years of Queen Victoria's reign up to the First World War, but despite the quantities produced the movements – particularly French examples – and many of the cases were exceptionally well made. As with so many mass-produced nineteenth-century clocks, until recently marble clocks were despised by both collectors and dealers. Twenty years ago a colleague of mine was offered for free every black marble clock sent into a local auction room – on condition that he collected them and took them away. The arrangement worked well until he found that train fares and the absolute necessity of hiring taxis made the deal uneconomic!

Material for the black cases was quarried in both Belgium and North Wales, where a variety of slate is found that, when suitably cut, dyed and polished, reveals a depth and lustre close to that of marble. Occasionally more exotic materials were used, including green onyx, white alabaster and a yellow-brown limestone. The movements are generally of French or sometimes German origin and often provide the only clues for accurate dating. It is very unusual to find an English movement in a marble clock of this period, and an English name appearing on the dial is certain to be that of the retailer. Indeed, close examination of such a signature will normally show that it is painted on top of the enamel glaze, and in many cases it will have partly or completely faded away. Searching through old trade or street directories at the local library may reveal the dates when the retailer was in business, but failing this, further information can sometimes be found on the back of the movement. If fitted with a bell for striking, the bell will

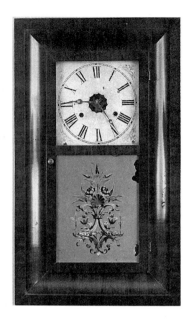

American ogee wall clock, 25 inches high, of about 1880. These now sell for between £50 and £150, depending on the condition of the decoration on the door panel.

CARE AND REPAIR
————— 1 —————

○ On marble and stone clock cases the joints can come apart. Take out the movement and dial before refixing the case with water-soluble glue.
○ Remove dirt from marble by wiping with a cloth wrung out in a mild solution of washing-up liquid. Wipe dry immediately.
○ Remove grease from marble with cotton wool soaked in benzine. Wipe dry immediately.
○ To improve dulled black marble apply repeated thin coats of black shoe polish.

See also p. 155.

probably obscure any stamps or marks, and first you must remove it. Punched or engraved numbers are of little help, because not much is known of the production figures and corresponding dates for the various factories. However, a maker's signature can be looked up, and award stamps may be useful if correctly interpreted. Awards were usually presented for a particular design of movement, or even for achievements in production output, and do not refer to any particular clock. However, by this method it may be possible to establish the date of manufacture to within ten years. German movements are normally of lower quality and dating is more difficult, but they are usually late nineteenth-century.

Now we come to American clocks, many thousands of which have been re-exported to the United States during the last ten years, with the result that the more unusual types – even of these mass-produced models – are becoming scarce. An idea of the quantities involved and the cheapness of these clocks can be gained from the well-recorded production figures of Chauncy Jerome, one of the many makers who revolutionised the industry in America by introducing machinery capable of stamping out the parts. In one day three men were now able to produce enough wheels for five hundred clocks. The complete movement for an 'ogee' wall clock (left) cost less than 50 cents, the case about 30 cents and the remaining parts 10 cents – in the 1840s the complete clock sold for less than $2. A hundred and thirty years later – in 1970 – the situation had not changed greatly, and the same clocks, by now antique, could be bought in street markets for £2 10s. I used to be able to half-fill a garage with about a hundred clocks in six weeks, selling them all at £3 apiece to the same American missionary preacher, who claimed that antique dealing was his hobby – a smart hobby, as any reasonable example is now £100. Bracket and shelf clocks have fared much the same, with the majority now fetching between £75 and £120.

There is usually a printed paper label stuck to the inside of the case of an American clock. Often this will bear the name of the maker and perhaps the date of a relevant patent, providing a reasonable idea of period. The movements, though simple in construction, are remarkably sturdy and seem to keep on running like an old-fashioned clockwork toy. The cases, if made of wood, can be successfully restored, but anyone considering buying an example should make sure that the transfer-printed glass panel in the front is original – they cannot easily be replaced in England and definitely contribute to the value.

The story of German clockmaking throughout the second half of the nineteenth century is similar to that of America, with more than ten thousand people employed in the industry in the Black Forest alone. Undoubtedly the best-known product of this area was the cuckoo clock, but in reality the Black Forest clockmakers made a far greater proportion of movements and clocks for export and therefore styled to suit their foreign markets. Almost without

Late nineteenth-century German weight-driven wall regulator in the Viennese style, 46 inches high and worth today £300–400.

exception these 'contemporary reproductions' are worth considerably less than the original designs on which they are based.

The so-called Vienna regulator is a particularly relevant example – it ranges in value from £10,000-plus for a superb original (difficult to mistake!) down to £100 for a German clock quite inaccurately given the same name. The Vienna regulator was introduced in Austria before 1800, and although production continued throughout the nineteenth century, only a limited number arrived in Britain. The finest examples are always in very elegant cases, generally slim in outline, with enamel dials constructed in one piece; the movements are weight-driven, beautifully made and keep excellent time. Although later examples from Austria have more elaborate cases and a dial made in two parts, they still exhibited a high standard of workmanship throughout (p. 156). This is also true of the best German 'copies', but the vast majority of late Black Forest models are obviously mass-produced and invariably spring-driven (left).

In France the reign of Louis XV saw the introduction of decorative mantel and bracket clock cases made entirely of metal; this style continued to be developed, revised and even faked almost continuously up to the present day. There are still considerable differences of opinion about the materials used, which are variously described as brass, bronze and ormolu amongst others. As the majority of these clocks were originally gilded or lacquered, it is usually impossible to determine easily the chemical constituency of the metal; indeed, it is seldom important when trying to establish the date or value – with the particular exception of spelter or soft metal.

Brass (an alloy of copper and zinc) was certainly most commonly used, whilst bronze (copper and tin) was used on occasions, particularly in the eighteenth century. 'Ormolu' – from the French *or moulu*, meaning 'ground gold' – is used to describe both 'fire' or 'mercurial' gilt-metal and a metal made by alloying copper, zinc and tin. The latter was developed in England during the eighteenth century, and resembles gold in colour. During the second half of the nineteenth century 'soft' metal alloys were increasingly used, particularly spelter, a mixture of zinc and tin with a consistency and colour similar to lead. It casts well in a good mould, but is naturally very soft, can be difficult to repair, and looks very unattractive when the gilding has worn away.

Many of the popular designs from the eighteenth century were revived during the Victorian era, often smaller, in an altered form and invariably of lower quality. However, since few people have the opportunity of examining original examples closely, it is not always easy to judge the date from the case alone. A very limited number of eighteenth-century French clocks were imported into Britain, but their rather 'rich' appearance never really suited English taste. It is best, therefore, to start with the assumption that the clock on the mantelpiece is probably mid-nineteenth-century, and

Walnut-cased striking longcase clock by England's most famous maker, Thomas Tompion, about 1685. Today it would be worth at least £50,000.

hope to be pleasantly surprised. The following pointers suggest a nineteenth-century clock: (1) A movement of the type used in many marble clocks and bearing similar punched marks, a small punched signature, or a series of punched numbers on the back-plate. (2) A Brocot-style regulator, or a pendulum mounted with a double hook, particularly if the pendulum is original and numbered. (3) The use of a balance wheel escapement on the backplate, similar to a carriage clock. (4) Any clock made of spelter or soft metal. If you find none of these details, further research could prove worthwhile!

Generally, even a relatively modest genuine eighteenth-century clock would be worth around £1000. The nineteenth-century 'copies' range from £250 up to £3000, although spelter examples are usually worth about half the price of a 'hard' metal clock. Decorative porcelain panels inset into a clock would probably double its value; these plaques are usually described as Sèvres — which they are almost certainly not if the clock is nineteenth-century.

A romantic, if apocryphal, story is associated with the origin of the carriage clock. It is said that during his campaigns Napoleon, dissatisfied with the late arrival of his generals at staff conferences, ordered a series of small portable clocks to be made and distributed to his senior officers. Certainly a form of portable clock, known as a *pendule d'officier*, was made in France at the time, but otherwise the legend is unsubstantiated. However, once established, the portable or carriage clock became so popular that hundreds of thousands were produced, mainly in France, between 1850 and 1925. Some original sales catalogues listed prices singly, per dozen and even per gross. They were not primarily made for use in carriages, a fact supported by the existence of so many highly decorative cases, and by the lack of contemporary reports of the traffic jams that would surely have existed if there had been as many carriages as clocks! Principally, the carriage clock was the first reasonably priced timepiece that could be easily moved around the house, or used whilst travelling.

All the usual criteria concerning quality, decoration and originality apply when evaluating this type of clock. Because the standard models were made in such substantial numbers, prices can be assessed quite accurately by means of tables which add increments according to the quality of the case, the complication of the striking mechanism or the addition of calendar work. For instance, a champlevé or cloisonné enamel case and dial would put up the price by £500 or more. Calendar work would add another £150.

In the past a number of people have written in to ask why longcase clocks feature so infrequently on the *Roadshow*. There are two answers. In the first place, they are really not something that can be loaded into the back of a Mini, nor are they particularly welcome on the bus. The second and more pertinent reason is

A selection of fine-quality French carriage clocks from the second half of the nineteenth century.

CARE AND REPAIR
2

○ Beware of cleaning a metal case. If uncertain of the material, leave it. Clean brass with non-abrasive metal polish. For bronze see p. 132.
○ To improve dulled wooden cases, first try wax polish. If that fails, use an antique furniture cleaner on 0000 steel wool and rub with the grain.
○ You can clean the working parts of American and German clocks yourself, but all others need an expert.
○ Never oil a dirty clock. When cleaning, make sure the movement is completely unwound before dismantling, then clean it in benzine before reassembling. Put one drop of suitable light oil (sewing machine oil will do) on each pivot point and in the pallets of the escapement, but none on the wheels.
○ Don't open the backs of watches with a sharp knife. In fact, don't touch them at all! All watch repairs should be left to a specialist.

For expert advice contact the British Horological Institute, Upton Hall, Upton, Newark, NG23 5TE

See also p. 152.

that, despite the understandable reverence with which a grandfather clock is always regarded by its owner – to many people they are symbolic of age and antiquity – the vast majority are so similar in construction and origin that we would inevitably find ourselves repeating the same information on every programme.

It is easy to forget that, before clocks and watches were available at prices to suit everyone's pocket, the ordinary grandfather clock was the most accurate timekeeper for all but a select minority. In the hundred years following the invention of the long pendulum anchor escapement, in about 1660, the majority of longcase clocks were made in London, very much on an individual basis. However the Industrial Revolution saw the establishment of clockmaking centres in the provinces, particularly Birmingham, and the industry separated into three distinct parts to allow for mass production. Movements were manufactured to standardised patterns; dials, mostly painted, were available to the customer's choice; and the cases were often made by local joiners or cabinet-makers. Usually the name on the dial will be that of a local retailer or

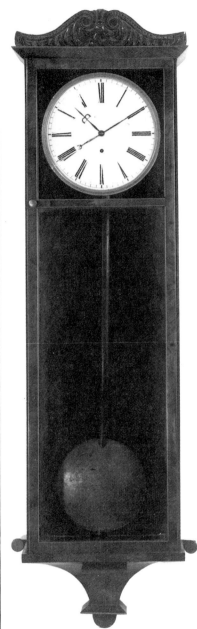

Mahogany-cased Viennese regulator of about 1840, selling for about £200 today.

clockmaker/repairer, and the cases vary in style according to where they were made. In the north they tended to be broad and tall, often with elaborate cross-banding and veneered inlay. Mahogany was the predominant veneer for clocks made in areas close to major trading ports, as it was often used as ballast on ships returning only partially loaded from the Americas. In contrast, clock cases from the south-west were usually in oak or softwoods such as pine, and generally of smaller size.

In the category of watches, the *Roadshow* turns up both the greatest rarities and some of the most commonplace objects – silver 'granny' watches. The survival rate of these simple watches is extraordinary – we see as many as a hundred in a day. Fifteen years ago they were sold by weight in the street markets; dealers would pour them on to the scales and charge the value of scrap silver, their profit being the difference between the weight of silver used and the weight of the complete watch – average price £2.50.

The majority of these watches, both the small ladies' model and the larger gentlemen's size, were manufactured in Switzerland, which dominated the watchmaking industry throughout the nineteenth century – and, of course, for the first half of this century, after the introduction of the wristwatch. In their 1899 catalogue the London firm of S. Smith & Son of the Strand advertised a Swiss ladies' watch with engraved silver case, enamel dial and cylinder movement for £1 5s; these were the equivalent of a wristwatch today, being affordable (albeit only just) by most working families.

Although most of the gold examples have been melted down over the years – many to support the nation during wartime – silver ones have been handed on, tucked away in drawers or jewellery boxes. However, on more than one occasion a much used cardboard box, stuffed with cotton wool, has revealed a watch of considerable technical or decorative value, usually a pleasant surprise for the owner. Indeed, potential fortune-hunters should take heart from the watch on p. 151. Valued some years ago at about £600, it sold recently in Geneva for nearly £750,000.

In general, repairs to the working parts of clocks and watches should be entrusted to a professional, and the names of suitably qualified clockmakers in your area are available from the British Horological Institute. However, many of the clocks I have described are still of small commercial value, and professional restoration may prove to be uneconomic. In the case of a damaged movement from a French decorative or marble clock it is sometimes possible to find a complete replacement, as many of these clocks were broken up years ago. I have a friend who bought hundreds of marble clocks when no one else wanted them. He paid 50p each, kept the movements and used the cases to build a garden wall. The movements are now only worth about £5, but the complete clocks fetch upwards of £30; still, he has an interesting, if expensive, view from his sitting room.

ENGLISH PERCUSSION SPORTING GUNS AND RIFLES

BILL HARRIMAN

Bill Harrison with a beautifully decorated truncheon.

Top of page A Birmingham-proved 10 bore live pigeon gun of about 1840, usually fitted with a ramrod (above); and (below) a Birmingham-proved 8 bore gun made in about 1850 for the South African market, where the deep butt was called Babbejaansboud *(baboon's thigh).*

English percussion guns and rifles are the type of gun that people bring me most frequently to look at. My long-suffering mother first bought me one in 1969, and the passing years have turned me from an unruly but fascinated schoolboy into an obsessive collector. These guns were designed to shoot game, and date mostly from the first half of the nineteenth century. They are loaded from the muzzle with a charge of powder, wadding and shot, and the charge is then seated with a ramrod. It is ignited when the hammer strikes the copper percussion cap, causing a flash to pass down the nipple into the powder. Barrels for shot are smooth, whilst those for bullets have rifling grooves to impart a spin which increases accuracy.

The chances of finding a percussion gun in an attic or farm building or at a country auction are good, and in my opinion their value, whilst quite low at present, may well rise dramatically within the next few years. Collectors of long guns tend to disregard them in favour of eighteenth-century flintlock fowling pieces or military weapons such as rifles or muskets. These are now very highly priced, so people will inevitably turn to the cheaper percussion gun sooner or later. Ten years ago it was common to hear the derisory comment, 'Well, it's only a percussion gun, isn't it. . . .' Now the tide is turning.

A thumbnail sketch of the English gun trade, centred on Birmingham, will help to put the guns themselves into context. First of all, confusion can arise when a gun is signed with what people assume is the maker's name. When the *Roadshow* visited Preston in 1986, for example, a gentleman brought me a shotgun of about 1860, signed 'James Burrow Preston'. Naturally he was very enthusiastic about the local connection, and firmly believed that it had been made in the town. Actually the gun had been made in

Birmingham and only retailed by Burrow. A bit disappointing perhaps, but this is almost always the case.

Apart from that, in the Birmingham gun trade of the mid-nineteenth century the term 'gunmaker' itself is misleading. The division of labour was so great that a completed gun passed through the hands of some fifty different craftsmen. The trade directories of the time list thirty major specialists, and other smaller ones undoubtedly existed. This fragmentation seems bewildering today, conditioned as we are to the machine-dominated production line, but in those days it enabled a rapid response to be made to changes in market forces. In lean times many worked in associated trades and only returned to their gun-making specialities when demand rose, for example in wartime. The craftsmen fell into two categories. 'Material men' made the components – barrels, locks, stocks, ramrods, sights, nipples and so on, whilst the 'setters-up', such as percussioners, stockers, ribbers, screwers, lock filers and engravers, assembled them into completed guns.

Barrel forging was the most important process. This involved winding a ribbon of iron and steel around a mandrel and hammer-welding it into a tube at white heat. The forge reached maximum efficiency at around noon, and it was then that the best tubes were produced. Others of varying degrees of quality were forged during the rest of the day as the forge heated up or cooled down. In this way all grades of barrel could be supplied in a cost-effective manner.

Two 'rook-and-rabbit' rifles: a 70 bore with 16 groove rifling and finely figured stock (above), and (below) a 70 bore Needham patent breech-loading needlefire rifle. Note the damascus on the barrels.

The cheapest barrels, produced with welded seams running longitudinally, were less robust than the coiled versions. Old horseshoe nails, called stubs, were the raw material; Continental ones were preferred. By 1840 stub twist barrels had been superseded by damascus twist, named after Middle Eastern pattern welding. For this the forging process was unaltered, but both iron and steel were used to give a stronger grain. Several types of damascus exist. The best tubes, stub damascus, contained both stubs and scrap tool steel. Next, but of inferior quality, were barrels made of second- or third-quality scrap, 'threepenny skelp iron', 'twopenny' or 'Wednesbury skelp' (Wednesbury is a town north-west of Birmingham). The poorest barrels, using the cheapest scrap – delightfully termed 'sham damn skelp' – were often skilfully painted to imitate the delicate patterning of damascus. Unscrupulous makers veneered poor barrels with a thin layer of quality damascus to deceive the inexperienced purchaser. After forging, the barrel was ground and bored to its final dimensions and the breech fitted. So expert were the Birmingham grinders that their barrels were often as true as if they had been turned on lathes.

Before final finishing, the barrels were proof-fired with a large charge of powder and shot to test their strength. If they passed, they were stamped with proof marks. The London Proof House was founded in 1657, and the Birmingham one in 1813; both are still in operation today. Many people who have brought guns to the *Roadshow* are under the mistaken impression that gun barrel proof marks are similar in meaning to silver hallmarks. Not so;

A selection of accessories: cap tins, a shot charger, two cappers, nipple keys, powder measures, a wad punch, a bore gauge and a blue glass artificial pigeon, precursor of the modern clay pigeon.

High-quality engraving on the patchbox cover of the Cogswell double rifle shown in colour on p. 163.

hallmarks guarantee purity of silver, proof marks safety in use. The same marks will be found on best stub twist tubes as on those of sham damn skelp.

Gunlocks, the mechanisms that discharged the weapons, were assembled from carefully forged components, mainly by Black Country firms; the most famous of them were the Brazier family of Wolverhampton, who exhibited gunlocks at the Great Exhibition of 1851. Cheap locks were made from die-stamped components. Best-quality furniture – that is, items like trigger guards, butt plates and ramrod pipes – was made from swarf (iron and steel filings); this was often a source of beer money to the workmen who collected it. The cheaper furniture was cast. Silver furniture on a gun of this period is most unusual.

Stocks were normally of Circassian walnut (*Juglans regia*). The finest were cut from the tree base with its tight, gently curved grain; the remainder of the tree provided ones of lesser quality. The poorest were of beech stained to imitate walnut.

When lock, stock and barrel were united, the gun was said to be 'in-the-white' because all the parts were bright from polishing. Most guns were engraved, and it is important to realise that engraving is not synonymous with quality. This myth was created by gunmakers who sold various grades of guns and scaled the quality and quantity of engraving accordingly. Though this practice gave the impression that engraving was expensive, its cost rarely exceeded 5 per cent of the total. English engraving was restrained and limited to fine acanthus scrolls interspersed with gamebirds, gun dogs and, on rifles, deer.

Finishing involved three processes. To prevent any further rust the barrel was browned using nitric acid and mercury sublimate. The furniture was heated in charcoal dust to blue it, and the locks colour-hardened by baking them in bone dust and old shoe soles. It is important to acquire an eye for these original colours, as some skilled modern restorers can imitate them closely. Only experience will enable you to differentiate between good renovation and original finish. As a rule of thumb, original barrel brown has a delicate greyish tinge and charcoal blue the same iridescence as a peacock's feather. Colour hardening, with its subtle blend of blues, browns and greys, always puts me in mind of a thunder-laden sky. Some modern oils can attack charcoal blue, and it is best to use a silicone spray to prevent rust. Be warned, too, that sunlight fades colour hardening and can bleach the colour of a stock.

During the early nineteenth century game was always 'walked up', using pointers, and shot whilst 'going away'. Game driven over the guns was unheard of. Colonel Peter Hawker, the famous wildfowler, soldier, author and hypochondriac, had his own favourite method: 'Sadly in want of a brace of birds, so took out my duck gun, "Big Joe" at dusk, crawled up to three partridges that were feeding and floored the trio at 95 yards with a four ounce Eley cartridge. . . .' He wrote his classic work *Instructions to*

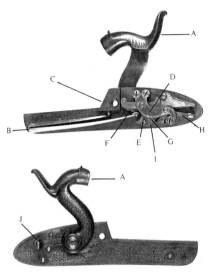

Above *Anatomy of a gunlock.
A=hammer, B=mainspring,
C=lockplate, D=bridle,
E=tumbler, F=swivel,
G=tumbler detent (rifles only),
H=trigger scear, I=half-cock
notch, and J=half-cock safety
bolt.*

Young Sportsmen in all that relates to Guns and Shooting in 1814, though the revised 1838 edition is more useful.

Nobody can say who actually invented the percussion cap. In 1807, the Rev. Alexander Forsyth obtained a patent for guns ignited by mercury fulminate. Percussion caps were on sale as early as 1816 in Joseph Egg's shop, and Joshua Shaw was granted a US patent for them in 1822.

In England, the size of a gun is expressed as a numbered bore rather than a decimal fraction. The system was based on the number of pure lead balls, of an arbitrarily selected diameter, that weighed exactly one pound. For example, balls of which twelve weighed one pound would always measure .747 inch each in diameter. Hence the gun that fired balls of that size became known as a 12 bore. The most popular type of gun had double 30-inch barrels of about 14 bore. The best had platinum breech plugs which blew out sideways if the gun had been overcharged; this prevented the barrel from bursting and injuring the user. However, single-barrelled guns were made in greater quantity and formed the basis of the Birmingham trade. In the English market they were bought not by sportsmen but by those who needed guns to exterminate vermin or to put meat on the table. Consequently, a single-barrelled gun of good quality is far rarer than its double-barrelled counterpart.

Three types of single-barrelled guns exist. Pheasant shooting in coverts produced guns that handled quickly and still threw a good weight of shot. They are normally 12 bore and may have had barrels as short as 26 inches. Wildfowling presented special problems, with difficult, high-flying and tough targets such as duck or geese. Consequently guns assumed leviathan proportions with bores from 10 to 4 and barrels often in excess of 40 inches. The flintlock was often retained, as its priming pan flash caused sitting birds to rise, their outspread wings presenting a better target for the shot pattern.

Good (above) and poor (below) sporting guns, with accessories including a powder flask retaining most of its original lacquer.

CARE AND REPAIR

- Assume all guns are loaded until you have proved they are not.
- Don't use any other cleaners, chemicals or tools than those mentioned below, and don't over-clean.
- Before cleaning, remove the barrels and locks with a gunsmith's turnscrew, which won't damage the screw slots.
- To prevent fingermarks wipe guns after handling, or wear cotton gloves.
- On metal parts, remove surface dirt and light rust with 0000 steel wool soaked in light oil.
- To remove stubborn rust scrape with a copper coin.
- Clean stocks with 0000 steel wool soaked in meths, then rub in a coat of boiled linseed oil using the ball of your hand.
- Never take locks to pieces because the temper of lock springs makes them brittle and dangerous to remove without the proper tools. Leave locks to experts.
- Don't cock and fire percussion guns because the hammer and the nipple can be brittle.
- Store long guns pointing downwards to prevent oil staining stocks.
- Clean leather accessories with hide food.

For expert advice contact the Historical Breechloading Small Arms Association, % Imperial War Museum, Lambeth Road, London SE1 6HZ

The third type was produced for the 'sport' of shooting live pigeons released from baskets, the precursor of clay pigeon shooting. Heavy wagers were made on these matches, so shooters used the maximum possible charge to increase the chance of a hit. This resulted in heavy guns of about 10 bore with barrels averaging some 32 inches. Their chief feature is the lack of ramrod pipes under the barrel, because separate loading rods were used. When in the 1870s Alexandra, Princess of Wales, expressed her distaste for the practice it was largely discontinued in favour of artificial targets.

British sporting rifles, that is, guns which fire bullets as opposed to shot, fall into two categories: heavy-calibre for deer stalking, and lighter 'rook-and-rabbit' rifles for small game. Stalking rifles have single octagonal barrels ranging from 20 to 12 bore. They are fitted with simple sights for ranges seldom greater than 250 yards. The locks are often fitted with safety bolts to lock the hammers and detented tumblers to speed the hammer fall by preventing any sticking at half-cock. Two main styles of rifling are found. Polygroove (eight to fourteen grooves) or two-groove Brunswick, using winged bullets. Both became difficult to load after a few shots, because burnt powder fouling built up.

Rook rifles are merely scaled-down stalking rifles averaging 90 bore and sighted to 100 yards. It is rare to find a good-quality rook rifle, probably because in England most game was shot with shotguns – unlike in America, where small-calibre rifles of good quality abound. An interesting breech-loading variation of the rook rifle is the Needham Patent Needlefire rifle, which is easily identified by its screw thread breech block and long needle to the hammer nose. Double-barrelled rifles were used little in Britain but frequently in India and Africa, where a second shot against dangerous game could mean the difference between life and death. Many rifles have 'set triggers' which reduce the pull and make for better shooting: these have tiny adjusting screws and give a sharp click when pushed forwards or 'set'.

The advent of the railway enabled the shooter to travel in search of sport, and as a result guns and their requisites began to be protected by cases, normally of oak or mahogany. The best are bound with brass and contained in heavy leather slip-covers. Their interiors are lined and partitioned in green baize. Often the lids bear the trade label of the maker or retailer. These can be very attractive in themselves and also provide a lot of useful information such as addresses.

The multitude of accessories used with percussion guns offer great opportunities to the collector. They are undervalued at present, probably because few people know what they are, and I am sure they will become a major growth area. For the beginner, accessories make a good starting point for a collection as they are relatively inexpensive, take up very little room and make an attractive display.

A 24 bore best-quality double rifle by B. Cogswell, 224 Strand, London, 1850–60.

There are five main makers: James Dixon, G. & J. W. Hawksley, Bartram, William Davies and Sykes. Beware of flasks signed by the last-named – good modern copies exist and may be passed off as genuine. Flasks for both powder and shot form the largest group, and are a collecting field in themselves. They range from high-quality pieces with morocco leather-covered bodies and nickel silver chargers marked 'Quickloading Fireproof', to what Colonel Hawker calls 'trumpery Sheffield flasks'. Shot flasks have leather bodies and two types of charger: 'English', with a spring-loaded cut-off, and 'Irish', with a scoop. Avoid polishing flasks if they have original lacquer, and don't smoke near any flask until you are sure that it is empty. Should you find any gunpowder, surrender it to the police who will dispose of it safely.

Percussion cap tins often have brightly coloured labels which are most attractive. Spring-loaded brass or nickel silver magazines for percussion caps, known as cappers, are desirable, especially if snail-shaped. These enabled the shooter to cap his nipple with gloved or cold hands. Nipple keys come in two main types: all-steel T-shaped with copper covers that unscrew to reveal a spare pair of nipples; and screwdriver-shaped with screw-in prickers to the ebony or rosewood handles. Shot chargers are double-ended containers that held a measure of shot for quick loading. They are normally steel, but examples exist in gilding metal.

The demise of the percussion gun began in 1835 when a Frenchman named Le Faucheux patented a breech-loading shotgun with a self-contained cartridge ignited by a pin. These were popular on the Continent but not in England. By 1860, George Daw had produced a centre fire cartridge that was little different from those in use today. The era of the muzzle loader was over, but they lingered on in the provinces and abroad into the 1890s and were still made in Birmingham well into the 1930s.

My advice to anyone contemplating collecting English percussion sporting guns is initially to invest in books and attend specialist auctions where you can handle specimens and gain experience. Only then should you consider purchase. The appeal of these guns for me is that they are so quintessentially English. Many have tried to imitate their elegant, thoroughbred lines and functional simplicity, but few have come even near. That so many have survived says much for the craftsmen who built them. A fine gun is a pleasure to handle, a joy to behold and a sound investment.

A selection of powder and shot flasks. The shot flask on the bottom right has an 'English' charger, and the shot belt on the left has an 'Irish' scoop charger.

CLOCKWORK MUSIC

HILARY KAY

Hilary Kay (right) explains to the owner of an early projector how the machine works.

There is only one sound which can produce a lull in the deafening hubbub of a *Roadshow* as quickly as that of breaking glass – the tinkling melody of a musical box playing somewhere in the hall. In the eighteenth century, when musical boxes were first produced, the only way for most people to hear music was to perform it themselves. The appeal of automatic music in the home was therefore irresistible.

The principle of the musical box lies in the automated chimes of carillon church movements, operated by a rotating iron drum fitted with steel pins, which date back as far as the fourteenth century. (A carillon is a series of stationary tuned bells struck by a movable hammer.) Small carillon movements were sometimes fitted to bracket clocks of particular quality, and these have been seen on the *Roadshow* in the past. Inside the cases of these clocks, the tuned scale of deep, saucer-shaped brass bells is usually placed just behind the rear plate of the clock, where the mechanism is powered by the clock spring. Beneath the bells is a brass cylinder with pins mathematically positioned so that the striking levers are lifted to sound the correct bell at exactly the right moment. Occasionally I have found these carillon clock movements mounted inside plain, easily portable wooden boxes, which could be described as the first musical boxes. Although they form an important link in the development of the musical box, the bells quickly lose their tonal accuracy and there is no damping device for the sound. This unholy union ensures that one out-of-tune note blends jarringly with the next.

Makers of pocket watches in Switzerland in the seventeenth century took the development of mechanical music an important step further with their use of slim steel teeth, each tuned to a different note and sounded by a revolving pinned brass barrel. The

Top of page *Early key-wound cylinder musical box by Ducommun-Girod, made in Switzerland about 1840. Note the grouping of six teeth on each section of comb.*

Rare autochange disc musical box made by Polyphon in Germany about 1900. Over 7 feet tall and using discs nearly 20 inches in diameter, this was the forerunner of the juke box.

mechanism was usually mounted beneath the mechanism of the pocket watch and operated by the same clockwork movement. The tune can be heard as the steel teeth are 'plucked' by the pins in the brass barrel as it turns. Tiny musical devices of this kind were fitted into a variety of other small objects – under the enamel tops of walking canes, within watch keys, and in patch and snuff boxes. These delicate objects, often made of gold with lavish enamelling, have only survived in small numbers, however, and are seen very rarely on the *Roadshow*.

The earliest cylinder musical boxes produced as solo instruments, rather than as novel accessories to something else, date from about 1810. They were made in Geneva and Sainte Croix in Switzerland, the locality which had become particularly renowned for clock- and watchmaking. Painstakingly constructed by hand, they were expensive luxuries only affordable by the wealthy.

Their plain wooden cases – unlike the later examples devoid of marquetry and wax-finished rather than french-polished – belie the treasure house within. Opening the lid of one of these boxes reveals the pinned brass cylinder with the spring barrel on the left and a scale of tuned steel teeth mounted horizontally parallel to the barrel. In the early days of development, before about 1830, the limited technology prevented the tuned steel 'comb' being made in one piece; small groups or even single teeth were tuned and mounted with screws on to the bed plate. At this time the ends of the brass levers to control start/stop and tune change/repeat emerge from the left side of the box below the key arbor (before about 1860 all musical boxes were wound by a large key; after this date a ratchet lever was mounted on the left of the movement, just over the spring barrel).

As soon as a long tuned steel comb could be made in one piece mass-production methods could be employed and larger numbers of musical boxes produced. This helped to meet the remarkable demand for these devices, although it had little effect on the retailers' prices. Once the demand had been established, manufacturers began to develop their lines, stimulating buyers to seek out the latest model with the most novel features.

In the 1840s musical boxes had one obvious, important limitation: they were restricted to the tiny repertoire on the pinned cylinder fitted when the box was purchased. Now, by more intricate pinning and increasing the diameter of the cylinder, more tunes or a longer piece of music could be accommodated. Usually known as overture or two-per-turn boxes, this development marked the first of a long line of adaptations, additions and innovations to the cylinder musical box over the next half century. Towards the end of the 1840s other instruments, such as groups of carillon-type brass saucer bells or small snare drums, began to be mounted within the wooden case. These additional instruments were operated by levers linked to teeth plucked by the brass cylinder, and accompanied the melodies.

Close-up of a cylinder musical box showing the pinned cylinder, tuned steel comb, and in the foreground the winding lever; the governor is at the far end.

In the early 1860s small, bellows-operated reed organs began to be mounted beneath the comb and cylinder. Though they are known as Voix Céleste (heavenly voice) movements, I have usually heard them in various stages of distress; the tune has been drowned by a bronchial wheezing from the bellows, and occasionally the reed organ is restricted to an unending single note throughout the melody, sounding for all the world like a small animal whining and breathing its last within its wooden coffin. Of course a new box would have produced a very different sound, as would a professionally restored one today.

The major contribution to the increase in the musical repertoire was the invention of a changeable cylinder system in the 1850s, enabling one cylinder holding six or more melodies to be removed and replaced by another playing a different group of tunes. This was a great leap forward not only for the buying public, who could now hear up-to-date operatic or music hall melodies, but also for the manufacturers, who could continue to retail cylinders for boxes sold perhaps many years before.

In time, the number of additional instruments and cylinders grew until it seemed as if a small orchestra had been squeezed into the wooden cases, which by the 1880s were rosewood-veneered on the outside, usually inlaid with marquetry, and occasionally decorated in addition with mother of pearl, buhl and engraved brass panels. They grew into large pieces of furniture when match-

Two-per-turn musical box with bells, drum and castanets, made in Switzerland by Nicole Frères in about 1872.

CARE AND REPAIR

- Keep away from sunlight and radiators because the wood will crack.
- Don't stress the comb teeth by stopping them in mid-tune.
- If lubrication is needed at all, use sewing machine oil very sparingly.
- Don't use sticky tape to repair any sheets that accompany the box.
- For care of wooden cases see pp. 16–17.
- Restoration is best left to specialists.

For expert advice contact the Musical Box Society of Great Britain, 40 Station Approach, Hayes, Bromley, Kent, BR2 7EF

ing stands were made to hold the additional cylinders which stood in Victorian parlours, and sometimes doubled as writing desks or side tables. Sadly, when their heyday passed many of these large instruments were 'adapted', their mechanisms removed and replaced by the fittings of an escritoire.

It is not always easy to establish the manufacturer of a particular music box since companies tended to use small trademarks, rather than their names, stamped on to either the top of the governor or the bedplate. There are exceptions, of course, and Nicole Frères nearly always placed its full name on the comb; Paillard Vaucher Fils and B. H. Abrahams sometimes marked the tune sheets mounted inside the lid with their initials – P.V.F. or B.H.A. Tune sheets themselves can be traced to individual manufacturers, and to help with identification a number of books have been published which illustrate both makers' trademarks and tune sheets.

It may seem strange that the popularity of the cylinder musical box dwindled in the 1890s, but mechanical music evolution took a sudden leap forward and rendered this style of box utterly outmoded. In 1885 the disc musical box was invented and production began in Leipzig, now in East Germany. These machines used the same type of comb of tuned steel teeth as those which had created the sound in cylinder boxes. The vital difference was a system of star-shaped wheels mounted alongside the comb, which, as the wheels were rotated, plucked the teeth by raised points on a metal

This simple disc musical box was made in Germany by Polyphon about 1900. It plays 15½-inch diameter discs.

disc revolving above them. It might not seem at first glance such an earth-shattering advance, but its effect was quite dramatic.

The most expensive component in the production of clockwork music had been the pinned cylinder; the craftsman pinning the cylinder had to be mathematically precise to ensure the accuracy of the original melody. With the use of a metal disc, which could have its points pressed out by machine, the most costly element of manufacture was eliminated at a stroke. Now at last a musical box could be made inexpensive enough for an average household to afford – and didn't the public show their appreciation! I am particularly fond of disc musical boxes, from the smallest with their discs of 5¾ inches diameter to the grandfather of them all at an incredible 32 inches diameter. I dislike the task of changing pinned brass cylinders on their predecessors. Will I be able to get the cylinder out of its resting place? Will I knock the pins and destroy the melody? Will it fit into the mechanism?

Two of the most prolific manufacturers of disc musical boxes were Polyphon and Symphonion; one of these factories, indeed, became so well known in Britain that disc musical boxes used to be described as 'polyphons'. Auction catalogues from twenty years ago sometimes carry the garbled description 'An 8¼-inch

Carved and inlaid musical hall chair made in Germany in the late nineteenth century.

Symphonion polyphon', just as today 'hoover' describes every vacuum cleaner and every vacuum flask has become a thermos.

Demand having been established within a very few years of its invention, the evolutionary path of the disc musical box closely followed that of the cylinder device. A zither attachment was added to some machines in 1896; tubular bells, a type of dulcimer, cymbals, drums and bar glockenspiels in time became options available to the more adventurous buyer. In a similar way, the design of the case and the internal mechanism differed from model to model. The majority of the disc musical boxes that I see have their mechanisms mounted horizontally and are contained in cases designed to be placed on a table to be seen and heard. Generally the machines which play large discs are vertical free-standing models, sometimes mounted above matching disc storage cabinets with their discs powered by a periphery rather than central drive mechanism.

The strength of sound produced, coupled with further inventiveness, produced machines widely used in cafés and similar public places. The most common of these are the $19\frac{5}{8}$-inch diameter Polyphon disc musical boxes, which played a complete revolution of one disc for 1d. Perhaps the rarest are the forerunners of the juke box: when the customer had indicated his choice of disc from a list inside and inserted his coin, the relevant disc holding the tune would be selected from a dozen others and automatically moved into the correct position to be played (p. 165). In America these machines were operated by the insertion of a nickel (5 cent piece) and became known as nickelodeons.

For me the pinnacle of disc musical box development is the Symphonion Eroica, a machine which plays three 14-inch diameter discs in synchrony. Once heard, I can assure you, such a machine is never forgotten, but it was very expensive even in about 1900 – far beyond the means of many families.

The demand for clockwork music was eventually totally eclipsed by the talking machines, invented in the 1870s and widely available as inexpensive devices for home entertainment by the end of the nineteenth century. Who wanted to hear the mere tinkle of tuned steel teeth when the most famous operatic or music hall star of the day could entertain you with songs in your own sitting room?

Over the years I have seen hundreds of small, hand-operated musical boxes, often in cylindrical nickel-plated casings; they are known as manivelles, since they are hand-wound. Produced in thousands from the 1880s to the time of the First World War, their particular Achilles heel was the fragility of the winding mechanism. If the handle was turned in the wrong direction the mechanism broke, and I am sure that many manivelles were thrown away as a result.

Musical holders for Christmas trees enjoyed a period of popularity after the introduction of trees by Prince Albert from his

*Musical longcase clock with
11¾-inch discs by Symphonion.*

native Germany in the mid-nineteenth century. The holders gripped the base of its trunk and actually revolved it slowly as a melody sounded, showing every part of the decorated tree to best advantage. These novelties must have been very popular, since they have survived in relatively large numbers.

Another novelty, from the later nineteenth century, gives a whole new meaning to the children's party game of Musical Chairs. Either a disc or a cylinder musical movement was concealed within the seat of a particular type of beechwood hall chair, and the tune played whoopee cushion-style when the unsuspecting seated themselves. I have seen relatively few of these chairs, and they are certainly singled out by collectors today. A fine example like the one on p. 169 would be eagerly sought after.

I am particularly fond of one type of turn-of-the-century photograph album which from the outside does not appear unusual in the slightest. The embossed leather bindings open to reveal delicately lithographed cardboard leaves with spaces for inserting family portraits, but hidden at the back of the book is a small cylindrical musical movement activated by opening a brass clasp. Turning the pages of the family album becomes a rare form of entertainment when accompanied by a sentimental melody.

Well into the twentieth century a bewildering assortment of objects were fitted with diminutive musical movements. Fruit bowls tinkled into life when raised to offer an orange, cigar cabinets revealed their contents to a tuneful accompaniment, and ceramic jugs and teapots sounded 'D'Ye Ken John Peel' or 'Tea for Two' as they were lifted to perform their duties. A pottery chamber pot – perhaps decorated within with a head-and-shoulders portrait of Hitler – would blare morale-boostingly the National Anthem or 'Land of Hope and Glory' as the contents were emptied. All are now collectable, or will be soon. Even the currently desirable early musical boxes in their plain wooden boxes were once left to moulder in dusty attics. Whenever I am asked to value objects at a client's house I keep an eye out for them, and after many years I reckon I can spot one by its box alone – but not always.

One day an Italian gentleman brought a plain wooden box to be valued at the saleroom where I work.

'Oh, that's interesting,' I said, without opening the lid and, wearing my scientific instrument expert hat, continued, 'Would you like me to value your sextant?'

Adopting a slightly puzzled expression, he replied, '*Si, grazie, signorina* – I was not sure how to call it for you.'

Lifting the lid, I understood his bafflement and blushed at my howling malapropism. The case actually contained a musical box with an unusual difference: above the mechanism was an automated picture of a lively human coupling!

'Don't worry, *signorina*,' he said with a twinkle in his eye. 'I understand. No sextant please, you're British!'

SCIENTIFIC INSTRUMENTS

SIMON BULL

When I first went to work as a trainee at an auction room, I quickly found myself faced with the problem of having to value objects about which I knew very little – obscure nineteenth-century scientific instruments were definitely top of the 'difficulty' list. However, support was at hand from the head of my department, whose expertise had to cover everything from coins through instruments to African art, because at that time there was not enough interest in these subjects to warrant having a specialist in each field. At an early stage, a lady brought in an extraordinary 'scientific device' and I called in my colleague to help. The conversation went as follows:

'Good morning, madam. Hm … ah yes … one of those. I haven't seen one of those for years. Excellent example, though, nineteenth-century, and in fine condition…. It's used for measuring, of course, using these engraved scales. I think it should fetch £20–25. Would you like us to put it in a sale for you? Fine. Thank you very much.'

Out of earshot, I asked him what it was. 'Haven't a clue!' was the answer. I think it made £27, but I still don't know what it was used for and I have never seen another.

I recounted that story to illustrate both the baffling variety of specialist instruments that were manufactured in the past, and the dramatic increase in interest in the subject during the last ten years. Important scientific apparatus has always been collected and highly prized, in particular examples dating from the seventeenth and eighteenth centuries. However twenty years ago hardly anybody wanted nineteenth-century instruments, and their value was based solely on their decorative appeal – hence my colleague's ability to provide an accurate valuation without the slightest idea of the object's use.

Top of page *Very rare brass and mahogany quadrant made by John Bird about 1775.*

Wimshurst machine or electrostatic generator in mahogany with lacquered brass contacts, about 1870.

For practical purposes nineteenth-century instruments can be divided into three identifiable categories: laboratory and educational instruments for pure research and teaching purposes; professional instruments for use in connection with a particular job; and utilitarian instruments for everyday use.

The main source of laboratory instruments must still be the store cupboards at universities and schools, although most of their contents have been broken up after being declared obsolete. Many people will remember the old-style electrostatic generator, which produced blue sparks and a painful reminder of the power of electricity. Fine examples, particularly in wood and brass, are now greatly sought after – though more for their decorative appeal than for their scientific importance. Air pumps fall into the same category. They were designed to assist with experiments into the behaviour of gases, and to demonstrate the existence of a vacuum. A famous experiment conducted at Magdeburg in Germany in the seventeenth century involved removing the air from two large hemispheres placed together, before attempting to pull them apart with teams of horses; schoolchildren perform the same test with a much reduced version of the equipment. Instruments for measuring electricity, which have only recently begun to interest collectors, include galvanometers for measuring electric current; voltmeters and potentiometers; better examples of the Wheatstone bridge, used to determine resistance; and various types of voltaic cells (early batteries).

The rapid expansion of trade, relentless exploration of newly colonised lands and exploitation of natural resources by the British throughout the nineteenth century led to an ever-increasing demand for accurate and relatively inexpensive instruments by the new generation of practical scientists and professional men. They included sailors, architects, surveyors and members of the medical profession.

For Great Britain, as an island nation, sea power and the ability to navigate efficiently and safely were of primary importance. Leading the world in the Industrial Revolution was of little value if manufactured goods could not be speedily delivered and the raw materials needed by our factories imported with equal reliability. Instruments for navigation and accurate hydrography (charting of the oceans and coastlines) were therefore required in considerable numbers, but the problems associated with their construction were only solved at the end of the eighteenth century. In order accurately to plot a ship's position at sea it is necessary to know both the latitude (the distance above or below the Equator) and the longitude (the distance east or west of the port of departure). For centuries, skilled pilots had relied on a combination of dead-reckoning and the use of simple instruments such as the compass, quadrant and back-staff. Finding a ship's latitude required the accurate measurement of the angle between the sun or Pole Star and the horizon. This was achieved in the late eighteenth century

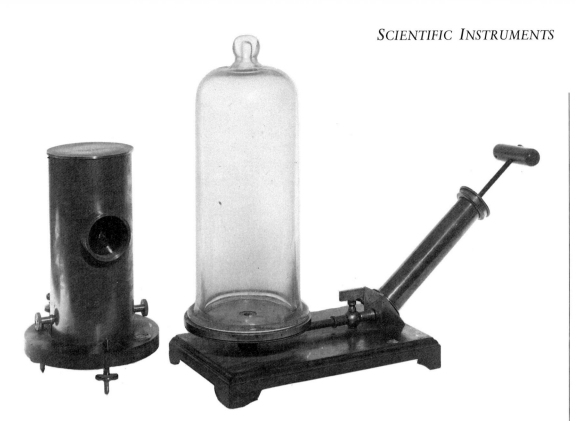

Vacuum apparatus, with a glass bell jar, brass fittings and a mahogany base, made about 1850.

with John Hadley's invention of the octant, so called because the arc of the measuring scale was one-eighth of a circle.

The sextant (one-sixth of a circle), a more accurate version of the octant, which it replaced in the 1780s, has continued in use up to the present day. It is still carried on board all ships in case of a breakdown in the electronic navigation systems. Whereas octants were usually made of wood, often ebony, with brass fittings and the scale engraved in bone or ivory, sextants are made exclusively of brass, with some later models in gunmetal. You will seldom find an eighteenth-century example of either instrument, as both are becoming increasingly rare. However wooden octants of standard pattern were cheap to produce and continued in use on small boats until the early twentieth century, while the demands of war saw mass production of sextants at about the same time. Originally these later examples were oxidised (a form of black finish) to reduce reflections off the metal, and came in a fitted wooden box with additional eye-pieces. Over the years the Admiralty has sold off large stocks, and many captains owned their own, so they turn up frequently. A particularly unpleasing practice in recent years has been to buff up the brasswork – thereby destroying both the scientific and antique value – and turn the instrument into a lampstand.

Finding longitude was a far more complex problem, and the search for a solution occupied the time of governments, scientists and craftsmen for more than two hundred years. In 1714 Parliament passed the Act of Queen Anne, offering a prize of £20,000 to anyone who could devise a practical method of finding longitude to within 60 miles. Numerous schemes were proposed, many of extraordinary complexity or just plain hare-brained, but the obvious solution was a clock capable of accurate timekeeping on board ship, even in rough seas. As the earth revolves once every twenty-four hours the time of noon varies according to the position of the observer, midday local time being when the sun is directly overhead. If a clock has been set to time at the port of departure, then the difference it shows, either fast or slow of this local time, will indicate the position in degrees either east or west of the starting point. An imaginary line running around the earth passing through Greenwich in London is universally recognised as the meridian. The prize was eventually won by an Englishman, John Harrison, but it was not paid to him until 1773, after forty-eight years of work and only three years before his death.

Although Harrison's contribution to the story of the marine chronometer (the generic name for all such clocks) cannot be overestimated, it was the work of two other English makers, John Arnold and Thomas Earnshaw, which finally resulted in the large-scale production of a practical instrument by the end of the eighteenth century. Although only a few firms were responsible for the manufacture of the bulk of chronometers made in the second half of the nineteenth century, a wide variety of names appear on the dials; many of them are the signatures of chandlers, retailers and government suppliers. The majority have a going-period of fifty-six hours and were wound every day; in addition examples running for a week were made in some quantity, but these were mainly for private buyers. Early examples, particularly those dating from the eighteenth century, and later instruments that include unusual technical features are greatly sought after by collectors, and of course chronometers that run for eight days have a special appeal to people unwilling to wind a clock every day.

Late nineteenth-century compound microscope of lacquered brass, made by Ross, London. The separate mahogany case contains accessories.

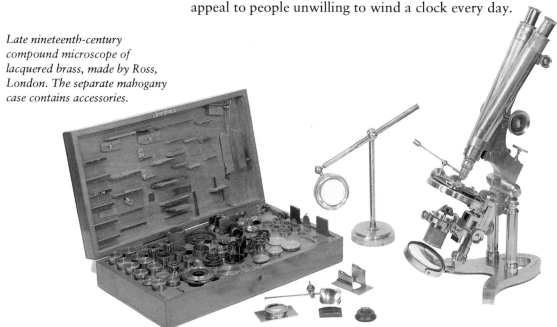

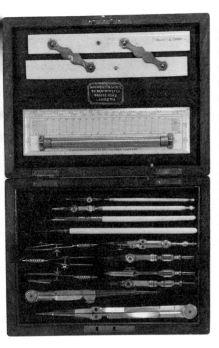

Set of nineteenth-century drawing instruments with ivory rulers and pens in a fitted walnut case.

Before leaving the field of navigation, there are one or two other frequently used instruments that are occasionally seen in salerooms. Of these, marine telescopes, which were usually the captain's own private property, have survived in quantity. Early examples were constructed with long wooden barrels and had a single focusing tube, which made them cumbersome to handle, or alternatively with cardboard 'draw' tubes, which suffered damage easily in damp conditions. The discovery of a way to manufacture thin and accurate tubing, combined with nineteenth-century advances in lens technology – notably due to the work of John Dolland – enabled neat 'multi-draw' telescopes to be produced. Later examples for use on board ship are often nickel-plated to resist corrosion, with a sliding shade at the objective end to minimise glare from the sun or sea. Binoculars are usually no earlier than twentieth-century.

Magnetic compasses were certainly in use during the fifteenth century, and consisted of a needle pivoted over a fixed card or 'rose'. Eventually the card itself was suspended on a pin, with a magnetised wire attached to the underside. The continual pitching and rolling of a ship at sea caused these light cards to spin erratically, and although considerable improvement was effected by mounting the instrument in gimbals, the task of steering a steady course in rough seas must have required considerable skill at the helm.

Again, the nineteenth century brought several improvements. The card was often floated on oil to reduce wobble; a new form of magnetic needle was invented by Lord Kelvin; and the instrument was housed in a free-standing wooden cabinet complete with internal lamps and an arrangement to counteract the magnetism of the new iron ships – the binnacle compass.

Finally, an instrument that I am surprised to see so frequently in private ownership is the mechanical log – not the captain's record, but a device towed behind the ship to indicate speed through the water. Invented by Edward Massey in 1802, it looks like a small brass torpedo; most examples are nineteenth-century.

Surveying and navigation are linked in that they are both concerned with establishing a location on the earth's surface. But while improvements in navigation required a major breakthrough in technology, truly precise surveying awaited only the appearance of much more accurate instruments. Surveying is largely a matter of measuring angles, and therefore the more accurate the scale on the instrument, the more reliable the measurement taken on the ground. For centuries simple instruments based on well-established principles had been used to mark out boundaries and survey land, but generally on a small scale. However, the early nineteenth century saw the arrival of the railways and the large-scale introduction of paved roads – both of which stretched over the countryside for long distances – to say nothing of expansion in the mining industry.

Surveyor's base theodolite made about 1930 by Stanley, London. Its late date would make it less valuable than an earlier example.

Discounting the numerous names given to surveying instruments designed to perform a specific task, there are only three basic implements, each of which was already in use during the seventeenth century. They are the theodolite, the level and the circumferentor.

The theodolite, invented in the sixteenth century and greatly improved by Ramsden at the end of the eighteenth, was designed to take measurements in both a horizontal and a vertical plane. The fully developed Victorian instrument – the form that usually appears on the market – was equipped with a magnetic compass, spirit levels and a telescopic sight, as well as small microscopes to read the very finely divided scales. Earlier examples are of lacquered brass, later pieces oxidised, and originally most had a tripod stand and fitted case.

Bubble or spirit levels are familiar to everyone, since they are still an everyday tool in the building trade. For the mining industry specific forms of level were required, in particular the inclinometer, designed to provide an accurate measure of slope; the dumpy level, much used for railway construction, was a robust combination of telescope and spirit level.

The circumferentor or graphometer was actually a form of compass, useful underground, which was sometimes called the miner's dial. It consisted of an accurate magnetic compass with attached sights of either pinhole or telescope form and reading off directly in degrees. The graphometer, a French invention of about 1600, performed a similar function using a half circle.

Other nineteenth-century developments included the prismatic compass, of which numerous examples were made for military purposes at the turn of the century, with luminous or mother-of-pearl cards for use at night; and the box sextant, a small, portable, drum-shaped instrument, again useful in military contexts. Of peripheral use in surveying are calculating devices and sets of drawing instruments; the latter, usually of superb quality with ivory rulers and squares, are still commonplace. Slide rules and computing tables were often designed for a specific purpose, and examples made for calculating excise duties on alcohol, timber measuring, nautical purposes and even sewerage flow have been seen. The cylindrical slide rule, although confusing to use, perhaps comes closest to the modern electronic calculator, since it can perform mathematical functions to four decimal places.

Until new ideas began to emerge in the eighteenth century medical science had remained unchanged in its basic thinking since the time of the Greeks, with all illnesses put down to an imbalance in the four 'humours'. The chemical properties of existing drugs were largely misunderstood, and cures for disease included such drastic measures as bleeding with leeches, cupping and purging, sometimes accomplished by the drinking of mercury! But it was the major improvements in the quality of microscopes during the nineteenth century that did most to advance medicine.

Nineteenth-century miner's dial in brass, fitted with two spirit levels and folding sights. Made by J. Casartelli in Manchester, it would also have been used by surveyors.

CARE AND REPAIR

~

o Don't remove old lacquer.
o Keep instruments in original boxes, if you have them, for protection and to increase their value.
o For care of wooden cases see pp. 16–17.
o Restoration is best left to specialists.

For expert advice contact the Museum of the History of Science, Old Ashmolean Building, Broad Street, Oxford, OX1 3AZ, *or* the Science Museum, Exhibition Road, London SW7 2DD

Early microscopes used a single objective, or combination of simple lenses, and were plagued by problems of distortion. The work of Joseph Lister, the wine merchant father of the surgeon Lord Lister, paved the way for the production of the superb Victorian instruments that survive today. As is often the case, the names of many different retailers appear on microscopes, but three firms were responsible for making most of the finest examples: Powell & Lealand, Ross, and Smith & Beck. In general microscopes from this period are of monocular or binocular type, made of lacquered brass and mounted on heavy stands to reduce vibration. They could be purchased in basic form, or cased together with a vast range of accessories including numerous powers of eyepiece and objective, various mounts and stages for holding specimens, and attachments for magnifying, polarising and splitting the light source. At the end of the century the German firm of Zeiss took over as leaders in the field of high-grade optics, but their instruments, usually black-lacquered and nickel-plated, are less attractive in appearance. For amateur and many professional applications, these nineteenth-century microscopes have never been bettered for quality.

Medical instruments have in recent years become a serious field for collectors. Complete sets of surgical instruments were made in considerable quantities during the nineteenth century; they are frequently fitted into elaborate cases, or simpler mahogany boxes if for military use, and contained knives, saws and tools for removing gun shot. Trepanning required implements similar to large, hollowed-out drills, and it was considered that drilling a hole in the head could cure epilepsy and headaches and even release demons! Before the nineteenth century dentistry was often performed at fairground booths. The implements used, called tooth-keys and forceps, also came in boxed sets.

I have called my third category of instruments 'utilitarian', but really it covers too wide a spectrum to be grouped under one name. Many people, indeed, may consider some objects in the group not to be 'scientific' at all.

During the nineteenth century a widespread fascination with the advances made in science and technology gave birth to a range of scientific 'toys', some of educational value, others simply entertaining. Included in this group are instruments which, although of scientific importance, were of dubious value, or out-of-date alongside the 'latest' technology.

The humble sundial may be included here, although it was still in everyday use in the countryside, and highly sophisticated variants such as the heliochronometer and dipleidoscope were developed for exploration work. Simple garden sundials were already being reproduced, often bearing false signatures and seventeenth-century dates. Another survivor is the induction coil;

Lacquered brass binocular microscope by Andrew Ross, London (left), of about 1860, and (right) a similar instrument by J. B. Dancer.

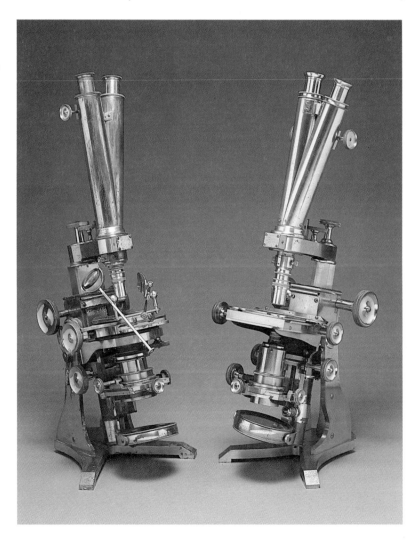

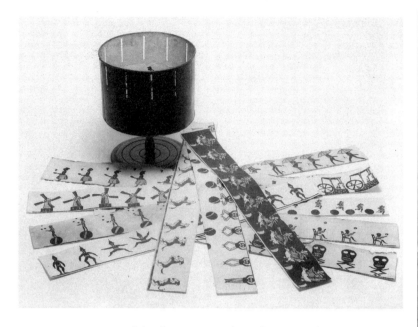

American Zoetrope. Made of black painted metal on a wooden base, it was one of many moving picture machines sold for home entertainment in the late nineteenth century.

Large stereoscope on mahogany stand, about 1880.

some were powered by batteries, others by a cranked generator. They produced a series of electric shocks claimed to be of great value in curing illness, but in most cases it is more likely that relief came to the patient as a result of the treatment ending! The mercury barometer remained a valued instrument for the explorer and mountaineer, but the invention of the aneroid mechanism, using an evacuated metal bellows to measure pressure changes, introduced a range of small domestic instruments, and professional examples used particularly for meteorology.

Among numerous optical 'toys' were the camera lucida, a device which employed lenses and mirrors to project a subject on to paper as an aid to sketching; the stereoscope, a viewer producing a three-dimensional image; and the magic lantern, forerunner of the film projector. 'Motion' pictures were available from a whole range of machines with exotic-sounding names. Perhaps best-known was the Zoetrope, introduced in about 1870, but its rivals included the Phenakistoscope, Praxinoscope and Choreutoscope! Even the commonplace yo-yo, diabolo, kaleidoscope and gyroscope, all still around today and fighting for survival against electronic Star Wars, were regarded as both educational instruments and entertaining toys.

On a recent *Roadshow*, I examined rather a nice telescope whose eyepiece bore a manufacturer's name unfamiliar to me. Sure enough, as soon as the programme was transmitted the letters started to arrive telling me of my ignorance – one came from the very manufacturer, still in business, though no longer in telescopes. Scientific instruments are like that: they encompass a huge range of complex objects, often collected by scientists themselves, and are definitely a field in which specialised knowledge helps.

TOYS AND AUTOMATA

HILARY KAY

Toys, now regarded as interesting antiques, were originally just part of normal family life; children played with toys whether they lived in a terraced house in an industrial town or in a substantial country manor. Despite their popularity at the time, surprisingly few early toys have survived their years of play by generations of children, and today the best are regarded as works of art which throw light on to a particular historical period.

One part of Europe which successfully exported wooden toys to other countries in the eighteenth and nineteenth centuries was the Erzgebirge region of Germany. This mountainous area, today between East Germany and Czechoslovakia, built up an unrivalled reputation for producing high-quality carved and painted wooden toys illustrating local life as well as objects of wider appeal such as Noah's arks, forts and nativity crèches.

At one particularly memorable *Roadshow* a lady arrived with a carved and painted wooden mid-nineteenth-century Noah's ark containing not only four-legged beasts from elephants to moles but also birds and tiny butterflies with painted paper wings. Her menagerie seemed endless as the table top rapidly filled with beasts in every shape and form. Noah's arks are one of the examples of the early toymakers' art which have managed to survive the passage of time. One explanation could be that these toys were amongst the very few amusements which children were allowed on a Sunday, because of their biblical connections. Suffering only one-seventh of the wear and tear of other types of delicate wooden toys must undoubtedly have helped them to stay intact.

In the early years of the nineteenth century factories were established which produced small objects in tinplate (a material composed from very thin sheet steel plated with an even thinner layer of tin), finished in brightly coloured lacquers. Their wares at this

Top of page Tinplate Pterodactyl monoplane made by Orobr in Germany about 1914. It has hinged wings and a clockwork mechanism driving a celluloid propeller at the rear.

180

Noah's ark, made of carved and painted wood in Germany in the mid-nineteenth century.

stage included funeral wreaths, canisters and household utensils, but before long the companies realised that it was more profitable to use less raw material to produce objects such as miniature kitchen equipment or dolls' furniture. Gradually these manufacturers expanded their wares to include a wide variety of metal playthings, and in the 1860s they produced the first tinplate trains in the world made to run on rails. But it was not until twenty years later that the mechanical toy industry really got under way in Germany.

From small beginnings an enormous international toy train industry grew. Bassett-Lowke and Hornby were the best known of the English companies, while Märklin, Gebrüder Bing, Georges Carette, Ernst Plank and Jean Schoenner manufactured quality trains in Germany. Originally toy trains were available in a number of different track widths, the most common before 1915 being $1\frac{7}{8}$ inches (48 mm), known as Gauge One; after the First World War the smaller Gauge 0 of $1\frac{3}{8}$ inches (35 mm) became more popular. Today railways of Gauge 00 ($\frac{5}{8}$ inch or 16.5 mm) are practically the only type of train set widely available.

This reduction in size may be linked to the reduction in scale of the likely purchaser's house. Before 1915 the only households able to afford these expensive metal playthings were professional or

Clockwork tinplate passenger boat made by the German manufacturers Gebrüder Bing of Nuremberg in about 1905.

aristocratic families who lived in large houses. As the twentieth century progressed, however, mass production techniques lowered the cost of the trains and allowed families on smaller incomes, who lived in homes of more modest size, to buy sets if they were made to an appropriate scale.

The first locomotives were powered by simple clockwork mechanisms, but soon the manufacturers experimented with live steam, which gave a more realistic feel to the toys. The boilers were heated from beneath by methylated spirit burners, and the connecting rod of the driving wheels was powered by the steam produced.

In the early years of this century a Northampton-based company, Bassett-Lowke, were responsible for importing and in some cases commissioning specific locomotives of English outline from the best German manufacturers. In time, this company progressed to producing fine-scale locomotives and ship models themselves, and were a thriving business until the 1930s when their production began to falter; in the 1950s they ceased production altogether. Bassett-Lowke model railways were produced in a number of different gauges for home use; larger engines, with good-scale detail, were also manufactured to be used on garden layouts or in endurance trials.

Perhaps it is because youngsters were probably supervised when playing with Bassett-Lowke trains that surprisingly large numbers have survived the years. At one *Roadshow* I was brought a 1920s' Bassett-Lowke locomotive and a train produced in Germany at about the same time by Märklin. The condition of both was quite outstanding considering their age, and their owner admitted that, although they had been bought for him as a present by his father, his father had played with them more than he had, and as a result their condition had been preserved!

Hand-painted four-seater open tourer made in about 1910 in Germany by Georges Carette. Its lifelike details include rubber tyres.

The company which most people in Britain connect with model railways is Hornby; these trains were made by the Meccano Company, owned by Frank Hornby, who began manufacturing them in 1920. At last an English maker had realised the potential market for railways amongst young boys, and succeeded in producing a range of merchandise to suit their pockets. Interest in Hornby trains was boosted by the publication of annuals in which the company cleverly merged sales patter with factual information on full-size locomotives. As the decades passed, the name Hornby became a byword for all toy train sets, and although the production of Gauge 0 railways ceased in the 1950s the company are now in production once more, producing models of Thomas the Tank Engine and his storybook friends.

Less common and highly sought today are other types of mechanical toy from the last hundred years which accurately mirror advancements in technology over the decades. The birth of the motor car was reproduced in tinplate, and its evolution from the horseless carriage to sleek saloon was faithfully recorded. The development of naval vessels, the first submarines and torpedo boats were all marked by toymakers; those manufactured for a particular export market were decorated accordingly and flew the flags of their country of destination. Man's early experiments with flying machines were copied in toy form. There were aeroplanes with flapping wing sections, and others with wings of celluloid or paper. Zeppelins, fighters from the Second World War and the rockets and spacecraft of the 1950s were all part of the repertoire; the last group included fanciful notions of intergalactic machinery which are pure science fiction.

Before the First World War pressed tin toys had details soldered on to the structure and were decorated by hand in colours baked on to the surface of the tinplate. This created a hard, enamel-like

The Great Bear, a clockwork Gauge 1 Great Western locomotive and tender made by Märklin in Germany in about 1909.

Two Dinky die-cast vehicles of the fifties and sixties, in mint condition and with their original boxes.

finish, which has a tendency now to chip off if the metal of the toy is dented or damaged. After this period the majority of toys had printed decoration rather than painted colours and details. Although the process of printing colours lithographically on to flat sheets of tinplate before it was cut and pressed to shape had been used in the 1880s for biscuit and other tins, it was not widely used on mechanical toys until well into the next century.

Manufacturers of tinplate toys seldom marked their goods with the factory's name in full; usually their products were stamped with a trademark which with practice can be identified easily. Sometimes toys emerged from the factories without even this small clue, but fortunately a number of original toy manufacturers' catalogues have been reprinted over the last ten years, and with patience unmarked toys can be classified in this way.

Besides toys which represent various forms of transport, some of my personal favourites are 'novelty toys' – vehicles of an unusual design or which move in an amusing way, or mechanised figures taken from characters in real life. The French firm of F. Martin produced a wide range of novelty figures; the German company of Philip Vielmetter made an outstanding toy of a clown artist; while another German manufacturer, Gunthermann, made delightful hand-painted toys of a particularly whimsical style. But the toys I find particularly amusing are those of the German company of Ernst Paul Lehmann.

The Lehmann factory produced its first mechanical toys in 1888 and the company is still in existence today, based on the outskirts of Nuremberg. Many of their toys are named after or represent members of Lehmann's family, or depict vehicles and characters of the time which particularly caught his eye. The quality of the lithography was good, giving additional detail to already complex tinplate pressings. One of the early toys was a group of two figures and a dog entitled *Familie Lehmann* in Germany and *Walking Down Broadway* elsewhere. In 1899 he produced a model of an English hansom cab containing two gesticulating ladies; entitled *Li La Auto Sisters*, it was named after two of Lehmann's sisters, Lieselotte and Laura. Another toy was entitled *Anxious Bride Nanni* and took the form of a wildly signalling lady, seated in a trailer pulled behind a mechanical three-wheeler which moved erratically. Another of Lehmann's sisters had the nickname of

Tinplate Anxious Bride toy by Ernst Paul Lehmann, made in Germany in about 1915.

Hookah-smoking automaton, made in France in about 1890 by Léopold Lambert. The mechanism is concealed in the base alongside the musical movement.

Nanni, although I don't know if she was driven to her wedding in this way!

Related to such toys, though produced more as after-dinner conversation pieces or adult amusements than as children's toys, are automata. French automaton makers in the later nineteenth century included Bontems, Decamps, Phalibois and Vichy, who each produced animated figures or scenes with a variety of complex movements. The mechanism is usually clockwork-powered with a series of cams operating taut wires joined to the articulated features of the piece. More effectively for the audience, wires often articulated the facial features, causing eyes to move, eyelids to flutter, the mouth to open and shut and the tongue to protrude. Sometimes automata incorporated bisque heads made by the better French doll factories such as Jumeau (see p. 20). Other, more individual, heads were made from papier mâché with articulated facial features assembled by the manufacturer.

I have been particularly lucky over the years to have seen two outstanding automata on the *Roadshow* – one in Bognor Regis and the other in Carlisle. They were visually very different, but inextricably linked in concept and internal design. One was a large standing figure of a flute player, who appeared to play the instrument as hidden clockwork-powered bellows created the whistling melody. The other was a seated Turkish figure dressed in harem pants with a hookah pipe beside him. When a lit cigar was placed in the top of the hookah, a mechanism concealed beneath moved the arm holding the end of the pipe to his lips as if to inhale; then – wonder of wonders – exhaled smoke appeared from his nose (again operated by a bellows system hidden away in the base). I remember him happily smoking his way through one of Hugh Scully's cigars!

Automaton of a negro magician, French, about 1890.

Opposite *Delicate cast-iron Girl Skipping Rope mechanical money bank, made in America by J. & E. Stevens Co. in about 1895. The legs and head move when a coin is inserted and a lever depressed.*

The number of different movements and their complexity has an important bearing on the value of an automaton; so too does the condition of the clothing and accessories, which should be good and original (often clothes 'crack' in specific places as a result of the constantly repetitive motion), and the quality and condition of the musical movement, which usually plays to accompany the action. Automata were commercially produced from the 1860s onwards, but the high point in their history was between about 1880 and 1910, when the biggest, best and most complex examples were produced. Gradually, as the twentieth century progressed, electricity began to replace the clockwork mechanism and automata were reduced to shop-window advertising displays or trade stimulators as the public looked to gramophones or motion pictures for their entertainment.

So far I have only discussed mechanical toys and automata made in Europe, but America too had a thriving industry. Significant numbers of certain American cast-iron toys can be found in Britain; they were probably used as ballast in ships returning to England with raw cotton for processing by the mills of Lancashire. In the mid-nineteenth century some American manufacturers of cast-iron agricultural equipment and domestic objects began to realise that there were other uses to which cast iron could profitably be put. Like the European tinsmiths, they found that by using a smaller amount of raw material and producing a toy rather than a ploughshare or cauldron a much larger profit could be made.

The American cast-iron toys which were imported in quantity into Great Britain were mechanical savings banks. These novelties, first seen in the 1850s, were cast in several individual sections which were assembled and screwed together, and usually had articulated features which moved as the coin was deposited. The wide range of different designs, coupled with their encouragement to the young to save money, ensured that the banks were as popular with parents as they were with children. Many are relatively easy to find today; others are much scarcer, perhaps owing to their more delicate construction, or because their design related to some short-lived political scandal. One word of caution, though: over the last fifteen years some of these banks have been manufactured extensively in Taiwan and exported. Although originally made as modern reproductions, over the years they have acquired a patina of age and can take in an inexperienced buyer.

For many of us, though, it is Dinky Toys, or their present-day equivalents, which take us back to our own childhoods. Dinky Toys were originally made by the Liverpool-based Meccano company as accessories to go with their Gauge 0 railway layouts and were produced to the same scale. Originally retailed as Modelled Miniatures, the first vehicles emerged from the factory in 1932; the following year the line was renamed Dinky Toys (from the Scottish word 'dink', meaning pretty, neat, small and dainty).

The appetite for the limited number of small trucks, cars and tractors available was ravenous and soon the company greatly expanded the range of toys; eventually the line included almost every type of vehicle – agricultural vehicles, commercial vehicles with product advertisements along their sides, emergency vehicles, service vehicles, army tanks, guns and personnel carriers, aeroplanes, ships, figures and road signs, as well as most makes and models of car of the period. After the Second World War some of the more stylish American convertibles – Cadillacs, Chryslers, Buicks and Studebakers – were reproduced in Dinky form. Now the general re-kindling of interest in the 1950s has made these particular models, together with larger commercial vehicles from the period, suddenly in vogue with collectors once again.

Other British manufacturers followed the Meccano company's lead. Lesney produced Matchbox Toys, and Corgi made die-cast vehicles, but neither held as great a share of the British market as Dinky, probably because of the attention to detail and quality of casting of Dinky Toys. Of course since this type of toy was produced in hundreds of thousands, and was inexpensive enough for a child to buy himself with his weekly pocket money, Dinky Toys – particularly those made after the Second World War – are not scarce. Bags and boxes of Dinkys are lugged in to each *Roadshow* by owners hoping to discover untold riches, but most Dinkys can only be valuable today if they are unusual, in an exceptionally good state of preservation – preferably in unplayed-with condition – and still in their original cardboard boxes! On early (pre-war) examples of Dinky toys look out for surface cracks or defects in the paintwork, which could mean that the toy is suffering from metal fatigue. At this date the alloy from which Dinkys were made was changed from being mostly lead to being mostly zinc. After the war the alloy was altered again, and this righted the faults.

Toy collecting is very much an on-going pleasure, and it's interesting to consider the toys we should be collecting now with an eye to the future. As an indication, look at those toys from past eras which are regarded as classics today because they seem accurately to reflect the historical significance of each decade: space toys from the 1960s which present a *Boy's Own Paper* view of interplanetary travel and reflect the realisation of man's dreams to fly among the stars; Cadillacs and robots from the 1950s, showing the early influences of rocket power and science fiction on car designers; and toy aeroplanes with bomb-dropping facilities and ranks of Nazi brownshirt model soldiers representing the horrors of the Second World War. . . .

Do you feel that the 1970s will be looked back on and remembered as the decade that saw the first moon landings or the break-up of the Beatles? Will the 1980s be recalled in the future as the era of development of the computer industry and micro-chip technology, or of the space shuttle? Make your decision and seek out those toys which you feel may best represent our lives today.

CARE AND REPAIR

- Clean only with a silicone spray polish and soft cloth, but don't rub any damaged areas.
- Never retouch or repaint. Original condition is more highly prized than restoration.
- Oil moving parts lightly with sewing machine oil.
- Don't wind the mechanism fully.
- Store fully unwound.
- Keep all original boxes and packaging but don't repair them yourself, particularly with sticky tape.
- Repairs are for specialists.

For expert advice contact the London Toy and Model Museum, 23 Craven Hill, London W2

GLOSSARY

Armorial porcelain Pieces decorated with a coat of arms, especially Chinese export ware.

Biscuit Fired but unglazed clay.

Bocage Ceramic leaves and flowers modelled to make a background support for figures.

Bone china Encompassed by the term *soft paste*; contains calcinated ox bones.

Calendar work Mechanism in clocks which indicates the date and occasionally the day of the week and the month.

Charge The load of a gun, made up of gunpowder, wadding and projectile.

Chasing Raised relief design made by working metal objects on the reverse with a blunt tool.

Cloisonné See p. 130.

Crazing Network of fine glaze cracks in ceramics, caused by differences in expansion and contraction between the body and the glaze during firing. The Chinese turned this normally undesirable phenomenon into a decorative effect.

Crizzling See p. 107.

Crocketing Projecting, leaf-shaped decorative feature in medieval Gothic architecture, also used on buildings and furniture of the eighteenth- and nineteenth-century Gothic Revival. See also *Gothic/Gothick*.

Damascus twist See p. 159.

Davenport Type of small nineteenth-century desk with sloping top and drawers in the sides.

Delft Tin-glazed earthenware named after the Dutch town and made mostly in England, Holland and Germany, often in imitation of Chinese porcelain. See also *Faience* and *Maiolica*.

Earthenware Pottery body that requires glazing to make it non-porous.

Embossing See *Repoussé*. Often described as high or low relief.

Engraving Decoration of metal with a sharp tool to produce a design of fine lines. Also any print made from an engraved steel or copper plate.

Escapement Part of the clock movement governing the release of the power stored in the spring or weights.

Etching Decoration of metal with patterns created by dissolving some of the metal in acid. Also any print made from an etched plate.

Faience French name for tin-glazed earthenware. See also *Delft* and *Maiolica*.

Famille rose Type of Chinese porcelain characterised by a strong rose pink colour in the decoration. See also *Famille verte*.

Famille verte Type of Chinese porcelain characterised by a brilliant translucent green colour in the decoration. See also *Famille rose*. The less well-known Famille jaune and Famille noire have yellow and black backgrounds respectively.

Finial Decorative ornamental shape at the top of objects such as covered vases or pieces of furniture.

Folded foot Describes the edge of the foot of a glass turned over to form a robust double rim.

Footrim See *Footring*.

Footring Very shallow round pedestal on the base of cups, glasses, vases and other similar objects, on which the piece rests.

Furniture (gun) See p. 160.

Glaze Hard, shiny layer on the surface of a fired ceramic object.

Gothic/Gothick Medieval style of architecture characterised by pointed arches, pinnacles and flying buttresses. Revived for architecture, furniture, silver and other decorative objects in the mid-eighteenth century (when usually spelt Gothick) and continued in the nineteenth (when spelt Gothic).

Ground Underglaze or onglaze background colour used on porcelain. Reserved areas left white are later painted in enamel colours.

Hard paste True porcelain, made from white china clay (kaolin) and china stone, and first produced in China in the seventh or eighth century. It was about a thousand years before a similar body was successfully made in the West. See also *Soft paste*.

Hardstone Minerals such as agate, jade, rock crystal, rose quartz and serpentine, also coral, often used decoratively in e.g. Oriental carvings.

Honey gilding See p. 80.

Imari Type of Japanese export porcelain made at Arita and shipped from the port of Imari. Its typical red and underglaze blue colours and gilding were much imitated by eighteenth- and nineteenth-century English factories.

Japanning European imitations of true Oriental lacquer.

Kakiemon Type of Japanese porcelain decoration named after its seventeenth-century inventor. Much imitated by the eighteenth-century European factories, it is typified by asymmetrical, sparse flowers and figures painted in bright enamel colours over the glaze.

Knop See p. 108.

Leather-hard Describes ceramics that have dried to a carvable texture, before their first firing.

Lock (gun) Mechanism which causes the gun to fire when the trigger is pulled.

Lock spring V-shaped piece of tempered steel which provides the *lock* with its motive power when a gun is fired.

Maiolica Tin-glazed Italian earthenware. See also *Delft* and *Faience*.

Majolica Lead-glazed English imitation of Italian *maiolica*.

Niello Black substance resembling enamel, composed of various metals and sulphur fixed by heat. It is used to fill, and thus enhance, incised decoration on silver.

Nipple (gun) Small tube screwed into the breech of a gun, on which the *percussion cap* is placed.

Ormolu Gilded bronze, eighteenth-century and later, used for mounts on fine furniture and on decorative objects, clock cases etc.

Parcel gilt Silver partially gilded. See also *Silver gilt*.

Parian Type of white nineteenth-century English porcelain imitating white marble, and therefore often used for busts and nude figures.

Patch marks See p. 74.

Percussion cap (gun) Small copper cap containing fulminated mercury, which explodes when struck and fires the gun.

Pew groups Eighteenth-century figure groups seated against a high-stacked settle, made in Staffordshire of saltglaze stoneware.

Pontil mark Rough scar left on glass where the iron rod that holds it during manufacture has been snapped off. On wine glasses, normally found on the underside of the foot. It indicates only that the glass was hand-made, and not necessarily that it is antique. Before 1780 all glasses had this feature.

Porcelain See *Hard paste* and *Soft paste*.

Pottery Generally used to describe objects made from a clay body other than porcelain.

Reduction (glaze) Glaze produced by being fired in a kiln which has been starved of oxygen. Unusual and unexpected colours, e.g. lustre glazes, can be achieved.

Repoussé Decoration in relief on metal, created by hammering on the underside so that the pattern projects on the top side.

Saltglaze Glaze with a pitted surface like orange peel, produced by throwing salt into the kiln during firing.

Scale Decorative background pattern used on porcelain and resembling the overlapping scales of a fish.

Scrimshaw Engraved whalebone or whale teeth, walrus or marine ivory, or shell carvings.

Seeds See p. 109.

Silver gilt Sterling (92.5%) or Britannia standard (95.8%) silver covered with a thin wash of gold, by means of either fire or electrolysis. See also *Parcel gilt*.

Slipware See p. 55. Slip itself is liquid clay.

Soft paste Porcelain made to imitate hard paste before its secret had been discovered in Europe. The ingredients are mostly white clay and ground glass. See also *Hard paste*.

Spelter Soft metal alloy, mostly tin and zinc, often used for cases of less expensive nineteenth-century clocks.

Splat Central rail or upright in a chair back.

Spur marks Small unglazed areas on the base of glazed ware, showing where the piece stood on spurs or *stilts* during firing. Also known as stilt marks.

Stilts Small pieces of fireclay on which glazed pottery or porcelain objects stand during firing, to prevent them sticking to each other or to the base of the kiln as the glaze fuses.

Stilt marks See *Spur marks*.

Stock Wooden handle of a gun, comprising forend, wrist and butt.

Stoneware Very hard clay body fired at an extremely high temperature, which makes the body vitrify so that it is impervious to liquids even when unglazed.

Stretcher In furniture, the horizontal piece of wood that joins and supports the legs of chairs and tables. In painting, the wooden frame on which the canvas is supported.

Thrown pottery Wares that are thrown on a potter's wheel, rather than hand-built.

Wares In ceramics, often used to describe useful items such as plates, cups and vases, as opposed to purely ornamental items, e.g. figures.

INDEX

Picture Acknowledgements

Asprey PLC: 7, 33, 113, 155
BBC: 4, 8, 25 below, 45 below, 60 below, 83 below, 91 below, 142 below, 150 below, 157 below, 164 below
John Bly: 11 left and right, 12, 13, 16, 32, 36, 38, 114, 117 above
Bonhams: 45 above, 46 above and below, 49, 52, 99, 101 above and below, 102, 104, 105, 142 above, 143, 145, 146–7, 147 above, 148
Bridgeman Art Library: 15 (Victoria and Albert Museum), 37, 39, 41, 43 above (Cameo Corner), 44 (Fine Art Society/Haslam & Whiteway, London), 179 below
Angela Burgin: 17
Chartfield PCC: 25 above
Christie's: 1, 26 below, 27, 28, 40 above, 42, 43 below, 47, 60 above, 61, 62 above and below, 63, 65, 66 above and below, 87, 106, 107 above and below, 108, 110, 111 above and below, 112 above and below, 116, 117 below, 118, 151, 154, 156, 174, 175, 177
Geoffrey Godden: 72
Gordon Lang: 119 below
Anthony Lester: 144
Christopher Lewis: 40 below

Simon Livingstone Studios, by courtesy of Weller and Dufty: 157 above, 158, 159, 160, 161 above and below, 163 above and below
Peter Nahum: 6
Percival David Foundation of Chinese Art, London: 121
Phillips Fine Art Auctioneers: 10, 14, 26 above, 31, 35, 48, 50–1, 57, 59, 69, 70 below, 71, 73, 74, 82 above, 91 above, 92, 93, 94, 97, 98, 103, 115
Henry Sandon: 58
Rita Shenton, London: 150 above, 152, 153
Sotheby's: 2, 18, 19, 20 above and below, 21, 22 above, 22–3, 24, 30 below, 53, 54, 55, 56, 67, 70 above, 75 above and below, 76, 77, 78 above and below, 79, 80, 81, 82 below, 83 above, 84, 85, 86, 88, 89 above and below, 90, 100, 119 above, 122, 123, 124, 125 above and below, 126, 127 above and below, 128, 129, 130 above and below, 131, 132, 133, 134, 135, 136, 137, 138, 139, 140 above and below, 141, 164 above, 165, 166, 167, 168, 169, 170, 171, 172, 173, 176, 178, 179 above, 180, 181, 182, 183, 184 above and below, 185 above and below, 186, 187
Victoria and Albert Museum: 120
Worcester Royal Porcelain Co. Ltd: 96